African American Women
with Incarcerated Mates

African American Women with Incarcerated Mates

The Psychological and Social Impacts of Mass Imprisonment

Avon Hart-Johnson

McFarland & Company, Inc., Publishers
Jefferson, North Carolina

LIBRARY OF CONGRESS CATALOGUING-IN-PUBLICATION DATA

Names: Hart-Johnson, Avon, 1958– author.
Title: African American women with incarcerated mates : the psychological and social impacts of mass imprisonment / Avon Hart-Johnson.
Description: Jefferson, North Carolina : McFarland & Company, Inc., Publishers, 2017 | Includes bibliographical references and index.
Identifiers: LCCN 2017042807 | ISBN 9781476666822 (softcover : acid free paper) ∞
Subjects: LCSH: African American women—Social conditions. | Prisoners' spouses—United States—Social conditions. | Imprisonment—United States.
Classification: LCC E185.86 .H378 2017 | DDC 362.83/9996073—dc23
LC record available at https://lccn.loc.gov/2017042807

BRITISH LIBRARY CATALOGUING DATA ARE AVAILABLE

ISBN (print) 978-1-4766-6682-2
ISBN (ebook) 978-1-4766-3047-2

Front cover images by M-image Photography/iStock

Printed in the United States of America

McFarland & Company, Inc., Publishers
   Box 611, Jefferson, North Carolina 28640
   www.mcfarlandpub.com

I dedicate this work
to the countless women and families
affected by mass incarceration.

Acknowledgments

There are important people who deserve mention and acknowledgment in this book. I would like to thank and acknowledge my husband, Geoffrey Johnson, for continuing to support every project that I endeavor. We are a bond and team. I further I thank my children Shaniece and Kevin. You both continue to be my inspiration to keep me going. Mom wants to make you proud. Finally, I want to thank Rachel Cartwright for your literary expertise and ongoing pep talks. You and I have been in the trenches for a long time. Finally, I would like to acknowledge Barbara Benoliel's mentorship—you are a tenacious and wise woman. Many scholars will contribute to making social change because they were under your tutelage.

Table of Contents

Preface

"When we dehumanize people in conversation, we give permission for them to be degraded in other ways as well"—Polk (2016)

Nearly 40 years of surging incarceration rates of African American men in the United States has affected African American women who partner with them. Psychological, cultural, economic, and social issues tend to overlap and converge in the lives of these women who experience the impact of a mate's incarceration.

The incarceration of the primary mate and breadwinner in the family can weaken even the strongest family unit. With this understanding, as I embarked upon this study, I was curious how African American women adjusted to the consequences of having an incarcerated mate while experiencing emotional pain stemming from a broad set of psychological and social factors. I also wanted to know how women were able to cope, and by what means? I found that when women are emotionally distressed, when their children are acting out, and when their family, friends, and support networks, all, have grown tired of hearing their problems, they hang on tighter to their relationships with their incarcerated mate. This relationship becomes their support network. These women also experienced social stigma, shame, and assumed guilt by association when partnering with an offender. Therefore, with the emotional and social strains of having a loved one locked away in prison, I wondered how women were able to maintain a job in the workforce under such stressful conditions. What are the impacts, the financial strains of managing a family, knowing that your position has likely become the head of the household and the primary support for your bills as well as the chief support for your incarcerated mate? A recent study indicated that 50 percent of Americans cannot withstand an unexpected $400.00 emergency expense because they are living from paycheck to paycheck (Gambler, 2015). Yet, women in this study found ways to survive. Each of these issues are expanded upon and explored throughout this book.

While the literature remains scant on how this population of women is affected by the imprisonment of the partners, the case studies set forth in this text can help to broaden the perspective on how these women experience grief and non-death loss, from separation by incarceration. To illuminate their condition, I provide a view through the lives of 20 African American women, who, at times, are faced with tumultuous, heartbreaking, and overwhelming circumstances. From their interview transcripts, we learn that even in their frailty, these women are committed to helping their families remain strong. Even the most resilient individuals may become worn and fragile after experiencing multiple crises. As practitioners, you may find that the most effective interventions come about through insights gained from hearing these women's stories firsthand, as conveyed through their case studies and their own words.

This book grew out of a doctoral research study. I interviewed a selected sample of African American women. The study took place in Washington, D.C., during 2014. My findings resulted in my creation of a context-specific grounded theory to explain this phenomenon occurring among the sample of Black women with an imprisoned mate: It is called *SIG-C Theory: Symbolic Imprisonment, Grief, and Coping.* Grounded theory is a method that is an ideal approach to use when a phenomenon needs explaining at a theoretical level (Charmaz, 2006). This method is generally used for research when there is an absence of theory to explain a context-specific problem (See Appendix B). While this study has theoretical underpinnings related to grief theories, the development of a network model helps to clarify the complex nature of this particular social phenomenon: women with incarcerated mates.

The results of my findings showed uniformity among these women concerning the psychosocial effects of loss. The main theoretical premise behind SIG-C is that women experience grief similar to mourning the death of a loved one, and that the manifestation of this grief, combined with shame, stigma, and stress, becomes what I entitle, a state of *vicarious imprisonment* (also referred to in a broader context in this book as *symbolic imprisonment*).

As the author, I offer my experience as a human services practitioner to shape the discussion points and strategies that practitioners can consider as an application to build rapport with clients and to develop effective interventions. By using this handbook, helping professionals can apply this knowledge as a practical, integrative approach to working with clients.

Practitioners can benefit from learning about the adversities experienced by the African American female. This book is designed to assist helping professionals and human services practitioners in understanding how African American women "on the outside" are affected on a psychological, social, physical, cultural and symbolic level when a mate is confined in prison. Using this text, practitioners will explore culturally relevant issues that describe the deleterious impacts of incarceration on women, their families, their children. With knowledge, practitioners can develop or tailor their interventions to support this group of women effectively.

Introduction

African American females and their families are one of the most vulnerable groups experiencing the collateral impacts of mass incarceration in the United States. This is largely because 1 in 15 African American men are incarcerated in this country (Kerby, 2012). These men are fathers, husbands, boyfriends, and relatives of these women. In Washington, D.C., where this study took place, 1 in 4 African American men are at risk of arrest and serving prison sentences (Alexander, 2014). Compounding the issue of incarceration, Washington, D.C., does not have a prison. Therefore, D.C. code offenders become a part of the federal system and are often transferred beyond 500 miles to serve their sentences in another state. While the literature continues to grow in areas related to how inmates are impacted by prison or reentry, and how their children are affected by incarceration, little is known about the well-being of the African American woman related to the phenomenon of having an incarcerated mate. This study explores the psychological, social, physical, and grief responses experienced by this group of women. This work contributes to filling the literature gap by providing a grounded theory that illuminates how non-incarcerated females try to adjust to life on the outside of prison without their mates.

The incarceration status of a loved one is often a private matter. The women in this study wanted their voices to be heard. As the researcher conducting this study, I considered the women who took part in this research to be co-creators of this research. I hope that their disclosures will foster insights that contribute to the well being of others like them. I believe that through the case study analyses included in this work, the reader will begin to recognize that women of similar status could be your co-workers, a supervisor, hairdresser, babysitter, or a dinner or lunch companion—yet in reality, you may not know their secrets and their hidden pain of having an imprisoned mate. If these women are your clients, friends, co-workers, or someone you just met, it is hoped you may, from reading this book, develop greater insights and empathy. If you are a helping professional, it is hoped that you may be better able to attend to their needs.

To share insights, I begin each chapter with a profile, partially or fully constructed from the interview transcripts. I stay true to their narratives, only correcting grammar for clarity as annotated with square brackets in the text. Most of the quotes remain verbatim, as stated to me during their recorded interviews. It is my goal to allow the voices of the women I interviewed to remain in their most authentic form.

Two of the women in this study pointed out that they felt that culturally specific support systems for affected women were lacking. I have learned through this study that, even with minimal support, beneath their pain is the resounding determination of African American women with incarcerated mates to save their marriages, relationships, families, and in some cases, their lives—these women have shown true grit.

As we examine this social problem, we may recognize that not to respond may cause more harm than good, as these women are a part of the social fabric of our communities, our workforce, and our society as a whole. When women are psychologically and physically healthy, they can be available and attentive to their children, productive at work, and, it is hoped, with fewer healthcare needs.

Finally, as I reflect, I recognize that rather than a singular traumatic loss, women in this study encountered multiple, overlapping losses. Often, these women moved from resolving one crisis only to encounter the next, rarely having time to adjust. For example, consider an altercation between their husband or boyfriend with another inmate at the prison. Or, perhaps the incarcerated husband recruited his mate on the outside to help file an appeal or to find an attorney. The crises seemed to be ongoing, and I found through my interviews that the women interviewed were always putting their husband's or boyfriend's needs ahead of their own.

I found that these women, vulnerable to their significant other's wants and needs, get lonely as well. This state of loneliness may be combined with varying emotions, such as fear, or feeling heartbroken, deceived, abandoned, and overwhelmed—all while grieving. The women in this study represent only a minuscule number of those suffering the collateral consequences and the legacy of mass incarceration. This population's plight is rarely a part of the national conversation on topics typically associated with mass incarceration or mass imprisonment.

Mass Imprisonment

Given that this book is centered on the adverse impacts of incarceration on female partners, it is important to understand the term mass incarceration, or mass imprisonment. David Garland coined the term, regarding the phenomenon of mass imprisonment of Black men in the United States, and detailed it in his essay, "Mass Imprisonment." Mass imprisonment describes the punitive practices of mass warehousing of whole groups of people in prisons across the United States (Garland, 2001). Garland indicated that the United States exceeds the incarceration rates of most countries, grossly departing from previous norms of punitive practices in criminalization. This radical phenomenon has been unparalleled since the latter part of the eighteenth century (Garland, 2001). Garland posited that the phenomenon is such a paradigm shift that it has the potential to alter the composition of specific population groups. He predicted that the practice of mass imprisonment could become so entrenched in the behavior and ideologies of our nation's criminal justice system that it becomes part of the social fabric of our nation. Sixteen years later, we witness the reality of Garland's predictions.

For African American women, this foreshadowing is most concerning. There are multiple avenues for both her mate—and her children—to be threatened by mass incarceration and to enter the criminal justice system:

• Through the *zero-tolerance school policy* where children are arrested by police officers and/or sent to court for tantrums or other infractions, creating a pathway or pipeline from school to prison, especially for children of color (Thompson, 2016);

• Through *walking or driving-while-Black* where children, women, men, are subject to arrest or death from being Black in America and/or are presumed guilty of a crime or a public threat (Bell, Hopson, Craig, & Robinson, 2014); and

• Through disproportionately high incarceration rates and extensive sentencing of African Americans compared to other racial groups (Abrams, Bertrand, Mullainathan, 2008).

These concerns form a backdrop if not an integration into the context of the African American woman's experience. Not every Black woman will endure these hardships and crises from the aforementioned situations. However, for some women, these issues are indelibly interwoven in the tapestry of their lives, and they are discussed in this book as part of a larger discussion about the complexities of mass incarceration.

While incarceration is an important means of formal social control, for prisoners there are social costs to pay when society as well as the criminal justice system renders indirect punishment on the prisoners' spouses, girlfriends, and families. Indirect punishment can result in stereotyping of women and their families through stigmatizing, shaming, and even through the application of rigid prison policy (e.g., intrusive and invasive searches, denied visitation, little or no physical contact between incarcerated parents and their children). To stay connected, as detailed in this text, vulnerable and often poor families bear the cost of paying exorbitant telephone rates, and enduring expensive long-distance travel to remote areas where prisons are typically located, all to maintain some semblance of a family unit.

The issue of whether 40 years of mass incarceration has definitively contributed to the destruction of the African American family is still under scrutiny by scholars who have studied the fragile family. However, there are schools of thought which purport that America's war on drugs was a war on people of color—the fuel that primed the engine of the prison industrial complex (Gustafson, 1991; Mauer & Chesney-Lind, 2002), and dismantled millions of poor Black families. Therefore, if this notion is even partly correct, the helping professional may find that, in addition to working with clients directly affected by a loved one's incarceration, it may also be important to engage the entire non-incarcerated family members in some form of intervention. These topics and others are provided in the following chapters, and are organized as follows.

How This Book Is Organized

Each chapter contains case study examples, themes and insights, and discussion.

• The **Case Study** examples provide a profile of the selected research study participants, using pseudonyms to protect their anonymity. Each case features a primary research participant. However, to show repeat themes, in each case example, I sometimes integrate quotes from other women in this study. Therefore, case examples may feature one or more of the women whom I interviewed. Most chapters comprise a summary drawn from an integration of field notes, verbatim quotes, relevant literature, historical events, current news, and other sources to establish a foundation of understanding when reading the women's stories.

- The **Themes and Insights** provide readers with an *interpretation* related to a topic brought forth through women's stories. Additionally, these sections contain examples of intervention and coping strategies, as well as rich examples and explanations of the major constructs of SIG-C theory, briefly explained earlier.
- The **Discussion** section concludes each chapter with a focus on the major themes and ideas for interventions.

The main themes identified from this research fall into 5 constructs or major categories (italicized below). These results have been codified and form the basis of the SIG-C theoretical model, where women felt:

1. grief, similar to mourning the death of a loved one *(Grief Akin to Losing a Loved One Through Death)*;

2. as though they themselves were serving their own prison sentences *(Vicarious Imprisonment)* or as though they were doing time on the outside;

3. manipulated and charmed by the inmate *(Charismatic and Controlling Encounters)*;

4. overlapping and co-occurring emotions *(Psychosocial Reactions to Loss)*, and

5. the need to use various coping strategies to survive the trauma of loss and to, ultimately, stay connected to their mate *(Metaphoric Rituals and Coping)*.

To contextualize these themes and findings, in Part I, I provide the case examples showing variations of how grief, vicarious imprisonment or social isolation as punishment, being controlled, and other emotions manifest in the lives of each of the women interviewed. The women's case examples illustrate that the psychological and social expressions of grief and loss overlap in the experiences of women, regarding their socioeconomic status, education, health, spirituality, relationships, race, and class. From these overlaps, it becomes apparent how difficult it is for these women to separate their daily stresses from the context of a mate's incarceration. In Part I, we also hear the voices of the women who share their experiences as wives or partners of incarcerated men. Some of the women are mothers; others are grandmothers. We learn of their struggles, as well as their tenacity in survival.

In Part II, I explore the theory of SIG-C (Symbolic Imprisonment, Grief, and Coping) through the lens of women's stories, and expand on examples. In Part III, I turn the focus to grief, coping, and ritual as well as to the challenges of working with a population of women who generally mask their grief. Part IV provides insights on culturally relevant conditions women contend with and offers insights on challenges specific to intervention. That part also covers the social consequences of mass incarceration, while the Conclusion discusses the implications of this work.

PART I

African American Women in the Age of Mass Incarceration

1

"The Fixer": Bring My Daddy Back!

We will each experience loss in our lifetime. How we describe that loss and recover is an individual experience. Sometimes a non-death loss can remain deeply tied to our identities. Maybe it is the human will to fight hard and give everything within our power to strive to regain footing and salvage what we can. Maybe lingering hope is what provides our will— "if we could somehow regain what has been taken or removed," life would be good again. That is how I interpreted Lotus' life. Her story is one of good times and bad, all mixed together as a representation of her life as *a fixer*. Perhaps, the absence of Lotus' significant other illuminates the part of her that longs to be fulfilled, nurtured, cared for—and healed. Non-death loss can deeply impact a person's life. One type of non-death loss is the incarceration of a significant other.

Case Study: Lotus

The first time that my daughter saw her father sober was during a prison visit. [Her daughter stated], "I know this is my daddy, but I don't know him. I never knew this to be him. He used to laugh all the time. I thought he was happy, when [all the while] he was drunk. Now I'm talking to a stranger." So, I [as her mother] didn't know how to deal with this—it hurt me. She always believed that Mom would fix it. Therefore, even in this case, [my daughter] thought that I would bring her daddy home. She'd wear and hug his clothes and cry and cry—dirty clothes and all. I would say to her, "You still have that dirty shirt on?" She would say to me, "Mommy, I know that you can bring daddy back! I want my daddy!" And she would put his clothes on and just hug herself or me.—Lotus

Lotus is a "fixer." She is the breadwinner and sole provider for her daughter and incarcerated husband. Her daughter believes that she can fix anything that is broken, including her daughter's father. Lotus is a 48-year-old African American woman with her life on hold. Her husband of 24 years is currently incarcerated and she has no idea when he ever will be released. Lotus lives in the Washington, D.C., area. This jurisdiction has no prison. Therefore, her husband is serving time in a prison located several states away. This condition adds to the strain of being married to someone who has little control over his life.

During our telephone interview, Lotus' sadness seemed to oscillate. She was sometimes reflective and sad, at other times, lighthearted. When we began our interview, I asked: "Could you tell me what you think is special about your relationship with your mate?"

Lotus' answer was initially directed towards herself. While laughing, she said "I liked to live on the wild side." Lotus said that when she was younger, she never missed a good party. Reflecting on her twenties and thirties, her friends thought of her as "the life of the party." Two decades ago, she married her best friend. They were together as a couple "off and on, for years." When they married, she recalled, "I already had a son." They later had a daughter from their marriage. The first few years of their partnership, she reflected, her apartment was the place to visit on a Friday night "to have kick-ass fun." Eventually, Friday night drinking crept into her husband's weekday habits. One day, she thought she smelled a beer on him as she made breakfast. Over the years, his alcohol consumption progressed in parallel with his increasing failures to stop drinking. His insults towards Lotus became meaner and more frequent. At first, there were a few verbal insults, and then it advanced to almost daily bickering and physical confrontation. A couple of times, Lotus said, she and her daughter left and went to a women's shelter, but always returned home.

She said, "by then we were invested too deep" to leave him. To *fix things*, Lotus said that she believed that moving the family out of the city was the answer. She thought that if they moved to a different neighborhood, a change of scenery and getting him away from his friends would make it easier to "sober him up."

So, Lotus and her family moved from their apartment in the city to a small but nice home just outside of Washington, D.C. "It was a nice place, with a little shed behind the house." To help take care of the home, Lotus found "a side job." Her husband continued to work construction. Lotus said she herself had never worked for long periods. However, to augment their income, she began working at the local hospital. The pay was good, but it kept her away from the house for longer hours than she liked during the week. However, having a job allowed her to pay the bills and "pick up the slack, where [her husband's] income fell short." She was also able to interact with coworkers and make friends. She eventually began to invite her new friends to her home on the weekends to party. During this time, according to Lotus, her husband was able to remain sober even while her friends came over. Then he was laid off.

Shortly after the layoff, Lotus began finding alcohol containers again, "in the shed, under the car seat, in the bathroom trash can." As his drinking progressed, he became even more aggressive and abusive. Years went by. His sobriety was intermittent. She said, finally, she could not take it anymore, so they decided to separate. She wanted to see if that would "fix things." This move, she felt, was not a permanent solution but a way to "shock" her husband into conformance. He went to live with a relative. Lotus described how, early one morning, while her husband was on his way to work, still not sober from the night before—driving while intoxicated—he thought he hit a deer; but as it turned out, it was a person. This was the beginning of Lotus' self-described nightmare.

During this part of the interview, Lotus's voice became penetrating and heavier as she shared the events leading to her husband's incarceration. In a justification of her relationship, she explained:

> We were separated for about six months prior to him being incarcerated. But, you know, he didn't live far from me. So, um, my husband was a chronic alcoholic. Okay? And so, I mean, he was the breadwinner. Um, I worked side jobs and things like that but, um, it was kind of like, um, taking care of him while he was taking care of me, so we were, basically, I guess, both of us were each other's crutches—to a certain degree.
>
> Um, it felt as though that I was in a state of shock [after his arrest]. And it was like my body was in a state of pandemonium and my mind was racing in a thousand directions. I felt as though.... I felt as though that I could do something about the situation and all at the same time, I knew that God Almighty was the only one who could fix this situation. You know. So, that's kind of basically it. You know? I know that I was just hopeless. There was nothing I could do about this.
>
> [When it first happened—the accident and subsequent incarceration] I really hid it well. I wanted to appear strong, as if I was the backbone, which I was.

Lotus's voice oscillated from intensity to unsteadiness as she expressed her sadness and reflected on how strong she had become, coping through the whole ordeal:

> [I] remind myself how strong I am as an individual and know that I have to live day to day for my daughter. It was, basically, knowing that I had a child to take care of. I had to work as much as possible, and so, basically, [my way of coping

was] work and my daughter—[and] writing letters and the telephone calls—[to my husband]—things of that nature.

And I'm all that she has and I push myself to keep going and be a better person every day. I guess it's just knowing that—thanking God that—I'm waking up every morning, to be able to do this! Only the strong survive!

I asked her how she felt about her husband's incarceration. She answered, "Like I said before…" [her voice dropped to a whisper to ensure her daughter could not hear her response]:

[I feel like] he did it to himself [the incarceration]. I kind of felt like [she took another long pause—a drag off a cigarette] Uhh … let me see here…. I kind of felt like he did it to himself and that basically the response from my friends or family, they would say that he did it to himself. I mean, I know that it was true. But I really didn't want to hear it, you know … but it really made me feel like I was just lost and alone with my thoughts. And the only one I could basically share it with … was him, in a letter or a telephone call. And then there was, if it was just through a telephone call then…. I only had a few minutes, to—you know—kind of speak about that.

Abruptly stopping in mid-sentence, Lotus called out her daughter's name— a searching voice—without covering the phone mouthpiece. She seemed to locate her daughter on the other side of the house, instructing her to "turn down the pot on the stove." She laughed—I laughed, too. She continued: "I'm teaching her how to cook spaghetti…. Like I said before, he was a chronic alcoholic. And I believed—well, I can almost say I know—if he was never incarcerated, then he would have definitely been dead."

Lotus experienced and exhibited a spectrum of emotions during our interview. She laughed and, at times, I thought that she was crying at one point. I then ensured that she was fine and wanted to continue. I imagined that when her life was not in turmoil, she enjoyed her interpersonal relationships with others. She had a way of finding the humorous side of things even when she spoke of sad events.

Lotus veered off topic multiple times, sharing events about her life, including that she is one of 10 children. I learned that she grew up in foster care. She recalled what it was like to have her family torn apart by divorce and the subsequent social services worker mandate to place her siblings in the foster system. She lamented that she did not leave the foster system until she was 16 years old. At that age, she said, school was not a necessity; her life away from a foster parent, who molested her nightly, was her priority.

During our phone interview, I thought I heard Lotus take a long drag on a cigarette—I heard her pause as she inhaled. She had previously asked me to pause as she reached for her "smokes." I think she exhaled before the next disclosure: "My daughter was a miracle baby," she said. According to Lotus, her miracle happened after she prayed earnestly to have this child even though she believed that she was infertile. "God had blessed me with my beautiful daughter." According to Lotus, her daughter adored her father and mother equally. We "were barely hanging on financially" when he was incarcerated. She said she found it hard to manage day to day even though she had a job. To make ends meet, she enrolled in an educational program at work that enabled her to receive specialized training and, with sacrifice, she became a certified professional, able to move up in rank at the hospital.

As she summed up, reflecting on her husband's incarceration and family impact, she indicated that she would never allow *complete separation* of her family. It is my understanding that even though her husband lived in a separate dwelling, he was engaged in their lives. Lotus was determined not to allow her daughter to experience what happened to her during childhood. "Family is too important." Her commitment to the relationship clearly demonstrated as she spoke of her dependency on her husband's phone calls to help stay connected. When his calls did not come in, she worried deeply:

> If I didn't receive a call, I would really be worried a lot. You know? I would … oh, a thousand and one thoughts would go through my head. And it would just be racing. What could be happening to him, or what's happened? Did he get [placed] in the hole or something? Has some incident happened, or is he being sexually abused, somehow? You don't know what's happening, you know? So, you're just in this state where you're just overwhelmed with worry and stress.

I then asked Lotus if she believes that she has changed since the incarceration occurred while they were married, to which she responded:

> Yes, I've gotten stronger. Um…. I've gotten better. Um, I have a lot of remorse. It's changed quite a bit. I—you know, when he got incarcerated, I went and I started a new career, do you know? And it helped me build upon myself as a mother, as a woman, and it made me stronger, and the more I did it … the stronger I got and the better that I felt about myself—after gaining more and more independence.
>
> I still feel anger. I still feel a lot of anger. Um. I got lots of it. You know? Like I said before, there's a lot of regret, you know, that I feel. I feel all depressed at times. Because of the fact—After my husband was [incarcerated], then it had changed a lot. You know? Minus the alcohol, the person—the same person's still there. I um … yeah. So, I'm feeling thousands of different emotions.

WHY NOT LEAVE?

When reading Lotus' story, one might ask why she did not leave her husband when he first started showing signs of verbal abuse, rather than to wait for his aggression to escalate to physical abuse or battery. To gain a perspective, to understand the nature of these relationships, it is helpful to examine issues relevant to domestic violence. The dynamics between couples where domestic violence is present may include the following elements (Buzawa, 2007):

- Conditions of stress may influence the degree of conflict;
- Separation between the partners may cause an escalation of behavior (i.e., due to suspicion, jealousy, or trust issues);
- Unemployment is a trigger for abusive behavior;
- Cohabiting relationships where ambivalence towards marriage may exist, and
- Social isolation where there is a lack of familial support systems.

These risk markers were present in Lotus' story. Financial challenges can be added to her stressful conditions. Additionally, Lotus hoped that her husband would one day remain sober. Instead, he became intermittently unemployed and began drinking again. His multiple failed attempts to achieve sobriety may have manifested as projected anger towards Lotus. Consequently, Lotus believed it was her responsibility to fix the situation and to "fix" him.

"THE FIXER"

Non-incarcerated significant others can feel as though they must take responsibility and solve their incarcerated mate's problems. Lotus stated, "We [are] each other's crutches—to a certain degree."

The term, "fixer," used here, is to illustrate this example of Lotus' perceived role and need to fix her husband's problems. She believed that she held the power and ability to fix him and make circumstances better for her family. Helping professionals may be able to tap into these strengths and resiliency and facilitate a process where Lotus may learn to focus on her own well-being. Lotus appears to have blurred lines of responsibility between what she owns and is responsible for versus that of her husband. She is often the one who rushes to remedy the situation or solve the family problem. By so doing, she perceives that her role is to bear the burden of her husband's shortcomings, as well as her children's issues.

When examining her role in the relationship with her alcoholic husband, the term "co-dependency" comes to mind. The *Encyclopedia of Health* describes the term *codependency or relationship addiction* as a psychological condition whereby, the affected person exhibits learned and unhealthy behaviors stemming from a history of abuse. This condition could also originate from being an offspring of an alcohol or drug abuser

(Hauswirth, 2015). This condition, referred to as *emotional over-investing,* also has characteristics consistent with (Hauswirth, 2015):

- Self-blame for not being able to *fix* other people, especially the alcoholic or perceived broken person;
- Denial and excuses—excusing away the issues of the addict;
- Obsession over other's issues while not spending time focusing on self, and
- Social-detachment and withdrawal.

Researchers have also referred to codependency as the affected person having an overindulgence and belief that someone else can help meet their emotional needs (Daire, Jacobson, & Carlson, 2016). To date, codependency is not included in the Diagnostic and Statistical Manual of Mental Health Disorders (DSM-V), as pathology or impairment. Therefore, clinicians should apply their professional training here. Although loosely defined, this descriptive set of behaviors helps us to understand common features that may be present when a woman is in a relationship at risk for abuse.

To understand relationship bonds further, an examination of attachments, as introduced (Bowlby, 1969). According to Bowlby, early relationships formed during childhood help to shape the lives of adults. Based on this insight, it is likely that Lotus' experience with molestation, abandonment, and being in foster care contributed to her need to cling to attachments even if the relationship was not healthy. She also may hold an ideal family image which is incongruent with her actual family situation and reality. Perhaps, this is the reason why she indicated, "We were invested too deep." Lotus might ultimately fear family breakup as analogous to losing control as a fixer.

"HE TALKED ME OUT OF LEAVING"

Lotus is not alone in trying to hold together her family. Other women in this study also shared their concerns about breakups. Women may stay in a relationship with an incarcerated partner, hinging upon the appearance that the partner is a changed man when imprisoned. Some of the women in this study indicated that their partner changed when he was sober while locked up; they felt sorry for him, he was dependent on them, or for other reasons. Justification for staying in a relationship is conveyed through Lotus' quotes and is demonstrated also by statements from two other women in this study, to whom I give the pseudonyms, Poppy and Violet:

Lotus: I mean, it's a known fact that, you know, women that date men [who are] always in jail, [Women] always say 'the only time you know me or had to give me attention is when you're in jail because you know that I'm going to be the only one to answer your collect calls or write you. The only time you can think about me is when you're in jail or you know this or that.' [However,] me and him work together when he went in, but when he went in and you know a whole bunch of stuff happened, there's this conversations that went on and, you know, I think he was finally realizing,you know, you've always been there for me regardless if we were together or not; you know it wasn't supposed to turn out that way but while you work in there, we wound up getting back together. The kids always want to see mom and dads finally back together. I don't know, it's just hard to explain sometimes when it's ... it's been 20 some years of ...it's had its good and it's had its bad...

Prior to him going in the system, I was ready to divorce him. I was going to send separation papers to him in the jail before he went to prison. But I spared him. He was desperate.

Poppy and Violet had similar thoughts:

Poppy: [I was] just waiting for this man to come home and do the right thing. He has been in and out of prison since he was 10 years old. I didn't mingle with men or no one else. It was just for him.

Violet: We'll keep having his back like we always have, you know; we love him, that's it. But his insecurities made him ... well, what he said was that his insecurities made him do that, and I'm thinking, "Okay. Well, you have me. I'm going to help you out. We're going to get through this."

Based on these accounts, from Lotus, Poppy, and Violet, it is difficult to discern if the men in these relationships are authentic. Some of the women in this study clearly indicated that they were about to discontinue their relationship and were talked back into staying.

"Family is important"

Feeling committed to remain in a relationship may be due to feeling the obligation to keep the family together. Although Lotus was not isolated completely from her family, there appeared to be an undetermined length of isolation and withdrawal after the incarceration of her husband. Recall that she separated from her husband just before his incarceration. However, the dynamics changed when her husband became dependent on her. She believed that she had to be strong for him, as detailed below.

> I wanted to appear strong as if I was the backbone, which I was. Many times, I hid it [the grief]; I hid it well. Because I really didn't want to.... I knew under the circumstances, where he was and what he was going through.

Lotus also reflected upon the importance of her husband's letters as a representation of their relationship. This affinity indicated that she still valued the communication between them. After 24 years, it may have been difficult for Lotus to consider being on her own. Additionally, as stated earlier, Lotus' past, suffering abuse and molestation, places her in a category at risk of domestic abuse as well. Her need for family cohesiveness may have influenced her desire to preserve their relationship as well as retain familial unity, even at the cost of abuse.

Children, too, may hear, witness, and be exposed to domestic violence. Verbal abuse can continue while the partner is incarcerated, whereby the inmate threatens the woman from his jail cell, thereby keeping the victim bound in the relationship.

Similar to the manipulation that Lotus faced, a woman, whom I call *Sage* and who will be introduced more completely in a later chapter, indicated how her incarcerated boyfriend mentally manipulated her:

> I feel like he really tried to get into my head and make me believe all of these lies—that's really why I cut him off. Like, I didn't talk to him for a good amount of time—three years—because I was just super brain-washed, like I didn't want to hear anything about bad news when it came down to talking to me or making a family or anything like that—I was just trying not to hear it. I feel like, that really broke me up because, now, while we're speaking in the physical ... right now in the present, I have a personal vendetta against him—*I feel some type, a way* [mixed feelings] towards him.

Here, Sage spoke of being brainwashed by her incarcerated boyfriend. She also detailed how she created distance from the relationship, but returned; a pattern similar to Lotus.' There appears to be a level of charismatic manipulation by the boyfriend/husband. She also spoke of her denial or not wanting to "hear anything about bad news," as if she wanted only to see and hear about good things. Additionally, telling is her decision about not wanting to discuss the possibility of having a family and children, as a reflection of her anger. This was a way to maintain or assert her control.

Both Lotus and Sage expressed anger and disappointment in their partners. In extreme cases, emotional stress can result in bodily harm or physical self-injury as discussed in Chapter 2.

FAMILY IN CRISIS

When a loved one goes to prison, families may feel an array of emotions yet have limited or no physical contact to resolve their emotional dilemmas. Through Lotus' narrative, we are introduced to the complexities of her life related to: (1) her exposure to the cycle of abuse and need for safety; (2) her role as a fixer; (3) her perception of the importance of family unity, and (4) her need to justify her relationship.

THE CYCLE OF ABUSE

In the present study, as with Lotus and with at least three other cases, I found clear evidence of women's interpretations of emotional manipulation and, perhaps, emotional abuse. For example, Daisy, an interview participant, shared her interaction with her mate:

> He can use manipulation, [in] a situation, I've always said that he has a way of putting words in your head and describing few things ... just getting you to follow his path I found that he makes [me believe] in him like a father figure, and I actually told him this one time. I said, "Okay, fine." And, you know, that's what he said that, you know, like if you have the parent-child relationship within the marriage, eventually the child is going to grow up. And you cannot have that relationship.
>
> He was [at times] controlling—control everything when he was at home. They [the children] had a father since her birth. I mean, he would get mad just like that. And I told him, I said, "You know, one day they'll grow up."

In my study, however, I did not learn of any case where any of the women were in imminent harm or danger. All cases were described as recollections of past behaviors of their significant others. However, each of these cases brings about an important concern and question: *How prevalent is the cycle of abuse in inmate-partnered relationships among incarcerated partner-relationships?* To answer this question is beyond the scope of this text; however, to ensure that women who experience this dynamic receive clarity about safety, it is addressed here.

Indicators of repeat abuse (verbal and/or physical) between intimate partners include in some cases the prevalence of substance abuse and alcohol use by the abuser or perpetrator (Cattaneo & Goodman, 2003). Through Lotus' story, the risk factors associated with abuse were apparent. Some people find it difficult to understand why a woman would possibly go back to a man who verbally or even physically abused her. Answering these questions is challenging and difficult, but, based on contemporary findings from the National Domestic Violence Hotline [NDVH] website, women might remain in abusive relationships because (NDVH, n.d.):

• The affected woman may fear for her life or children's well-being and she may be afraid to leave;

• She may not recognize that the abuse is abnormal. This could stem from having a history of being in abusive relationships where abuse appears commonplace;

• Embarrassment may prevent the woman from sharing her circumstances with others;

• She may not have a high degree of self-worth and/or self-esteem;

• She may feel that she is in love and that maintaining family bonds is the highest priority;

• She may have cultural barriers where leaving is perceived as too difficult;

• She may feel as though she has religious requirement to stay in the relationship;

• She may not have skills to gain employment and support herself, and

• She may feel that she is unable to make it on her own due to a disability.

Offering clinical and nonclinical advice for individuals who are at imminent risk requires real-time intervention; therefore, emergency authorities should be contacted. However, if you are reading this text and you or someone you know is a victim of domestic violence, there are international and national emergency (911) hotlines that can be contacted, as well as your local police department. For additional resources, see the Appendix C.

Only the Strong Survive

Through Lotus' story, we learn how vulnerabilities can affect a mother's views and her role in the family unit. For women, roles can become blurred and somewhat skewed. The line between influence and personal responsibility becomes vague. Lotus took on the role of "fixer" within the family unit. In her mind, her role was to fix all the ills or errors occurring in her family. In the process, Lotus' self-image was marred by failure and the unrealistic vision that she, somehow, could have changed her husband and repaired her husband's alcoholism.

Lotus also experienced stress, recalling moments of "pandemonium," and even feeling victimized by her husband's incarceration. At times, she expressed that she felt that the incidents surrounding her husband's incarceration had depleted her emotional strength. However, she was able to muster courage and train for career change, which enabled her to care for her daughter, pay the bills, and attend to her husband's needs—emotional and financial.

Taking Back Control

Lotus, as did over half (55 percent) of the women in this study, expressed feeling a loss of control at the point of her husband's arrest; for some, this lasted through the continuum of his sentence. The sense of powerlessness perpetuated the need for women to regain control, if not to dominate, in other areas of their lives. For one woman, regaining control meant maintaining a spotless household and subjecting her children to a rigid schedule. As a result, her family members grew concerned that she was becoming a harsh disciplinarian.

Two women indicated that they became fearful of not being in a relationship. There was a genuine sense of a fear of being lonely. This fear was more intense if children were involved. However, some mothers (at least 2), did not inform their children where their father was. These children just assumed the father was missing. Therefore, it is understandable why some women reported their children also felt they were to blame for their fractured family. Women also felt they were to blame, as if *they should have seen the early signs—maybe they could have prevented the situation from happening.*

Adjustment to a Mate's Incarceration

Adjustment to the absent husband and father may be challenging for all members of the family unit, even if the father did not previously live in the home with them. Typically, an intact family is interdependent. The family develops routines—a set of behaviors and expectations—to establish a sense of normalcy. The definition of normalcy is relative to each family. A view of normal" by one family may be abnormal for another.

A case in point: During my interview with Lotus, I learned that her relationship with her husband had suffered disruptions long before his incarceration. However, Lotus still viewed him as her husband and as a part of her family unit and household. She depended on his financial support and expected him to be involved in raising their children. Recall that Lotus said they had separated six months prior to his arrest; although he lived in a separate dwelling, he was nearby and visited often. In Lotus' words, he was "a chronic alcoholic," but he was also the "breadwinner."

From Lotus' disclosure, it is apparent that sudden separation from the primary breadwinner may place multiple strains on the family unit. Women in this position may find that they must take on a second job, start a new career, and, in general, find ways to retool and learn new skills.

THE COST OF SURVIVAL

Although Lotus was able to build a new career, not all women follow a similar path. A lady whom I call *Rose,* indicated that she had to go out and do things about which she was not proud. She suggested that in order to survive the financial loss, she had to engage in embarrassing or illegal activities:

> Sometimes I had to do things I did not want to, just because, at that time, it was a locked gate. He was my everything. He got locked up and I just didn't know what to do. I had to take care of myself. I was messed up. I was really messed up, because, again, he was gone.

When women feel desperate, this mindset may result in committing acts, such as mentioned above, where the woman feels ashamed of what she had to do to survive. It is possible that through their need to survive the crisis, the price to pay is the piling on of guilt and shame for committing acts that are beneath their own ethical and moral standards.

Themes and Insights

While Lotus is the primary participant featured in this chapter, both her story and the integrated quotes from other women illustrate how unique their challenges and coping mechanisms are to the context: mass incarceration.

A loss is not separate from the context in which it occurs. When people suffer loss, their world may not only look bleak, it may also feel bleak. Complicating matters are the social context in which the loss takes place. For example, Lotus could not separate herself from the possible shame of her husband killing another human being by vehicle. The social conditions that shaped Lotus' world also underscore her need for social support. Lotus indicated that she felt a sense of fear and this, coupled with her belief that it was her responsibility to fix others, generated her perception of the burden that her husband's incarceration was hers. Finding ways to cope is a natural response to separation and loss.

Psychological Impacts: Conflicting Emotions

Eighty-percent of the women in this study indicated that they felt as if they were serving a prison sentence of their own. This phenomenon introduces the self-defined concept of feeling vicariously imprisoned. Lotus experienced a range of conflicting emotions in addition to having a need for social isolation. On one hand, she felt strong and able to shoulder the burden of managing her household and even changing careers to earn more income. And on the other hand, there were times where she was fearful, withdrawn, and felt alone. Lotus felt conflicting emotions. She initially conveyed that she wanted to leave her husband. However, she felt a sense of obligation to remain in the relationship because of his incarceration. This type of obligation is, in a sense, a metaphor of Lotus feeling trapped in or imprisoned in the relationship. Perhaps Lotus felt guilty and resentful at the same time.

Social Support as Intervention

Social support, whether through informal networks or formal interventions, may assist women such as Lotus to overcome adversities and regain a sense of control and personal empowerment. A family member's arrest may leave women feeling as though they are powerless and helpless, as half (50 percent) of the women in this study indicated. Common sense tells us that the sooner that women can regain footing in their own lives, the less likely the effect of the feeling of helplessness will have on their lives and families.

Women may seek out support through multiple channels. The church, social services groups, grief support groups, and family relationships can be a source of support. Professional or paraprofessional assistance may include faith-based counseling, therapeutic relationships, professional coaching, domestic violence support groups, and psychoeducational workshops for women. Nonprofits groups can also network and serve as a source of support for women to achieve empowerment through community and advocacy groups. Nonprofits may also provide assistance through tailored services such as anger management, drug, and alcohol treatment, clinical and counseling services available in the community setting. Each of these groups or institutions has the promise of serving in some capacity to help reverse the adverse impacts of incarceration on families and communities.

Lotus would benefit from an intervention that helps her to assume greater personal control over her life. She would benefit from establishing defined goals and a strategy to help her to achieve a sense of purpose and, further, to establish the boundaries of her relationship. There are psychosocial conditions identified in Lotus' narrative that draw attention to the need for healing and self-care. Drawing from the philosophy of positive psychology, a strength-based approach might be effective. Note: The AARM® is an intervention detailed in Chapter 2, and is also fully described and illustrated in Appendix A, using Lotus as an example.

Professional judgment should always take priority when working with individuals who are experiencing trauma and crisis. Most helping professions have ethical codes that embody guidelines that ensure competency and practice when working within client relationships. Having said that, it bears emphasizing that when there are any doubts about how to properly serve the client, adhere to the specific profession's identified code of ethics, local laws, and seek out appropriate professional advice.

Discussion

Students and helping professionals may wish to explore the following areas as a strategy to help women focus on personal self-care and well-being:

• As with mourning a finite loss, when a significant family member goes to prison, the affected person or griever must find ways to understand the loss and develop ways to come to grips with the loss and adjust through learning new ways to cope with the absence (Marron, 1999).

• The family left at home may find that they toggle between resentment and grief. This is due to family members needing to take on roles identified by labels such as breadwinner, head of household, problem solver, protector, handyperson, and other roles that are generally shared or performed by the absent person. Therefore, it may be wise to focus on anger management and even conflict resolution, depending upon priorities identified by the client or affected woman and family members.

• Family counseling may also be a wise alternative.

QUESTIONS TO PONDER

1. At what point should a helping professional intervene in Lotus' life to ensure her safety and well-being?

2. Using a strength-based perspective, how might professionals build a trusting relationship with women similar to Lotus?

3. How might Lotus' entire family benefit from support services provided in a community context?

4. How might Lotus' daughter's ritual of wearing her father's shirt provide a means of comfort?

5. How can clients who are suffering the absence of a loved one use ritual?

6. As a helping professional, how do we ensure that we do not conflate Lotus husband's problems with issues that Lotus must resolve?

2

There Goes
the Neighborhood

The name "Aster" is a pseudonym that I gave to an interviewee who articulated in the best way that she could how her life had been severely impacted by both her husband and children's incarceration. She struggled a bit with conveying her thoughts in a cohesive manner, so rather than providing verbatim quotes here, I string together a picture of her life by integrating her summary, my field notes, and her interview transcript. For clarity, I integrate a historical context related to the geographic area, Washington, D.C., to fill in the blanks so that we begin to understand why her history is so important to understanding her life and its significance to the *war on drugs*. Further, through Aster's story, we learn that having an incarcerated mate can result in adverse economic, social, psychological, and physical issues, which all tend to coalesce. This complex set of phenomena can cause women such as Aster to assess their lives at some point, and begin to ask from an existential perspective, what life is all about.

Case Study: Aster

Aster is a 63-year-old African American woman, who cannot remember a time when she was not grieving the loss of someone, some family member, incarcerated. While being interviewed, Aster described how she felt that almost her entire life reflected one traumatic separation after another. On top of her buried pain and grieving, Aster holds the guilt of gaining over 50 pounds during the past 10 years. She says that she "hates the way her clothes fit." She has currently experienced hair loss, so she wears a wig. "Who cares," she said. "Everyone else in church is wearing one." According to Aster, her days are spent reading the Bible and praying for her incarcerated family members. She laments over the loss of those she holds most dear, but has no control over the circumstances, her imprisoned children, and husband. "They are all locked up," she said.

Aster blames herself for her children's incarceration. She ruminated that this guilt never leaves her mind. She says she is reminded of her loss everywhere she goes, even at church, especially when she observes families who are fortunate enough to worship together. She envies these families, and she wonders what she could have done or should have done to prevent her family's incarceration. These thoughts circle around in her mind until she feels completely miserable. Survivor's guilt consumes her as she searches for answers within herself but "comes up short, every time." Although a deeply spiritual woman, Aster said she "is losing [her] faith—tired of struggling—tired of praying—tired."

Aster has lived all her life in Washington, D.C., a city once coined as "Chocolate City" because of its high population of Black residents. During 2015, a survey conveyed that, of Washington, D.C.'s 601,000 residents, 305,000 are Black, 231,000 are White, and approximately 65,000 are Non-White Hispanic or categorized as Other (Suburbanstats.org, 2015).

WASHINGTON, D.C., CRACK DEALING AND GENTRIFICATION

Aster and her husband raised their children in their home, located in Washington, D.C., during the height of the crack cocaine era; specifically the 1980s through the late 1990s. This area of the country was a difficult place to raise children and maintain a healthy family, especially if you were poor and lived in the public housing projects. During that time period, crack cocaine proliferated throughout drug markets in Washington, D.C.; the drug was sold by dealers in low-income communities similar to Aster's. According to Aster, her neighborhood was one of the most depressed areas in the city. Based on Aster's recollection, a drive down a city block any time of the night or even the early hours of the morning would surely yield clusters of drug dealers making transactions publicly to those who craved this inexpensive drug. The geographic configuration of some neighborhoods in D.C. made it easy access for foot traffic and drug sales. At the same time, police raids were difficult because the configuration also supported *lookout* spots. Clients seeking to make a purchase from dealers felt secure, as police were often challenged gaining unencumbered access via police vehicle. For example, the dealers discovered they could place couches and other abandoned furniture as obstacles in the streets to slow down the police access via vehicles (Fenston, 2014).

Based on Aster's account, she lived in the heart of this type of neighbor-hood.

Amidst the backdrop of drug markets, heavy foot traffic, and derelict activities, children played in the streets, walked to school, and lived in communities of social disorganization. One might begin to wonder whether Aster's children ever stood the chance of avoiding this exposure to the drug-infested environments all around them.

To provide an even broader perspective, one which also aligns with Aster's reflection, one D.C. resident stated that when he was growing up, people were either selling drugs or purchasing them (Fenston, 2014). He began his career as a lookout or *watch-boy*—a young child who played in the streets and informed the drug dealers when the police were coming. At the time, he believed he had only two options for future job prospects: sell or be-sold-to. He decided to sell (Fenston 2014). It is difficult to tell whether Aster's children felt the same way. She indicated that she tried to influence each of her three children to stay in the church rather than to use or sell drugs—one by one, they became "caught-up" and either "went to jail repeatedly," or ultimately ended up in prison for selling or using drugs. They are now "all are scattered across the map." With this reference of being scattered across the map, Aster refers to her children being sentenced to serve time in a federal penitentiary because as stated earlier, Washington, D.C., does not have its own prison. Therefore, inmates from this area serve sentences as far away as California and Washington State.

As Aster enters her mid-sixties—an age where she imagines that others are enjoying retirement—she is alone, isolated from her family through no fault of her own. She is angry and bitter that life turned out the way it did, with her husband and her children behind bars.

For Aster, travel is difficult and costly. The cost of traveling to four different prisons in four different states is beyond her financial means. Additionally, as she calculates the cost of phone calls, prison e-mails, and even the cost to access kiosks that may provide video visits, all add up to exceed her social security budget.

Aster is also angry, for instance, because she does not have family in attendance with her as do other church members. She feels that she is missing out on life. She expressed that she cannot look forward to her boys giving her grandchildren to dote over because co-ed relationships are not possible in most prisons. Instead, she lives in a community that once had high incarceration rates and high crime. Her community was known for its drugs trafficking, high poverty, inadequate schools, and high unemployment—all occurring in the nation's capital—the epicenter of politics.

Aster's reflections and insights on how Washington, D.C., changed cannot be taken for granted. She said she believes that at the time of high crime and drug activities, politicians turned a blind eye to solutions that would have improved conditions and benefitted those living in crime-infested neighborhoods. Aster indicated she thought that rather than providing support and solutions for the residents, lawmakers decided to make a clean sweep through neighborhoods to arrest people for drugs, following suit with the rest of the nation's movement towards mass imprisonment of offenders as a part of the *war on drugs* (Collett, 1989).

Drug treatment was not the popular option. Instead, between 1980 and 2011, the federal prison population increased from 316,000 to 1.5 million, with another 750,000 in locally run jails (Kasparian, 2016), largely due to drug related crimes.

Aster finds it difficult to separate her current circumstances from her history because she believes that her past is responsible for her present life conditions. She recalled, in decades past, her neighborhood was one of the most rundown parts of the city—a place where turf wars took place and open-air drug markets thrived. Two decades ago, a significant number of apartments were Section 8, government-subsidized housing projects. These projects were notorious for their prevalence of *crack-prostitution* or (perpetrated by those identified by the street name, *crack-hoes;* meaning having sex in exchange for crack). There was low police presence. Berlin (2014) reported that these areas were considered a place where there were "Kids who grew up together [and] suddenly had guns ... and were fighting in the street" (p. 1).

To outsiders, Aster's world and present social conditions in public housing may be viewed as a neighborhood nuisance. She may be viewed as a victim of her own choosing, living in a public eyesore—right in the middle of a now thriving community. However, to Aster, this was home. Women like Aster, who remained in the same neighborhood for years after the crack epidemic, may not have the financial means, the education, or skill sets to leave public housing. Additionally, ex-offenders who return home from prison to their families may also find that they are no longer wanted or even allowed in the communities from which they originated.

This is because public housing regulations may prevent certain ex-offenders from occupying a government-subsidized dwelling. One challenge that this introduces for a family that is dependent on government subsidy is that they must choose between their relationship and housing.

As Aster reflects on her losses, all beyond her control, surely her community and social conditions highlight yet one more loss. She now finds herself in the middle of an existential crisis where she continually asks: What happened to her life? With the neighborhood thriving and changing, Aster fears possible displacement from her home, given the gentrification of the city.

SOCIAL CONDITIONS:
CRIME AND GENTRIFICATION

Aster's history and community conditions certainly have some level of impact on her life. Aster lives in only one of the approximately 56 public housing projects in Washington, D.C. These projects account for more than 20,000 residents who occupy 8,000 units (D.C. Housing Authority, n.d.). Aster said the new neighborhood is upscale and has mixed dwellings; comprised of townhouses and condominiums are all around the perimeter of the public housing projects. All of these new residential areas are conveniently located near mass transit subway and bus routes. She said these modern dwellings appear to be sprouting up all around her home, which is now located in the middle of public housing projects, surrounded with "shiny, tall, mirrored buildings" and contemporary urban sprawl. There are food markets, charter schools, and bicycle rental racks, and public transportation to get across town. Aster appears to be a bit envious of the new amenities provided for the new residents.

The patterns of gentrification are quite revealing in understanding why people like Aster remain in the housing projects. The patterns of residence can be understood through The Office of the Chief Financial Officer of Washington, D.C., who examined behaviors of tax filers to understand gentrification and to further detail who established residency in D.C. and who is likely to leave the city and move to the suburbs. This office found two interesting patterns, based on tax return filings: poor families were more likely to move out of the city, while educated high-income individuals were likely to move in and stay in the city (Office of the Chief Financial Officer [OCFO], 2015). Income earners with annual incomes that were below $14,000 were more likely to leave the city (OCFO, 2015) because they could not afford the high rents. However, women such as Aster may not even be in a position to leave the city to find residence outside the projects or be able to move to areas such as Virginia or Maryland suburbs. As Aster indicated, she has a fixed income and limited ability to find affordable housing inside or outside of the city. This condition probably adds to Aster's anger, envy, and belief that she is "stuck."

Change did not happen overnight. To restore social control, city workers boarded up abandoned properties to prevent drug users from designating these spaces as *crack houses*. This change took time. As Aster indicated, neighborhood gentrification happened over a couple of decades. Her husband and children were a part of the arrest and cleanup.

As a final reflection, Aster said, "Life has changed and I learned a lot. With her husband being in there [in prison], you see a lot going wrong—I guess with my husband and sons in there [prison]. My son was in there for six years and he got out and went back on a technical [violation]."

After decades, Aster appears to be still suffering much pain. To have her family torn apart and to believe that she could have saved them was, and is, difficult for her. As I interviewed her, she spoke in a low, raspy voice. She told me that in the past, her income always hovered at or below minimum wage; now she receives a social security check. This money pays her rent. She divides her disposable income between prison accounts for her incarcerated husband and incarcerated children, and the rest goes to church tithing.

Aster did not reveal much about her educational background. However, she said she used to have an active role in her church where she maintained records for one of the church ministries. While this work seemed to have given her meaning and purpose, she has pulled away from active engagement. As we returned to our discussion on her husband's incarceration, it became clear to me that both time and multiple life crises had taken a toll on her relationship. She seemed to reflect more on her children, the neighborhood, and how she felt. Aster also indicated that she struggled with her spirituality and she felt as though she was losing her faith–"mad at God." Aster described how one day she stood in front of a window, reflecting on her life. She felt so much anger and pain at that moment, that she "punched [her fist] through the glass."

Themes and Insights

To understand what intervention might serve Aster as a client, we can examine the psychological impact and examine her coping strategies. We should also consider an intervention that may help to open the lines of communication and help her to establish goals of building a support network.

Psychological Impacts:
An Existential Crisis

Aster is 63 years old. She, seemingly, has spent half of her life alone, supporting incarcerated family members both emotionally and financially. Her quality of life has declined over the years and now she is having an existential crisis. She is angry and bitter with her incarcerated family members, her community, and even with God. She admits that she is envious of other people in church who have an intact family. Perhaps she feels she should have been granted the privilege to have that type of life. She also appears to be having a spiritual crisis of sorts. Recall that she indicated that she was tired and hinted at her faith being questioned. An intervention might include exploring Aster's support system at the church. Through this spiritual connection, she may find a sense of purpose and meaning in her life.

Grief and guilt from separation and loss of her incarcerated family members are prominent emotions in Aster's life. Aster may feel abandoned and angry about being left alone. However, she is a survivor. She has made it through the tough times of the Washington, D.C., drug epidemic. Aster appears to spend a great deal of time alone without the support of extended family. An interventionist may wish to explore how she could build or establish a stronger support system especially during times when she is lonely.

Aster's bitterness and anger conveys that she has a deep sense of frustration and, further, that she feels disempowered and stuck. Interventionists or helping professionals might work with Aster to uncover ways to work through her anger and to begin setting goals for her life and make new meaning. Also of concern is that she limits her social interaction as she mostly remains inside her household. In a way, it appears that she is punishing herself by staying indoors. She may also isolate from the public to protect herself and her image. As we review Aster's case, we sense that she is resentful that while her neighborhood has transformed, she is bitter that change did not occur when her family needed rescuing from the drug wars and crime. She does not feel welcome in her own community. Helping professionals working with women similar to Aster's may wish to determine if her anger poses a risk for self-harming as well.

Coping Strategies and Intervention

Aster's suffers from stress and anxiety, and she indicated that she has gained weight. Helping professionals may wish to discuss the possibility of physical fitness and exercise with Aster where she can adapt to a healthier lifestyle. Physical activities may alleviate her stress and anxiety. Activities outside of her home may also prevent her from feeling physically isolated and alone. Helping professionals should also be concerned about her physical injury as a priority. Based on Aster's story, her anger appears to be based on her loss of opportunities in life. Goal setting may help with this issue, but there is concern that self-inflicted injury could place her as a high risk of harming herself.

The effectiveness of coping strategies and intervention may be dependent largely upon a person's current self-awareness, priorities, and concerns. Therefore, helping professionals may wish to use an integrative approach for intervention strategies. In my own practice in working with women with incarcerated mates, I have used what I refer to as the Awareness, Assessment, Reframe, and Matched-Response (AARM®). I designed this intervention as a to that I use during psychoeducational workshops as explained below.

AWARENESS, ASSESSMENT, REFRAME AND MATCHED-RESPONSE (AARM®) MODEL

As a means of establishing effective communication, raising self-awareness, and establishing role clarity, I developed the AARM® intervention model. The propositions that underpin the use of this model are:

1. **Adverse Events May Influence Guilt and Women's Roles Become Blurred:** Women similar to Aster may believe that their lives are governed by their environments. This is generally referred to as an external locus of control. Aster believed that the drug-infested environment in her neighborhood influenced her husband and children going to prison and that she had little control over her life events. This left her feeling bitter and, at times, helpless. It is unclear whether Aster has always been in the role of provider and supporter to her family, but, in her current role, she is the breadwinner or sole supporter of her incarcerated family. Self-evaluation theory holds that a person's self-appraisal is based on how people view their roles in their environment as it aligns with their self-esteem, emotional stability, and emotional constitution (Johnson, Rosen, Chang, & Lin, 2015). Therefore, triggering events such as arrest or incarceration of a loved one can stimulate thoughts of being a target of ill fate. Faulty reasoning may also lead women like Aster to take ownership of a problem (that is not rightfully theirs to solve) as if *they* somehow are to blame for the outcome of their mate's incarceration. Aster certainly has stepped into the role of provider for her family. Faulty logic can also lead to self-blame

and feelings of failure—mainly because women may feel that, somehow, they are able to control the behavior of others. This misguided logic may also influence *emotional thought loops* where the individual continuously replays thoughts in her mind about how she could have and should have done things differently. However, this thinking only reinforces the notion of the individual's perceived shortcomings and failure, which reduces effective coping. Interventionists working with women similar to Aster, may wish to explore to what degree the person feels guilty or responsible for their significant other's incarceration.

2. **Affected Women's Emotional Well-Being is Believed to be Predicated on an External Source:** Consistent with the previous proposition, women similar to Aster believed if only their mate was not incarcerated, they would be happy. For example, Aster would find herself envying others in church. She also felt victimized as if she was left all alone or abandoned by her family. However, Aster appears to still have hope that one day her family would be released, and together. Anything short of having her family at home seems to mean that life is not worth embracing. This thinking brings about what some scholars refer to as all-or-nothing thinking (Uncommon Knowledge Ltd, 2001–2016), where events are either all wonderful or all bad—no in between.

3. **Distorted Reflection Leads to Faulty Expectations:** Aster cannot control people outside of herself. Therefore, she is likely to feel as though she is failing each time she creates this expectation to do so. Her loss is proportionate with her reflection of accumulated loss, failed attempts to save her family, and overall misfortune. The more that she believes that she could have modified the past in some way, the greater the consequence of a failed attempt and delivery. Therefore, as she reflects on her past, her thoughts of being able to save her family is a distorted sense of ownership of the problem. This distortion is commensurate with feelings of guilt for not saving her family. This status is likely a contributor to her feeling the need to punish herself by limiting her activities, staying at home, and feeling angry and victimized.

An Intervention

Based on my workshops, the AARM® model can raise awareness and help individuals clear distorted thinking. I use this tool to generate a discussion about roles and responsibilities and help affected women develop a sense of who really owns the problem. This exercise also works well with goal setting.

When holding my sessions, I encourage women to engage in an introspective examination of what they are feeling specific to having an incarcerated mate. What I have found, more often than not, is that the issues involving the mate's incarceration (e.g., court hearings, sentencing, financial support, personal safety), are all-consuming and overwhelming, which reinforces distorted thinking of who own's their mate's problems. Conversely, I found that 80 percent of the women disregarded their own priorities and advanced their mate's responsibilities and personal choices as a primary concern. If the women's roles, priorities, and sense of self becomes blurred with their mate's lives and affairs, it is understandable how they might be prone to emulate his state of social isolation. As a note, in this study, I refer to this phenomenon as *Vicarious Imprisonment (A subset of* Symbolic Imprisonment, Grief and Coping Theory), as explained in Part II of this book.

This entanglement of who owns the problem and what priority should be given is not always easy for women to determine. The women with whom I spoke appeared strong, with determination and grit. Their natural instincts are to care for others and, first, fix things outside of themselves. As a result, there is little attention paid to what they are really feeling. When they do pay attention to their own thoughts, when they self-assess, they find that they have placed so much responsibility and blame on themselves for failing to change a situation (for example, of their mate's status) that they tend to feel and express that they deserve punishment. To achieve healing, it becomes important to raise self-awareness and clarify roles and responsibility as a first step.

An Example of the AARM® Model

The following is an explanation of the AARM® intervention model. To illustrate its use, we can apply it to Aster's scenario. Helping professionals may use this model as a communication tool. Affected women may use this tool as a means of establishing clarity about their role in a relationship. The goal is to identify what appears to be distressing the individual, establish clear boundaries of responsibility, and develop reasonable goals to foster well-being.

Before helping professionals, clergy, or other professionals begin the AARM® exercises, it is important to establish a foundation of trust. Trust may be gained through building a rapport through empathetic listening, with limited self-disclosure. I generally like to ask women to share what they feel comfortable sharing and as a result, women tend to open up and share their feelings as if it is a form of relief and catharsis. Generally, trust-building and rapport occurs when women determine that I am genuine and that I guard their confidentiality as a priority. After a rapport is established, the helping professional can facilitate the following steps.

Step 1. Raise Awareness: The first step involves raising self-awareness. The activity used to stimulate role clarity is entitled *Circles and Roles*® (see Figure 2.1). The participant will perform the following simple steps:

a. Describe a circumstance that you would like to change for the better. Try to limit the description to one or two sentences. Write this statement at the bottom of a blank piece of paper (preferably 8 × 11 inches) or a whiteboard.

b. Draw a circle on the left side of the paper or whiteboard. This circle represents one's life view.

c. Think of the people who are involved with the situation and create one circle that represents each person (Guidance: use nouns [person, place, or things]). Allow ample room between circles and the edges of the page.

d. Draw outward spokes or arrows extending from each circle (see Figure 2.1). Next, label these spokes or arrows as verbs or adjectives that describe each person's role, identity, and responsibility (related to the context of the situation described in step a). All labels are appropriate. There is no wrong label.

Note: At this stage, do not try to solve any problems. The purpose is to understand how Aster, or you, or your client sees the context of the situation (see Figure 2.1).

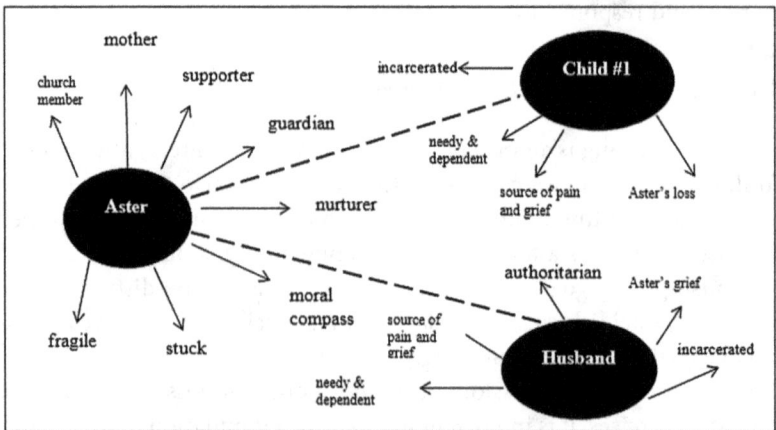

Figure 2.1. Circles and Roles (Current State—Aster's World View). Circles represent nouns; dashed line depict relationships; spoked arrows point to adjectives and verbs describing roles and perceived responsibilities or circumstances.

I generally refrain from asking women in my support groups to tackle big problems at the outset, but rather work on smaller problems to build a rapport with the client. Clients must feel comfortable and safe to share their experiences. Establishing a nondirective trusting environment is critical. The power of the AARM®️ model is that it is not an evaluation or an assessment, but rather a means of discussing the situation(s) women may be encountering. The client decides the most important topic for discussion.

Step 2. Assessment: This step involves a facilitated exploration of the linkages and relationships identified in the diagram the client has drawn. From this discussion, you and the client can explore each of the labels and their intrinsic roles and meaning. Probe questions might include:

a. Think about your roles or relationship with the people or entities you identified in your circles. What do these labels represent?

b. Who assigned the responsibility attached to each label?

c. What would happen if the perceived owner of the role did not fulfill his or her responsibility?

d. What role did you play in the presenting issue of concern?

Guidance: As a reminder, try not to solve problems at this stage. Remain focused on gaining clarity about relationships and the meaning of the labels. Annotations as notes on the diagram can clarify these interpretations.

Step 3. Reframe: Role clarity begins with reframing the situation through a lens that is not filtered, cluttered with inaccurate distortions. Therefore, appropriate probes to help (you or your client) gain this clarity may include answering the following questions to begin reframing thoughts specific to the labels.

a. How would you modify these roles in a manner that is consistent with your future goals?

b. If these roles were in alignment with your goals or desired results, how might these labels change or look different?

c. How could you relabel these attributes with labels that are consistent with your goals?

d. Mark through existing labels and replace with your desired labels.

Step 4. Match Response: This step is action-based. The following probes help establish goal setting.

a. Which of these labels belong to you, alone?

b. Of those roles that belong to you, which ones can you perform with complete autonomy?

c. What is the first step necessary to accomplish this goal? Repeat for the second, third, fourth, and so forth and so on.

Items a and b help the client to differentiate between having influence for change and actually being able to make change. This step should be facilitated with a discussion about who actually owns the problem. Proceed cautiously as a helping professional because the client may become guarded about her "problem ownership." This could be because her helping role and problem-solving role is linked to her identity as a mate. Additionally, try to ensure that her priorities are realistic and achievable. It is not necessary to redraw the diagram if new labels are needed. The diagram will evolve to match reasonable and realistic goals. Additional probes to generate thoughts about goal setting include:

- What reasonable steps can you take, given your current resources?
- To achieve your goal, what influence is reasonable to promote this change?
- What are the steps that you can take that are consistent with your desires or goals?
- How might your actions differ from the actions of others?
- How might your actions differ from that which you have tried in the past?

Example of a Possible Outcome: Aster will decide what issue she wants to focus on as her priority. Her diagram/drawing is a tool for provoking discussion or thoughts about the identified situation in need of attention. This drawing serves multiple purposes. Aster can safely explore her world, roles, perceptions, in a manner that is nonjudgmental. She decides who is presented in her life view. This is a clue as to who are the important people involved in the situation.

If a helping professional is facilitating the process, he or she will learn more about the client's worldview, presenting challenges, and values assigned to significant attachments. You, the professional, may learn about her perceived roles and responsibilities. The important first step is to begin the understanding about who Aster perceives herself to be. It is possible that, as a helping professional, you can help Aster to see how she lacks a support network. She may then explore how to expand this network in a manner that would increase her quality of life.

Clarity: About the AARM® Process

As shown in Figure 2.1, the Circles and Roles is used as a tool to facilitate a broad discussion about one's personal worldview. I used Aster's data to show how she might perceive herself: a church member, mother, supporter, guardian, nurturer, moral compass, or stuck, and fragile. Each label can be very telling. From this diagram, Aster might ask herself: What is causing me to feel stuck? This may open a line of thinking and communication about why she feels angry, immobile, and helpless. Perhaps her answer is a lack of financial means to leave the neighborhood. It is also possible that she feels that she is stuck in the relationship. Notice that her role as wife is not listed. This could be telling, as well. This may indicate that she no longer wants to be in the relationship. However, this diagram is a query rather than an assumption tool.

When creating the diagram, the women are encouraged not to focus on drawing a perfect design. This tendency may show up because those who feel responsibility for "fixing" things may also feel the need for perfection. Additionally, it is important not to overly focus on the labels. The point is not to focus on right or wrong. The exercise is nonjudgmental and non-evaluative. This exploration helps women to establish a foundation for role clarity. There is no right or wrong role assignment.

Another use of the Circles and Roles® is to draw the "as is" or "current state" circles that represent what her roles are currently. The next step would be to create the desired "future state" circles of roles. This exploration may provide insights into what ideal roles could be in a world where the presenting problem is solved or more congruent with the future goals.

For example, perhaps Aster may label a spoke depicting a wish that her child would earn higher education. A probe question might be: How might your child acquire higher education? Her answer may include, "he could earn a GED while in federal prison." This discussion may help Aster to realize that it is her child's responsibility to earn the education—she can only influence his decision. Additionally, through this discussion, Aster recognizes that she bears no responsibility or limited responsibility for her son completing the GED. This also helps to raise awareness about self-perceptions. She may then proceed through steps 2 through 4 of the model to decide upon appropriate steps to respond to the situation. The helping professional may facilitate working through these steps using an iterative set of steps, and it is not necessary to follow the steps in order. However, it is important to raise awareness first. One final note of caution is that women who are *heavily grieving* may not be ready to perform this type of exercise. Therefore, I repeat that establishing a foundation of trust and rapport is critical before working with the AARM®.

In summary, the AARM® is a simple communication tool, not a clinical intervention. The awareness piece of the model helps women to ask: What is going on here? What am I really feeling? The assessment is concerned with the woman asking herself: What am I able to do in response to this problem, and to be able to examine the pros and cons associated with the situation. The reframing is an action that firsts ask the women to make a plan of action "using a clearer definition of her new role" or clarified role and sphere of influence. This action moves the women from being stuck to a place of empowerment to make decisions. Finally, as she reframes her thoughts and actions, she moves from a state of disempowerment to that which is moving towards a solution. *Note: Even the contemplation of a goal is a success for women who feel stuck. This step is worthy of acknowledgment, because to do so moves one from a state of immobilization to small steps towards awareness and action.*

Integrative Approach. The AARM® and *Circles and Roles®* are compatible with other interventions, such as spiritual counseling. Intervention may be individualized and integrated. I have found that the AARM® is easily applied. Aster expressed having an existential crisis of sorts. Therefore, a helping professional may wish to address how spirituality fits in to the process of role clarity and meaning making. When roles are clarified, the distortion tends to be cleared, and guilt alleviated.

Spirituality as Coping. Clergy, clinical counselors, even leaders of local support groups could provide intervention for women with incarcerated partners. Using a strength-based approach or an integrative approach, there is opportunity to help Aster to redefine her role in life and to find new meaning in a world where she no longer has access to her children and husband.

Over half of the women in this study (55 percent) indicated that spirituality was an important coping mechanism. Women's references to God varied:

- "it's just knowing that—thanking God that—I'm waking up every day."
- "I'd pray and I just ask God for strength; I would smoke some marijuana."
- "Believe it or not, through my family and my church. I, is still ... the one thing is, I've always told everybody and I believe— When it gets to be to a point that you can't handle it, put your hands up, throw it to God and let God deal with it."

Discussion

While understanding Aster's emotional state is fundamental to providing an intervention to contribute to her healing, we cannot ignore her environmental conditions. It is reasonable to understand why Aster is angry when we examine the social conditions stemming from the crack epidemic and the drug war that she endured during the 1980s and 1990s.

Box 2.1. Background and Context the War on Drugs in Washington, D.C.

During the 1980s and 1990s, Washington, D.C., had a serious drug problem. Crack cocaine was so rampant in the city that in September 1989, President George Herbert Walker Bush went on national television, declaring the nation's capital a "battle-zone" in the war on drugs (Fenston, 2014). To express his concern to the American public, while he was seated in the Oval Office, television cameras zoomed in to focus on the content in his hand— a plastic baggy of the off-white, soap-like substance known as crack cocaine (Fenston, 2014). The bag of drugs held by the sitting president, confiscated by law enforcement, was said to have come from drug dealers located across the street from the White House, in Lafayette Park. While this display by the president was dramatic in substantiating his battle cry, others indicated, "This is crack cocaine, was … seized a few days ago in a park across the street from the White House.… It could easily have been heroin or PCP" (Isikoff, 1989, p. A01).

… [O]btaining the crack [as a prop for the President's White House televised briefing] was no easy feat. To match the words crafted by the speech-writers, Drug Enforcement Administration agents lured a suspected District drug dealer to Lafayette Park four days before the speech so they could make what appears to have been the agency's first undercover crack buy in a park [Layfette Park] better known for its location across Pennsylvania Avenue from the White House than for illegal drug activity, according to officials familiar with the case.

In fact, when first contacted by an undercover DEA agent posing as a drug buyer, the teenage suspect seemed baffled by the agent's request.

"Where the _____ is the White House?" he replied in a conversation that was secretly tape-recorded by the DEA. [Michael Isikoff, *Washington Post* Staff Writer, Friday, September 22, 1989, Page A01].

Whether the president's actions were staging or truth, public officials, and lawmakers targeted certain areas of the city as *hot spots* for possible drug sales. At that time, crack was more affordable at ($5.00 or $10.00 for a pea-size portion) than powdered cocaine, the elite drug that may have cost $50.00 for a similar amount (Fenston, 2014). With the cost so low, it was affordable for young and old to access and consume. This drug was also highly addictive and produced a sense of nirvana in its users: "Smoking crack produces an intense, euphoric high, but it's gone in five or ten minutes, leaving users desperate for more. This is part of what made crack so profitable for dealers: there was a steady stream of return [in] customers" (Finston, 2014, p. 2). As a political response to President Bush's request, Washington, D.C., Police Chief Isaac Fullwood's law enforcement officers began massive arrests of close to 800–900 people on weekends alone (Fenston, 2014).

In summary, Aster's social condition, the impacts on her psychologically, and her physical responses to separation and loss are contributors to her isolation and withdrawal or *Symbolic Imprisonment*. In her state of withdrawal, Aster tends to refrain from seeking external support, even from the church. Her anger has escalated, whereby she may be facing a higher risk of self-inflicted physical harm. It is also possible that her existential crisis is a sign that she has lost faith in the church and God, which has been her spiritual support for so long. Aster feels fear and anger. She feels as though the community is changing and fears that it is just a matter of time before she is displaced, given the emergent gentrification. She speaks of the changes in the neighborhood occurring all around her.

At this stage, it may be meaningful to move away from Aster's specific story, and close out this section with an historical overview, a description of the scale and conditions of the drug epidemic in Washington, D.C. (See Box 2.1.) The so-called "war on drugs" in Washington, D.C., and the nation occurred within the time frame of Aster's reflective story.

Practitioners should not discount the role in which understanding a client's background to determine how issues such as drugs, housing, and incarceration could intersect in her life and exacerbate her concerns as a grieving wife and mother.

QUESTIONS TO PONDER

The following questions are discussion points for helping professionals to examine as you reflect upon Aster's case study and consider appropriate interventions.

1. What strategies will you use to bracket biases specific to incarceration, prison, or drugs in order to provide effective intervention for Aster?

2. What are the social conditions that led to Aster's resentment?

3. Given what you know about Aster, what steps would you take to facilitate a discussion about Aster achieving positive change and improved well-being?

4. What are ways that Aster may transform her resentfulness to empowerment?

5. How might Aster find relief from her seemingly *Symbolic Imprisonment (a.k.a. vicarious imprisonment)*?

6. Explain how Aster may or may not progress toward involvement in civic or social advocacy as a means of empowerment?

7. What are reasonable goals for Aster to set on a short-and long-term basis?

3

The Cost of Remaining Connected

Financial burdens placed on a non-incarcerated significant other can come at a high economic and psychological cost, especially for those who are emotionally invested in these relationships. Families generally pay significantly to stay connected to a loved one in prison. The exorbitant costs associated with out-of-state phone communications, for instance, add to the complexities and difficulties for women trying to maintain their relationships with incarcerated mates. Letter writing is one form of communication, but even this method has restrictions in states such as Maryland that ban families from sending greeting cards and other paper products that could be used to transport contraband. In this section, we learn more about the emotional side of staying in contact, as we read through Willow's story.

Case Study: Willow

Willow is a self-identified African American female who is over the age of 18. She does not provide her exact age as she agrees to informed consent. Willow does not have any children. She lives in Washington, D.C. During our interview, it appeared that she needed to talk about how her relationship made her feel about herself.

Willow stated that, at one time, she believed that she was a strong Black woman, able to withstand all sorts of adversity "but this prison thing was too much." She said that each time a crisis occurred which was associated with her boyfriend's incarceration, it chipped away at her fabric, and her confidence, and "left her bare—raw—unprotected." She described her experiences of failing to support her confined boyfriend as a constant reminder of being the incompetent young girl she used to be while growing up. For instance, visiting the prison was a challenge. Sending him clothing sometimes resulted in not providing the right size or color apparel. Consequently, failing to meet her boyfriend's expectations left her with haunting thoughts of worthlessness that crept back into her psyche and, mentally, she felt reduced to a child-like status. These feelings were based both on her self-perceived shortcomings and her boyfriend's insults. This was especially true when her boyfriend argued with her during the expensive collect phone calls made from prison. She reflected that the irony of it was that she was indirectly paying for these personal assaults via funding his prison commissary, which enabled her mate to make the calls. To Willow, the reasons for the arguments did not matter because, regardless of topic, he made her feel that she fell short of being a "good woman."

Willow said her boyfriend blamed her for all that went wrong. He was upset because she could not arrange a prison visit. He was upset that she did not blend in well with his family members. He was upset that she did not put money on the books or prison commissary as often as he liked. It was "all her fault." Willow said she did not know his family that well and, besides, they did not like her. Willow deeply reflected on how challenging it was for her to deal with her boyfriend and his demands:

> Well, when he first went to prison, we interacted very frequently because he was right at the DC jail. It was easy for me to get back and forth over there. He called me every day. So, we communicated a lot. [During] the visits, you sit behind a glass and you're on a phone. I used to go Wednesdays and Fridays and it would be a half an hour visit. So, we communicated a lot and then, just like that, it went on, where I could say [it was] maybe a year. Then he was sentenced and sent to Kentucky.
>
> When he went to Kentucky, we communicated, but the phone calls were our communication; it got lesser. I guess because it was different financially—it all attributed to [feeling] the separation.
>
> [I recall] one time when his mother and them was going up there [to the Kentucky prison] to see him. I had put in a business trip [at work], but for some reason, it was some things on my [criminal] record that wasn't allowing [the prison] to put me on the visitor list. So, I had to go downtown to get all these papers and file motions and all this stuff to get this stuff off my record and, oh my god—so he's calling and stressing me out about sending these papers down there and coming to Kentucky with his mother and them. But I'm so mentally drained by the situation with my son [newly incarcerated], I really didn't have the energy or the motivation to go down there to these courts and [file] all these motions and do all this stuff.
>
> But I wasn't able to explain that to him. If I'm not mistaken, I told lies, like he'd call and [ask me] did I go down there, and I'd say: "Yeah, I went and they're giving me the runaround."
>
> So, that put friction on the relationship. I was never—I could never just say to

him the truth and ... he didn't really understand it, when I'm like, "This is too much for me. I can only deal with one thing at a time."

Either I said it [that I can't deal with this] and he didn't understand it, or maybe I didn't even say it [clear enough], but I wasn't able to communicate with him openly, so it really seemed like I was closing him off.

SADNESS AND LIES: A VICIOUS CYCLE

Willow said that she felt like a liar. A new loss interrupted her world. Her son went to prison. She explained that she felt that she should have prevented her boyfriend's incarceration. Now, her son was in prison and she just couldn't do things the right way. To Willow, it was all her fault and the associated guilt was exhausting her. Besides, she said, she also had her own problems to remedy concerning an item showing up on her own criminal record. This sanction prevented her from visiting her son and boyfriend in prison. It appeared that issues of her past had come back to haunt her. Now, exposed to her boyfriend and his family, she did not want to go back and forth to the courts to pursue having her criminal record expunged. Maybe she was afraid, or perhaps her lack of follow-through was an excuse to back out of the relationship. She felt overwhelmed, with too much going on at the same time, while trying to financially support two people in prison.

THE NARCISSISTIC MATE CAN BE CONTROLLING

Incarceration strains relationships. Relationships can become unbalanced when the incarcerated man or non-incarcerated women must negotiate new ways to reciprocate each other's gestures of love and work through arguments. For example, prison phone calls have a 30-minute restriction. There is generally a 30-second warning before the phone is disconnected. This can be disconcerting, to say the least, if a couple is in the middle of an important discussion or argument. Further complicating issues are the often encountered narcissistic behaviors of the inmates. Viewed from the woman's perspective, I interpret and entitle this phenomenon, *charismatic and controlling encounters*. Willow and 75 percent of the women in this study indicated that their husbands or boyfriends were sometimes caring and during others, self-centered, focusing solely on their own needs and wants, as a few of the women shared here:

"He was a gentleman when he needed to be; he will do that to, like, all the women he wants to be with, you know, it was just—he was real. He was real when most people call him to be real, he was real…. Regardless of all the bullshit and all the baggage in the past, it just made me feel like, you know, that's my man."

"So, at certain times, I was like, 'Would you like to be plastic or real?'"

"He was—controlling, control everything when he were at home."

"He's such a good person, and he's very smart."

"and he can manipulate words, he can manipulate words and he can manipulate people"

"someone who makes me happy and understands me better than anyone else…"

Willow tried to establish boundaries by pleading with her boyfriend to allow her time to regroup and adjust. His response was to continue to badger her about his needs. The women mentioned above and others in this sample discussed how their mate's personalities were dichotomous. At times, they were wonderful and charming; at other times, manipulative and controlling. Here, in a brief exploration, we find that individuals exposed to the narcissistic and controlling tendencies of their mate may encounter behaviors where the mate:

- is socially dominant;
- acts more intelligent than others (Gabriel, Criteli, & Ee, 1994);
- responds to negative feedback by denigrating others, and
- exploits others and fails to consider the other person's feelings and needs (Bayse, Allgood, Van Wyk, 1991).

Women who are vulnerable and feel guilty for their mate's circumstances may be prone to manipulation. One of the more challenging aspects that families of inmates face is when the narcissistic behavior displayed by their incarcerated loved one overshadows the emotional needs of the family. (Bayse et al., 1991). This double-edged sword tends to pose difficulties for women. On one hand, they feel the need to be loving and supportive of their confined loved one; on the other hand, they no longer want to tolerate the manipulative and controlling behavior. This duality can create a cycle of attraction and withdrawal. However, the women reflected that completely walking away from the relationship may be even more challenging. Severing a relationship when the partner is confined appeared to cause 89 percent of women to feel guilty, and frustrated. As such, these women felt obligated to stay in the relationship. Lotus expressed sentiments similar to Willow's. Recall that Lotus had separated from her husband and became involved again because of his incarceration status. As she indicated, "He needed me."

For Willow, severing her relationship was not easy. She felt guilty for not keeping her boyfriend off drugs and for not keeping him off the streets. She indicated that she played back the events of the arrest leading to his incarceration several times in her mind. Consequently, her list of failures and shortcomings grew into a constant stream of negative self-talk. At the time of her interview, Willow felt that she had to choose between maintaining her relationship with her incarcerated boyfriend or her newly incarcerated son—she literally could not afford to do both.

> He got the impression that I was closing him off. However, I'm really screaming for help, asking him to "Look, just give me a minute. Understand what I'm going through with my son." For instance, when I was going through that and him being locked up and I'm going through what I'm going through with my son, I wasn't able to focus to write letters to him anymore.
>
> I wasn't able to focus to go look for cards or to take pictures, so, instead of just saying, "Look, I'm not focused to do this stuff," I would probably lie about it. "Oh yeah, I sent you a letter and some pictures," or "I'm going to do it" and never did it, and, you know, that caused anger on his behalf, thinking like I'm just totally deceiving him when, realistically, I'm going through this incarceration situation with my son and I can't deal with [him].

MAINTAINING FAMILY RELATIONSHIPS

When a significant loved one goes to prison, it places strains on the relationship and added pressures within the family unit. The barriers to maintaining family connections during such crises can render families vulnerable. For women like Willow, the strain is not always apparent. According to 65 percent of the women in this study, during life-changing events, both good and bad, the pain of separation and the loss of their mate is exacerbated. The husbands or boyfriends with whom they still share a semblance of a relationship are not physically there. However, the demands of life continue, and they must go on with living while their mates are locked away. For example, funerals, joyful weddings, births, graduations, and other events happen while the incarcerated person serves time. They must problem-solve, address ongoing personal issues and family changes, even under duress, and somehow get through these experiences. These events are reminders that the family is fractured and, somehow, incomplete.

When asking study participants to recall happy moments, each of the women paused a long time before answering. Several of the women also cried. This reaction was difficult to interpret. Through theoretical sampling (addressing emergent questions through additional participant interviewing), I later found out that this reaction was likely a result of a combination of both good and bad memories. Their reflections triggered conflicting emotions that left them feeling both nostalgic and sad as they ruminated on a time when smiles, and perhaps, happiness, were unencumbered.

Willow indicated that it was a struggle to manage her emotions and maintain contact with her boyfriend, who is located in a Kentucky prison over 7 hours away from Washington, D.C. Several times during our discussion, she reiterated her concerns with finances. She continued:

> A lot of times [prison expenses] put me in debt. It put me in more deeper of a financial bind. Of course, a lot of times, I had to juggle my money so that I could put money on the phone or so that I could send him money into his canteen so he could call, and then it was like an extra struggle for me because then my son got arrested.
>
> Well, when my son got arrested, oh, God, it was just so much. It was [too] emotional and then it's like you go through so many different emotions that you're like sad, then, you're mad, confused, struggling financially.
>
> You just go through so much and I think with myself, I really lost focus completely—but I couldn't like balance it out where it felt—I couldn't deal with my boyfriend locked up and my son being locked up. So, I just blanked out the boyfriend being locked up and was solely concentrated on my son's situation. So, of course, that put a strain on [our] relationship as well.

Willow's experience is similar to that of others who bear the financial burden of supporting loved ones and offenders (e.g., See Box 3.1). This financial obligation of caring for an incarcerated loved one may last for years.

PHONE CALLS ALLEVIATE WORRIES

Lowery (2015) found that non-incarcerated women who support loved ones in prison regularly find themselves making difficult choices between allocating funds for prison visits and telephone bills, and paying household expenses.

Reflecting on previous chapters, we can see that balancing financial priorities with the needs of the inmate is a difficult choice. Recall that for Lotus, a phone call was a means to find out that her husband was safe. Also of note is that she wanted to leave her husband prior to his incarceration. However, her fear and concern about him likely kept her bonded to the relationship. Her guilt caused her to stay in the relationship to support him.

Exorbitant Phone Bills: I Paid to Say Hello

Moving away from Willow and Lotus to share other women's experiences, at least one woman in this study indicated the use of creative solutions to stretch the budget. For instance, sometimes it was necessary for the inmate to make back-to-back phone calls. This is because each phone call had a 30-minute duration. However, there were times when even more

---

Box 3.1. The Cost of Connecting

Communications companies that monopolize the prison industry lure family members into paying high rates associated with telephone and other telecommunications technologies. These industries earn revenues from a market comprised of struggling families who feed into the promise of instant access to their loved ones via prison e-mail, phone calls, and video conferencing. Incarcerated persons more than likely earn little or no wages.

Although there is no national survey that captures inmate net worth, we can reasonably assume that most inmates are not financially independent. Some inmates earn wages from prison employers such as UNICOR. Prison employment yields wages between $0.12 and $1.15 per hour. Employment opportunities include manufacturing office furniture, license plates, signage, clothing and textiles, and other products (Federal Prison Industries, 2015).

It becomes apparent why there is a natural linkage between inmate dependency on women as outside financial support systems.

Telecommunications company website advertisements often depict communication offerings, where smiling family members are situated in the comfort of their homes, holding a laptop, telephone, or other communication device. The inference is that the user will be happy, have instant access to your incarcerated loved one. Using Willow as an example, we could estimate her costs as:

- A 30-minute call from Washington, D.C., to Kentucky is estimated at $.25 × 30 minutes = $7.50 per call.
- If Willow called her husband 15 days out of the month, using his calculation, her bill would be approximately $112.50.

In this example, Willow would likely need to pay the additional surcharges, as well. If she were to call her son (although we do not know the location of her son), she might pay an additional $50.00 in phone charges per month, which is approximately $170.00 total.

---

time was needed or perhaps the inmate wanted to speak with multiple family members. Therefore, a second call would come with additional costs. Generally, the cost of calls is capped at between .21 and .25 per minute. To offset being charged exorbitant phone fees for multiple phone calls at one time, some of the men were able to make one phone call and have the recipient use their 3-way calling feature or call transferring so that multiple calls could be utilized, using limited first-time fees. One woman elaborated,

> They make phone calls and stuff. Sometimes we can get a three-way. I send that money for [his] needs and to feel that you are not being harassed by anyone.... I'm not really going to write a letter, like I said, maybe every other month ... somehow I might get to talk to [him] and make sure he is all right.

Another woman said,

He calls at ten fifty-five at night. He calls me in thirty-minute intervals and we talk for thirty minutes. In addition, I go visit him, not as much as I should, but I have priorities, so the last time I visited him was, maybe, about three weeks ago. In addition, that was…. I had not seen him in six years.

Not everyone is willing to pay the exorbitant costs of prison communication. An example is a grandmother who was not included in this study, but from the Washington, D.C., area, who fought the exorbitant phone rates (See Box 3–2). She decided to seek remedy by challenging the overseer of the telecommunications companies, the Federal Communications Commission (FCC, 2013).

All calls from the prison facilities have a time limit. The "cost of calling is substantially higher than the cost of providing long distance" (Securus Technologies, n.d.).

Prison telecommunications companies generally seek to appeal to families or loved ones and design their advertisements specifically for vulnerable audiences. For instance, Securus Technologies advertises "AutoPay and TextPay," an option when your phone account reaches a $10.00 balance; the phone company will notify the prisoner's family member of the billing option to add money to accounts. The Securus phone system collect calls are operator-assisted. Surcharges generally apply. This cost is in addition to the per-minute phone call charges.

It appears that telecommunications companies use advertising to

---

**Box 3.2. Federal Communications Commission
Ruling on Exorbitant Phone Calls**

During 2013, the Federal Communications Commission capped exorbitant phone rates at $0.21 per minute for standard out-of-state calls, which enables families to remain in contact. This "action addresses a petition filed nearly a decade ago by Martha Wright, a Washington, D.C. grandmother who sought relief from exorbitant inmate calling rates. Since then, tens of thousands have urged the FCC to make it possible for them to stay in touch with loved ones in jail" (Federal Communications Commission, 2013, p. 1.). According to the Marshall Project advocacy group Martha, would find herself making a trade between taking medication and calling her grandson who was serving an 18-year sentence. She indicated that prior to the FCC capping the rates, inmates such as D.C. transfers could not make contact with legal counsel or even afford to speak with their children and family members. The FCC also set out to cap in-state fees and add-on costs. On October 22, 2015, the FCC's goal to cap the increased fees, ancillary charges, and add on costs to a single call that could skyrocket upwards 40%. However, the U.S. Court of Appeals issued a stay on March 7, 2016; therefore, as of this publication, the prison phone businesses are fighting this.

appeal to families as a way of soothing their fears and concerns about inmates who are outside of the Washington, D.C. area and where these members become guilt-ridden because they are out, free, and able to earn incomes yet unable to visit the prison where the loved one remains incarcerated. Take, for example, the marketing appeal of the following advertisement:

> Secure Instant Mail is our answer to putting you in control of communication. What this means is for you is no more waiting to hear or share important news. Instead, share your important news when it happens by sending an email message whenever you want!

The advertisement infers that there is freedom to call and communicate whenever desired. Although a loved one may send an e-mail day or night, the inmate may not receive it for weeks if he is detained in a segregation unit or if he does not have access to the e-mail system. Family members may literally buy into this myth of instant gratification and happiness.

There are also costs and privacy issues associated with sending e-mails. Family on the outside must adhere to prison policy as well as communication policy. E-mailed communications are still subject to the surveillance of prison personnel. Companies such as JPay also claim ownership of:

- e-mail video
- photographs
- poems/books, other written work
- any data transmitted through their services (Electronic Frontier Foundation, 2015).

A distraught wife, worried about her imprisoned husband, may not read terms and conditions in a lengthy contract. For example, Lotus indicated that if she did not receive a call from her husband, she feared that he was in segregation or someone had sexually abused him. The phone call served as her assurance of his safety.

Anxious people may simply click the "accept" button and sign up for the service offering. She may not realize that the book that her loved one has written, or the poem, or photographs, all belong to the telecommunications company.

THE BURDENS OF MAINTAINING CONTACT

"[I]f morality represents how people would like the world to work, then economics shows how it actually does work."—Levitt and Dubner (2005, p. v.)

The burden of maintaining relationships via long distance communication seems to rest solely on the shoulders of the families or women who are heads of household. The costs are high, and families risk exposure to exploitation via telecommunication companies who make profits by charging exorbitant rates to vulnerable inmate families.

Women in this study also voiced concerns about maintaining phone contact because of their fear of inmate abuse. The risk of prison abuse varies by facility and type. The D.C. Corrections Information Council is a federally appointed District of Columbia entity whose function it is to visit, inspect, and monitor facilities where D.C. inmates are placed throughout the country (Corrections Information Council [CIC], n.d.). During 2015, the staff-to-inmate ratio was 4:5092, meaning four people were responsible for inspecting 114 facilities across 35 states, with a finite budget of under $300,000. In addition to performing inspections, this body is responsible for managing complaints that align with concerns expressed in an earlier chapter, by women such as Lotus. These women have genuine concerns that may or may not be unfounded and unrealistic. An example of documented concerns from a correctional facility in Lewisburg, Pennsylvania illustrated that (CIC, 2014):

- D.C. inmates were subjected to harsh and excessive punishment by corrections officers, whereby these prisoners have been assaulted in locations without cameras (p. 3);
- Staff retaliation against D.C. inmates is high, and the use of restraints, segregation/isolation, and other punitive practices are high;
- Staff were found to be tampering with mail from family and even legal resources, whereby family members have difficulty communicating.
- The staff and corrections officers make it difficult for family members to visit and "multi-year" phone denials have been put in place for some inmates (p.3).
- Inmates have been denied psychological treatment, and their medications have been withheld.

The challenges inmates from Washington, D.C., face do not end with these conditions, alone. The economics of a prison visit involve more than just securing transportation, according to one of the women in the study. Olive indicated:

> The prison is located in a small town. There are a lot of truck drivers who pass through and stay in that town. I am a young woman, traveling alone to this far away prison. I stay in hotel rooms—not even the nicest places—cheap motels that are at least a hundred dollars a night. It is a long way from my home, over six

hours, so I can only go once a month. When I do go, I stay the entire weekend. The costs add up. So, I'm usually spending two to three hundred dollars on hotel rooms.

If family members are traveling, including with young children, the costs are increased and the requirements may become more challenging. Table 3.1 covers some of the basic considerations that women and families may have to consider when they are planning an out-of-state prison visit. Prison visitation is also challenging. Contact visits can be limited between family and the inmate (see Box 3.3).

**Box 3.3. The Loss of Physical Contact
Begins with Jail in Washington, D.C.**

Women from the nation's capital are at risk of facing unique consequences of a loved one's incarceration. When a person is arrested in the District of Columbia, the physical separation begins with the jail sentence. Any D.C. Code offender/inmate awaiting trial loses his (or her) ability to make physical contact with a loved one. All social visits are facilitated through video conferencing. Visits can be scheduled onsite at the jail or via Internet. To use the system, at a minimum, family members are required to be Internet-savvy, use e-mail, and have some understanding of computer technology to register. Visits are conducted at the jail facilities. Although the advertisement of the system alludes that the visit takes place in a comfortable and convenient environment, these visits are monitored and take place in a sterile environment in a corrections-setting, the jail, or designated locations.

Themes and Insights

Social Conditions

When a woman is suffering, the extent of her recovery from the ill effects of a partner's incarceration may depend partially on her financial position. Social theorists have found that people who are poor—living below the poverty level—tend also to live in jurisdictions that are plagued with crime and high incarceration rates (National Research Council [NRC], 2014). Women and children who live in impoverished neighborhoods are exposed to a piling-on of multiple risk factors that can lead to income deficits and economic strains. Individuals who are mothers and who have incarcerated partners have been found to even face the risk of homelessness (National Research Council, 2014). This condition may be a result of a loss of supplemental income from a significant other.

In contrast, a person with greater economic wherewithal may have access to resources that fill the income gap left by a significant other's incarceration. Already disadvantaged families may find it hard to overcome the new financial strains brought about as an economic imbalance. Additionally, not all affected women are able to augment their employment or even develop a new career focus to make ends meet.

Unfortunately, cities with high crime and trending incarceration rates also have high unemployment. For example, Chicago has an 11.2 percent unemployment rate; Detroit City, MI, is at a 24.8 percent unemployment rate [Bureau of Labor Statistics, 2010]). Washington, D.C., where this study took place, averaged 9.8 percent unemployment during 2010. It then surged to 13.4 percent during 2015 (Bureau of Labor Statistics, 2010; Marans, 2015). By 2016, the unemployment rate decreased to 6.5 percent at January 2016, (Department of Labor Statistics, 2016). These unstable financial conditions can add to the struggles women face because of their individual financial status. This adds to the burden of geographic separation for the non-incarcerated mate.

African American Women: Jobs and Employment

To gain a general sense of the financial status of African American women, we can examine the job roles and opportunities available for this group, and their ability to earn income. To do so, we look across the national landscape and find that Black women are employed as helping professionals in domains such as human and social services (29 percent), followed by employment in the retail industry (11 percent) as the highest sector (BlackDemograhics, 2015).

The women in this study, concentrated in the Washington, D.C., metropolitan area, have financial situations that are not so different from the financial conditions conveyed in national statistics. Although my study was not designed to capture income demographics or occupation information, through interviews, I was able to discern the types of jobs they have and how well women were able to withstand shifts in income when their significant others previously contributed to the household.

Women in this sample held occupations that mostly mirrored the national profiles as well: retail, healthcare, human services, social services, and the legal and education professions. At least one woman in this study was on disability and another was unemployed. Some of the women sought part-time employment to maintain a lifestyle to which they were accustomed. Another woman indicated that she had to resort to living in a shelter for a period because she lost her means of employment.

My general sense is that women were willing to seek work rather than to depend on social services because they felt obligated to take care of themselves, their mate, and their families. As Lotus stated, "I had a child to take care of.... I had to work as much as possible."

Income is an important determinant in maintaining a relationship when a loved one is confined. However, we know that Black women's income levels can vary, as shown in in Table 3.1.

Based on the generalizations contained in Table 3.1, income levels have narrowly increased for Black women over the past three decades. Black women contend with unequal wages, compared with other groups. These trends show that between the years 1980 to 2002, Black women's hourly wages grew from under $9.00 per hour, upwards to slightly under $11.00 (Dozier, 2010). By 2015, the median income for Black women approached $33,533 annually, but still positioned them at 20 percent lower than their Non-Hispanic, White female counterparts. The unemployment rate for this group ranged between 6 percent and 8 percent, compared to the national average of 4.9 percent (BlackDemograhics, 2016).

**Table 3.1. Black Women Demographics:
Income, Earnings and Employment**

- Fifty-three % of Black women in America were heads of household (Guerra, 2013).
- During 2015, Black women earned 20% less than they earned their White female counterpart (U.S. Department of Labor, 2016).
- The median income for Black women was $33,533 compared to $41,822 for White females (U.S. Department of Labor, 2016).
- Black women were found to have higher unemployment rate than all other women in the U.S. [between 6 and 10%]. During 2016 the average rate for African Americans was 8.3% compared to national average of 4.9% (Black Demographics, 2015).
- Black women made up 6% of those who were employed in private sector jobs and held 1 in 10 public sector positions (U.S. Department of Labor, 2016).
- Twenty-Nine % of Black women lived below the poverty level (Black Demographics, 2015).
- Black women earned 68 cents to a dollar compared to 78 cents to a dollar by their White female counterpart.
- Median wealth for Black women was $100.00 and $0.00 for unwed mothers (Guerra, 2013).

Of note, a woman's income can also determine how well she is able to maintain or acquire adequate housing for her family. In Washington, D.C, during the year 2015, 22 percent of the general population earned income below $22,000, annually. Women who were living below the $22,000 mark likely faced tremendous housing disadvantages unless they were living rent-free or received federally subsidized housing. For instance, in Washington, D.C., the cost of renting for a single mother, with one child, can vary from a minimum of between $500.00 to $1,500 per month (Liggett, 2015). At least 58 percent of the population in Washington, D.C., are renters (Ligett, 2015). Impoverished areas of the city such as the projects or in government-subsidized housing have the lowest rent.

EMOTIONAL IMPACTS

Helping professionals may wish to consider how the emotional and psychological factors covered in this chapter can affect the African American woman, as well as other household members. This is especially of concern if the woman has experienced long-term exposure to these conditions.

For example, at least two women in this sample were in a relationship with a "lifer" (i.e., a person serving a life sentence in prison). A woman who plans to spend the rest of her life in a relationship with an incarcerated man serving a life sentence may need to consider ways that she can maintain a quality of life consistent with her personal goals and her well-being.

Fear. There can be a number of reasons to experience fear related having a loved one in prison. According to women whom I interviewed, the fear can go beyond a prison visit or the fear for a loved one's safety. It may also include:

- The fear of living alone for the first time without a male presence;
- Fearing the financial struggles of being "head of household";
- Fear of never having the same relationship, given the strain and separation;
- Children may fear a parent who is absent and the child may fear maintaining bonds with someone whom others perceive as a participant of criminal activity;
- The wife or girlfriend may be afraid that the inmate will become "turned-out," which means they may change their sexual orientation or become bi-sexual because of limited options to be in an intimate relationship;
- There may be fears of what others will think of them as a couple;

- A fear of the unknown may be the most significant and debilitating kind of fear.

PRISON VISITATION

While prison visits are stressful to women, they can also be rewarding. Women expressed the fear of being turned away from a visit, or arriving late. If the spouse herself has a criminal record, she may not be able to visit as easily. Women also expressed feeling singled out for not wearing the right clothing, or not adhering to subjective dress codes. Other considerations are listed in Table 3.2. Rosemary described her circumstance:

> There was a guard who just did not like him [her husband] and didn't like him for many years, so he would look at me and say, "You know what? You're parked in the wrong spot. You need to go move your car." Okay, so I go move my car and I'd come back. "Yeah, you can't wear that today. We don't let girls in with those kind of pants." So, I go change my pants. You know, there was one thing after one another. [There was a] girl wearing the same pants right behind me.

Table 3.2. Prison Visitation Travel

Consideration in Preparation for Distance Travel to Remote Prisons	Cost Consideration
Transportation	Cost of bus, flight, or costs of car travel. This travel may include the cost of local transportation in the destination city. For example, if local transportation does not go to the prison, a taxi or other forms of transportation may be required.
Vacation from Work	If visitation is on weekdays, and the visit requires multiple-hour travel, vacation or time off work may be needed.
Childcare	If children are not visiting the prison with caregivers or parents, there may be a cost associated with childcare.
Hotel/Motel Costs	Overnight stays near hotel or weekend stays are based on the local costs and associated fees.
Ensure Visitor Is on Visitation list	Inmate updates list and is effective within 30–60 days?
Clothing	Depending on the facility, the dress code restrictions may mean that women will need to have special clothing, otherwise be denied a prison visit.
Inmate Commissary Account Deposits	Visitors have the option of placing money on the inmate commissary account. This may be an added expense.
Food	Food for overnight and weekend visitation.
Inmate Status	Inmate may be placed in segregation because of a violation or infraction.
Visitor Security Clearance	The woman may have a criminal record that prevents her from a visit.

Most prisons are not a nice place to visit. Some of the earliest prisons were designed to generate feelings of unease. Based on the work of Jeremy Bentham's study, originating from the early 1700's, prison models were constructed to evoke the illusion that the people within are under surveillance. The architectural design of the facilities left no hidden spots or privacy (Semple, 1993). Even the illusion of monitoring can generate the feeling of surveillance—even if no one was looking.

There appears to be a delicate balance between choosing to visit the prisoner or stay within the safety of one's home. The decision may include trying to maintain physical contact while dealing with the humiliation of a prison visit. To show the complexities of this decision, note Jade's journal entry that conveys her innermost thoughts as she contemplates what prison visits meant to her.

> Today, I don't have any patience for those badass kids running around the prison visiting room as I wait for my visit. Having a bad case of PMS makes it difficult to flip on and off the happy switch. I'm on my period and I think the damn bathrooms at the prison have video cameras disguised as smoke detectors. The bathroom's smell is gagging. The smell of bleach and cheap soap, like the police substation— it reminds me of the night of his arrest. That is a familiar smell that I will never get used to. How the hell can anyone sneak a prisoner out of a damn bathroom that is on the other side of the prison visiting area and segregated by a turnstile and a metal detector? I hate the idea of going in that godforsaken bathroom that has the smell of prison-issued soap. Sometimes, there is toilet paper on the floor in the stalls. I don't want my shoes to touch the tiles. But I can't hold it. The drive was too long.
>
> It is bad enough that I have to go through the metal detectors and empty the contents of my pocket to be examined for contraband. Everything associated with prison seems to subtly strip you of your dignity. This is how they remain in control. Strip you of your rights while you are on their premises.
>
> I take the tampon out of my jacket pocket and place it in the wooden box, with my watch, earrings, and a piece of costume jewelry that is not gold with my locker key. The guard picks up the box for inspection, tips it corner-to-corner as the tampon rolls to the side, and slides it onto the counter top beyond the metal detector. All of the other corrections officers look at the object and pretend not to see the cardboard cylinder. It's my turn to clear the metal monster [detector], and I make it through—because I know the rules. No metal buttons, belt buckles, hair pins, shoes with metal plates in the soles and the ultimate: no underwire bra. I clear to the other side.

Whether we focus on Willow's conundrum, deciding whether to go to Kentucky, or on Jade's perception of limited privacy and embarrassment, a visit to a prison can generate feelings of unease along with the desire to see an incarcerated mate.

Discussion

COPING AND INTERVENTION

A possible intervention strategy may include using the AARM® and Circles and Roles® mentioned earlier to help Willow manage her perceptions, roles, and responsibilities in the context of her relationship with her boyfriend and her son. By applying this communication tool as a mechanism to provide her with clarity of her perception, responsibility, and future goals, Willow can discover the specific triggers that are contributing to her distress.

Perhaps a natural starting point for intervention is to understand her feelings related to her need to discontinue her relationship. Willow may also wish to address her financial concerns and its spillover effects on her life. Part III covers grief extensively, and this condition is a prominent feature in Willow's life. Here, the use of William Worden's "tasks of mourning" may be an applicable intervention and may be helpful in understanding the range in which women feel nonfinite grief.

Although Worden's focus primarily is on finite loss or loss due to the death of a loved one, I have employed several of his "tasks" in my support groups, based on each woman's self-report. Worden (2009, pp. 39–56) advises:

- Task 1: Accept the reality of the loss;
- Task 2: Process the pain of grief;
- Task 3: Adjust to the world without the absent person (Worden uses the term "deceased." I substitute with the "absent person"); and
- Task 4: Find an enduring connection with the absent person in the midst of embarking on a new [role] in life (I modify Worden's description here by adding the word "role").

Here, the helping professional will facilitate a discussion about the meaning associated with the absent person and the significance of this loss. Again, the Circles and Roles® is used to help aid this discussion and to raise awareness about the roles and the relationship before and since the incarceration occurred. In Task 2, it may be helpful to refer to the Circles and Roles® diagram to facilitate a discussion to help the client to express her pain and grief.

In Task 3, the use of the AARM's® assessment and reframing steps may help to provide a focus on identifying and taking on new roles and focus. Finally, in Task 4, Willow can set goals that are consistent with living in a world without the incarcerated loved one for the period of absence.

ECOLOGICAL METAPHOR

The stories of Aster, Lotus, and Willow, as well as of other women cited earlier in this work, show intersectionality regarding African American women's socioeconomic status, education, health, spirituality, interpersonal relationships, and even social networks and status. This system of *interdependence* contends that within the context of a person's life, there are networks of interrelated parts, all connected and related in some manner to the larger whole (Kelly, 1966). If one part of the equation becomes out of balance, it can have cascading impacts on the other parts of the system.

The *ecological metaphor* (Kelly, 1966) is complementary theory to family systems (Bowen, 1985), as well. In brief, both theories explain how families operate as a system. When one part of the system is incapacitated, the other parts suffer the impacts until the system adjusts, makes compensation for its loss, and regains stability or falls apart. This dynamic helps us to understand how women who have lived apart from their mate, in separate dwellings, experience distress when their mate serves time. In essence, when the partner is incarcerated, the family or relationship cadence is interrupted and becomes out of balance.

QUESTIONS TO PONDER

1. Willow may not recognize that she is grieving. How might you use Worden's tasks of mourning to help facilitate a discussion about acknowledging her personal loss?

2. What are the coping strategies that are used by Willow?

3. How can the Circles and Roles® activity help Willow open up about the guilt and shame that she feels, specific to telling lies to her boyfriend?

4. How might you broach a discussion about the interpersonal relationship between Willow and her boyfriend's family?

5. What strategies might you use to facilitate a discussion specific to income, budget, and helping Willow to balance her priorities?

4

Relationships, Children and Loss

Our success in personal relationships can influence how we view our lives as individuals. Moreover, how we reflect on our relationships can shape our perceived happiness and can color our world as sad or happy (Jackson-Dwyer, 2014). In this chapter, we explore incarceration and its impact on relationships and children. We consider age-appropriate discussions and alternatives to having conversations about paternal incarceration with children. With the focus on family, in this chapter we explore how to build strong relationships, establish continued bonds and address loss.

Case Study: Hazel

Hazel, is a 34-year-old African American woman. She has one child—a daughter. She is unsure how to categorize her relationship with her mate when asked about her status. She said that she preferred not to use titles. However, as with other women in this study, at times during the interview, she referred to her mate as her husband. Hazel met her mate shortly after graduating high school. They were both under 20 years old when they fell in love. Later, they had a baby girl; this child was their bond. Some years following, her then-boyfriend received a 10-year prison sentence. Hazel said that she was loyal as he served his time. This was a difficult period for her, she said, emotionally, financially, and even romantically as she struggled to live without her significant other.

She learned through his absence that adjustment to a crisis event is not a linear progression. It appeared that the struggle of overcoming one issue required looping back and asking oneself, how did this happen? How did I end up in this relationship? What is really in it for me? At times, women similar to Hazel do not know what steps to take to move beyond a crisis. A crisis could be related to how to explain to children where their incarcerated father is. Perhaps the child was told an untruth, and now the mom feels it is time to tell the truth. Sometimes, women remain "stuck" in a cycle of lies, confusion, and made-up stories to cover for the life they do not have. At times, they do not know how to move forward, as we see in Hazel's reflections:

> He was ... locked up when he was 19 and released when he was 28. So, it was a lot of time between us. We knew that we were going to be together. Well, it was hard because, at the time, we had a daughter together. So, it was hard financially, and it was hard emotionally, and it was hard just explaining to my daughter [where her father was all of that time]. You know, he left when she was a year old, until she was about,—I think she was about seven or eight [when he came home]—if I'm not mistaken.
>
> When he came home, it was kind of hard to explain to her as she got mature what was going on. It was hard because, um, basically I would have to take trips down there [to the prison] almost every weekend. He was incarcerated in North Carolina. So, it was a [long trip] and sometimes I would take it every weekend just to show my commitment. The *trust* part was hard and the financial part of trying to stay committed was hard, emotionally.

During the ten years that Hazel spent supporting her absent husband, her life was on hold. It also appears that "fibs" or "little lies" have an expiration date. It is apparent that Hazel withheld the truth for years from her daughter. This is a common practice where parents tell their children that their father is in the military or in another country (doing something noble). However, eventually, they end up telling the truth or the child grows up and finds out the truth. This untruth can cause problems within the family. It appears that Hazel finally needed to tell her daughter about her father and they began to visit the prison together.

Perhaps Hazel's change was due to her self-reflection on the difficulties of managing a father-daughter relationship during his absence. Perhaps she recognized that the family's basic loss was greater than her own loneliness—that her child was also missing her father. Her daughter was experiencing loss, as well. The separation due to incarceration did not diminish the need for her family to remain a cohesive unit. Jackson-Dwyer (2014) defines a relationship as a configuration of two or more people having strong connections and where there is an element of having influence over one another. This description is fitting and describes Hazel's family. For instance, even though her husband was not physically located in the same household, it is clear that he played a key role and had influence in the family's life.

Although Hazel avoided discussing her husband's incarceration with the children, this period of loss could have been a teachable moment for her child. Various losses inevitably will occur over a child's life span. Parents can use examples to help children understand the meaning of separation, even with incarceration. Parents can teach their children ways to cope and redefine their new roles in the family as they adjust to the absence and loss of an incarcerated family member.

WAYS TO DISCUSS INCARCERATION WITH CHILDREN

There are effective ways to discuss incarceration with young children. Having an age-appropriate discussion may be helpful rather than to leave the children to their own devices to assume what has happened and why the parent is gone. Sesame Street's *"Little Children, Big Challenges: Incarceration"* provides toolkits and guidance on topic-relevant discussions for young children (under 8 years old) with incarcerated parents (Sesame Workshop [SW], n.d.). Here, I consolidate some of the main takeaways. Using age-appropriate language, the non-incarcerated parent may consider the following questions to explore and ponder before having a conversation with the child.

Preparation: (Questions to consider when preparing for a discussion about incarceration with children):

- What does the child know about incarceration?
- What did the child see, related to the absent member's incarceration (such as the handcuffing and arrest of the parent)?
- What has the child heard about the arrest or incarceration?
- How do other family members characterize the arrest and subsequent incarceration?
- What has the child witnessed, related to the behavior of the non-incarcerated parent?
- How are the family priorities affecting the child's temperament and emotions?
- How are the child's peer relationships, in school or otherwise?
- What are the formal support systems in place to support the child after this discussion?
- Recognize that no other person can take the place of the absent parent. Therefore, stepparents and other new people introduced to the child during the period of the absent parent's sentence are not necessarily a substitute for the parental loss.

Having the Conversation

- Communication with children should be age-appropriate, but honest.
- Parents can begin by explaining the importance for taking responsibility for their own choices and bad behavior. Consequences are generally commensurate with the poor choice.
- Share your own feelings of sadness and let the child know that it is okay to feel sad. Children need to know that it is acceptable for them to cry and to grieve the loss of a significant household member.
- Be supportive and reassure the child that it is natural to miss the absent parent and that feelings of anger, betrayal, hurt, and even loneliness are understandable.
- Also, tell the child that you are there to support him or her and that you will take care of him or her.
- Encourage him or her to write a letter to the absent parent. If they are too young to write a letter, ask them to draw a picture.
- Allow the absent parent and the child to plan holiday activities, using the phone, letter writing, and participate in visitations on family days.
- Encourage healthy bonding time on the telephone, video conference, or during in-person visits.

Even after having age-appropriate conversations with children, mothers may still grow concerned about their children's well-being. This may add to the mother's stress levels as a secondary source of worry and concern. The incarceration of a family member and ensuing crisis may not be a one-time event. The stress levels within the family system may elevate even when a loved one returns home, or ensures parole. Incidents of this nature can generate another wave of grief. Although it is beyond the scope of this work, it is understandable how children might grow to be distrusting of significant relationships, especially if the child is reunited and separated then from a parent on multiple occasions.

Although a mate's incarceration can be a sad time for women, happy moments are not totally absent. Hazel recalled, fondly, one of the happiest moments in her life—her engagement at the prison: "He got on his knee and proposed, so even though, you know, others might not think that, it was a significant day." Although this day was a happy time, she lamented, the barrier of prison had stagnated the growth of their relationship because she could only speak with him by phone every other day.

THE FAMILY AND INCARCERATION

Conditions of a mate's incarceration may affect the mother-child relationship in different ways. Ninety percent (90 percent) of the women in the study had minor children. Having a husband incarcerated may cause women to have fears about their child's risk for incarceration—especially in the Black community, given the prevalence of incarceration in this cultural group. Women with these fears may feel overwhelmed with worry. The mainstream news reports can exacerbate and amplify the notion that these are valid concerns. Individuals who are of a specific demographic of race, economics, education, or postal codes in Washington, D.C., are at risk either of being a victim of crime or at risk of being incarcerated (*ABC News*, 2010).

The nation's top 25 most dangerous neighborhoods, identified during 2010, included residents who live within a specific zip code in Washington, D.C, indicating that these residents face a 1 in 9 chance of being a victim of crime (Wallet pop Staff, 2010). Moreover, a Black man living in this city faces a 3 out of 4 chance of incarceration in his lifetime if he is unemployed and did not finish high school (Braman, 2004). The possibility of these risks weighing heavily as a potential fear that women hold should not be taken for granted. Black women fear for their husbands and families.

Risks of incarceration are present for children, as well. The phenomenon, *school to prison pipeline* describes how school administrators have adopted a punitive zero tolerance policy for school-aged children (Schept, Tyler, & Brisman, 2015). This focus on policing children provides a direct path for youngsters to enter the criminal justice system. During 2015, there were 12 incidents involving children's arrests in Washington, D.C. (Martin, 2015). An extreme example includes a seemingly innocent act that led to criminal sanctions: the case that involved a D.C. elementary school student, who was charged with a "sexual" offense of harassment for kissing another child on the cheek (Martin, 2015, par. 3).

Jazmine is another mother who participated in this study. While Hazel tried to shield her daughter from finding out about her Dad's incarceration, Jazmine was overprotective of her sons, as illustrated:

> Also, I think that [with him being incarcerated it] made me closer to my children because I have all sons and I never want to see them in that position [incarcerated]. So, I would even go as far as have them sleep in the room with me just so I know that they're all right … it's like being closer to the kids was being closer to him, as well.

Jazmine's fears are real. The phenomenon of mass incarceration intersects with the lives of African American women in multiple ways, including from an environmental perspective, as learned through Aster's story. Some people believe that Black boys and men are becoming endangered through their rate of deaths and incarceration (Hunter, 2014)—and a life marked with the risk of recidivating. Even more sobering, the average life expectancy for a man who spends time in prison is 10 years after he leaves prison, while on parole or probation—especially if these individuals have health-related conditions (Katzen, 2013). According to Bureau of Justice Statistics (2013), men fitting these demographics face a 50/50 chance of violating conditions of their release and re-entering prison within 3 years after release.

Even when a woman's significant other returns home from prison, the couple may spend the rest of their time together living in fear and in doubt of regaining normalcy, and worrying about his potential violation of probation or recidivism.

FEAR OF INTERGENERATIONAL INCARCERATION

African American family systems vary in configuration and interactions, and the variations shape the unity found within the household. Researchers also contend that family systems differ based on the level of conflict occurring in the family unit, as well. (Clay, Ellis, Griffin, Amodeo, & Hassler, 2007). One study suggested that Black families experience less conflict within their units than White families encounter (Clay et al., 2007). If this is valid, it is unclear how this finding influences the family unit during an incarceration related crisis.

My research findings disclosed that all of the women indicated that the institution of family is important. The overwhelming majority of the women in this study had children. These women expressed love for their families; specifically, those who had children expressed the adverse impact incarceration had on the family unit in several ways, as illustrated through the following quotes:

- "I think that it made me kinda closer to my, my children."
- "I felt the need to hang on to the children even closer because they are a part of both of us and I did not want to see them in that type of situation, ever."
- "It doesn't take much at all to make me happy as long as my family is content and everything's going good."

Children are a by-product of their environment and family conditions (Mooney, 2013). Children with incarcerated parents face a higher risk of health issues such as asthma, attention deficit disorder, and obesity, compared to their counterparts with non-incarcerated parents (Turney, 2014b). In addition to compromised health risks, children can be prone to repeating the cycle of incarceration (Harris, 2013). With more than 10 million children with a parent or sibling incarcerated, the dynamics of imprisonment adversely affect the family system, and the children, in particular (Harris, 2013). The risk markers for intergenerational offending include but are not limited to (Sarri & Stoffregen, 2013):

- Poverty and or homelessness;
- Low or a lack of parental interaction and attention;
- Frequent relocation or change of caregiver and residents, and
- Childhood delinquency.

Detailing all of the impacts and implications of incarceration on the family unit can be a challenge. Children of the incarcerated are at risk for health-related issues and may themselves be at risk for future incarceration (Turney, 2014b). There are opportunities to explore this topic in detail as future researchers examine the impacts of over-incarceration in America.

A significant other's incarceration can strain and alter the dynamics of the entire family unit. Family units are interdependent and members of the unit influence each other's behaviors in positive or negative ways. The family unit is a system. At times, this system can comprise smaller subsystems, such as children, non-related household members, and even extended family. These units are self-regulating and operate in their own unique manner with established norms, roles, and expectations. When the family unit is in chaos and crisis, the whole system can become out of kilter.

This imbalance can affect young children, especially if the mother is emotionally unavailable. This deficit of emotion can influence and shape child development, social relationships, and the child's emotional development (Rosen, Ackerman, & Zosky, 2002). Therefore, it appears essential that women who are struggling with their emotions would benefit from intervention. This could have a positive impact on children's development as well.

BUILDING STRONG RELATIONSHIPS

Relationships strained by prison may make it difficult to maintain continued bonds with the confined loved one. To adjust, women can develop new ways to maintain continuity of their relationships. Jackson-Dwyer (2014) found that intimate relationships thrive when three key ingredients are present:

- Interdependence;
- Need fulfillment, and
- Emotional attachment (Jackson-Dwyer, 2014, Chapter 1).

Findings from my study suggest that women can use nontraditional methods to meet these requirements. Jackson-Dwyer (2014) suggested that proximity plays a large role in relationship maintenance. Some of the women in this study overcame barriers of geographic separation by using imaginative techniques. One woman, whom I call Mansi, used the following ways to express affection without physical contact:

> The physical separation, actually, for me … helped me to learn different ways of communication of affection, you know, when you even think of ways you want to hug someone if you love them or something. I think it made me think more outside the box. It made me, you know, it made me actually appreciate those small things, too; but it really made me think outside the box. It really—just to make the long story short, yes. … It seems like our communication, our blind wish has … broaden[ed] so much more—it [is] more in depth, and I mean, I feel a connection with him like I've never felt before. Just from words alone, you know. I think I kind of missed those before.
>
> But I mean, now, we have words, and I think they're getting deeper and I mean the communication is just like major, much more major for me. I mean, I feel a way deeper connection just by our communication through words, and I mean, it gives me to show a side of me of expression that I didn't show at once before.… I feel closer to him than I ever have before, and I feel like he's closer to me because I'm able to express myself in ways that I wasn't in the past.

Themes and Insights

Continued Bonds

There are similarities between techniques used to maintain bonds with a deceased loved one and the methods used by women in the present study to maintain bonds during periods of absence from an incarcerated loved one. The concept of *continued bonds*, often used to explain the behavior of bereaved individuals, is applicable here (Stroebe, 1992). This concept helps us to understand how grief maintenance techniques related to deceased individuals can be effective when these steps are applied as an intervention for women grieving their loss from an incarcerated person.

Research shows that there are benefits in developing a new sense of self *and* maintaining symbolic bonds with a deceased person (Strobe, 1992). Table 4.1, Maintaining Bonds, draws a comparison of similarities between issues of adjusting to the death of a loved one and adjustment to separation and loss with an incarcerated person.

Women in this study disclosed that they maintain bonds with their incarcerated loved ones, using rituals such as:

- wearing a favorite piece of their spouse's clothing;
- carrying his wallet, visiting places they used to go;
- eating his favorite food, listening to his favorite music, or
- taking up hobbies or activities that he now has found rewarding in prison, such as exercising.

Symbolic rituals may help grievers to find meaning in and adjust to a life without the absent person. Symbolic Imprisonment, Grief and Coping Theory is explained in Part II, which suggests coping via metaphors and using a proxy as a way to maintain continued bonds. Instead of daily physical touch, women were able to substitute the warmth gained through physical interaction by using creativity, such as: thinking of their mate at a specific time, listening to a collection of music, or even having a glass of wine and a romantic dinner with a symbolic representation of their

Table 4.1. Maintaining Bonds

Maintaining Continued Bonds with Deceased	Maintaining Bonds with Incarcerated Spouse
Maintaining symbolic bonds with the deceased served as a sense of comfort (Stroebe et al., 1992)	Maintaining symbolic bonds with the incarcerated mate served as comfort.
Hanging on to memories and fonder times using object/possessions as ritual to overcome loneliness (Stroebe et al., 1992)	Women used symbolic objects in rituals to bridge their need for physical contact (e.g., articles of clothing, photos, or jewelry).
Proximity maintenance involves the affected person seeking to maintain proximal closeness to decrease distress (Hazan & Shaver, 1994)	Some women considered relocating to be near the prison where their husband is serving their sentence. Other women visited the prisons weekly.
Women felt a strong sense of presence of the deceased and welcomed this hallucination as companionship (Rees, 1971)	Women used a proxy to maintain the spouse's presence; served as a source of comfort.
Weaker bonds produced less struggle to adjust; stronger attachment and unexpected separation produced greater distress (Stroebe et al., 2011)	Women who self-reported having less attachment to their boyfriends and husbands were able to recover from their distress more easily than those who were deeply invested in their relationships.

mate. One study reported that children of incarcerated parents used ritual to connect by looking at the moon at a designated time, knowing their parents were doing the same (Steinhoff & Berman, 2012). Others have used a place setting for the absent partner, or a handmade craft. Of course, there are also women who have used other men as a substitute relationship. For example, Sage, one of the women interviewed, married another man while her boyfriend was serving time. She acknowledged that she did not love the man she married and that she just wanted to pass time while her true love was in prison.

Unaddressed Loss

There are times where absence from an incarcerated loved one can be a reminder of other losses in one's life. Women with lower self-esteem may struggle with compounded feelings of loss. Hazel not only experienced current loss, but she also feared that she might not have a promising future due to her concerns over her husband. These losses may evoke repressed issues. Both Bowlby (1969) and (Baumeister & Leary 1995) argued that humans have an innate desire to maintain bonds. Bowlby indicated that these bonds begin as a normal part of childhood development within the parent-child relationship or, perhaps, between the secure attachment bonds established between caregiver and child. Baumeister and Leary (1995) found that individuals not only need to have relationship bonds, but the "belongingness hypothesis" suggests that humans *need* to have "strong and stable" relationships (p. 497). Further, relationships maintained through contact that is both frequent and nurtured with warmth have the best chance to thrive.

Psychological Impacts

Many women can experience the phenomenon of loss and react differently. This is why life events can challenge one person's assumptive world while another person may be able to move on with life resiliently. Some people deal with unresolved issues by using what The Bowen Center for the Study of Family [BCSF] (2016) refers to as *emotional cut-off*. Perhaps, emotions associated with issues such as unresolved childhood events are never properly addressed (BCSF, 2016). New loss may serve as a trigger of emotions related to unresolved issues. Sometimes, these issues compound feelings of grief and, possibly, guilt. Then, these emotions can trigger feelings of inadequacy, especially if a person has low levels of self-esteem. Karakurt (2012) investigated the connection between attachment, romantic jealousy, and self-esteem and inadequacy (p. 334), and found, in part, that individuals who have a high value of self (self-esteem) were less likely to feel inadequate. Incidentally, they were also less likely to feel romantic jealousy. Similarly, when new losses occurred in Hazel's life, these reflections on loss triggered other self-defeating thoughts:

> I was so disappointed in myself. When I look back on my life, I have found that I am carrying so much weight and guilt about things [that] I should have done differently. At first, I didn't want to admit this. I evaluated the way I parent, the way I connect or disconnect with family. I judge how I approach my relationship, and even my own eating habits. I start thinking about all the stuff that I did wrong then; I ended up in a circle of thoughts. I ran away from most of my problems. I hurt people who meant the most to me. I was so selfishly focused on me and my relationship and my needs. I needed to marry so that I could heal from the path of stuff I left damaged.

SURVIVOR'S GUILT

In addition to unresolved issues, I found that women may feel both guilt and shame similar to survivor's guilt, as illustrated in Olive's quote below:

> I feel guilt or shame even though I haven't done anything wrong. I feel ostracized from support, even though I haven't done anything to "deserve" not being supported. I may feel unable to relate to people in a healthy way; (i.e., jealousy of friends who have their partners "with" them or isolating so I don't have to discuss things. Sometimes, I become suspicious and mistrusting of them [my friends]. This is because I am anticipating being judged for my situation.
>
> Sometimes I am overly defensive about my relationship. I feel as though I need to "justify" my decision to be with my partner or constantly "prove" to people that I'm okay. I feel anxiety over money, or time spent out enjoying pursuits, telling myself that I "should" put his needs ahead of my own or I "shouldn't" be participating in things they can't also enjoy.

In her work, *From Guilt to Shame: Auschwitz and After*, Ruth Leys described a survivor of the Holocaust and Auschwitz camps as suffering from "self-destructive guilt...." [see Leys (2007)]. This is the type of guilt that brings about inward-directed behaviors such as self-sabotage, self-criticism, and negative self-talk. These conditions mirror the stories of women in this study. Leys (2007) stated, "[t]he victim becomes contaminated by the aggression directed against himself by identifying with it and passing on its sting" (Leys, 2007, ch.1).

A similar finding, illustrated in Tulip's interview transcript:

> The first few weeks following his arrest were unbearable; I had to function in choosing a lawyer, dealing with my bank to free up funds to pay for a lawyer. There is

no playbook to tell you what to do when your spouse is arrested. It was total and utter chaos in my mind. In front of people, I put on the business face and functioned, but on my own or talking to my friends, I would break. It was hard to do simple things like remember to eat or drink water. My diet was terrible. I smoked, barely ate meals, and lived off coffee.

It was ridiculous. After the initial chaos died down, I found myself in depression. I couldn't tell everyone where he was, so I had started to lie where required.

I felt isolated and alone, because some of my friends couldn't and still don't understand why I support him—so I isolated myself from them.

The majority (90 percent) of the mothers in this study reported they believed that they should attend to their husband or children's crisis first and heal themselves later. For example, as Tulip indicated above, she felt it was her responsibility to find a lawyer for her husband. This became her priority. In doing so, she admitted that she often forgot her most primary needs, such as hydrating and eating food. In her mind, too, it was her responsibility to navigate the legal system on behalf of her husband. The implications of continued and built-up neglect of the self or one's quality of life may lead to adverse health issues and unaddressed stress.

BODY SNATCHERS

It is common for grievers to isolate from support networks. Tulip withdrew from her family and friend network because she felt that they did not understand her and her deep feelings of self-described depression. David Evans, author of *Essential Interviewing: A Programmed Approach to Effective Communication*, suggested that helping professionals may be a logical choice for individuals who need someone outside of their informal networks to listen to them (Evans, 2017). In this case, the micro-skill of empathetic listening may be one of the most important roles that the helping professional plays. Employing empathetic listening to women in Tulip's situation can serve as an important first step towards their healing. Women may simply want someone to listen to, not solve, their problems.

Kenneth Doka described grief coupled with withdrawal and shame as "disenfranchised grief." In describing this phenomenon, Doka once compared the feelings associated with grief with a metaphor of the movie, *Invasion of the Body Snatchers* (Doka & Aber, 2002, p217), stating that grieving people tend to behave as though their body is occupied by a force other than their own. The affected person becomes disengaged, going through work, chores, and life as if on autopilot. This may be an expression of guilt-ridden behavior, which is only apparent to family members or to those who really know the affected person well. Although disenfranchised grief theory helps us to understand how grieving women may feel a sense of out-of-body experience, it fails to explain women's feelings of self-blame for the incarceration of a loved one. Therefore, it remains essential to understand the role of *Symbolic Imprisonment* as a co-existing component of grief.

The sense of being responsible for the mate's incarceration not only perpetuated negative self-talk, but also 60 percent of women in this study felt somehow responsible for solving their mate's problems with attorneys or attempts to remedy situations associated with prison life. This sense of responsibility most often occurred if they were in a relationship with a man who had a repeat history of going to prison. This sense of *ownership and responsibility* did not necessarily end upon the mate's release. A research participant named Poppy (whose profile appears later) shared the following narrative:

About January or February, he came back [home from prison]. He was slipping— I started seeing the "red signs," and I was trying to back away. He stole 6 years of my life. [I had] no contact with anyone else [while he was incarcerated]. [I was] just waiting for this man to come home and do the right thing. He has been in and out of prison since he was 10 years old. I didn't mingle with men or no one else. It was just him.

The street got more control over him than I did—I tried, but the streets got him. I helped him for more than 10 years. I was his first girlfriend. I had him going [on the right path] for a while; then drugs took control…. I had him going to a career center, working on resumes, etc. Then he was going to the drug counseling center.

I knew there were red signs. I loved him for six years and he came home, but he didn't do the right thing. I had anger and attitude. When he was gone, I would send him "green.dot" [pre-paid cash] cards here and there…. Now he is facing 17 years. I was shocked and betrayed. He said there was no love for me. He used me.

REENTRY OF A LOVED ONE

As noted, life for the Black female can be difficult even after her partner's release from prison. As we see through Hazel's story, hardships do not end upon the release of her mate. This may be one of the most endearing bonds of the woman's lifetime, but when the object of her affection returns and the bond is hampered by the challenges of reentry, she may fear that her life will never be the same. At times, the affected woman may believe that her world and identity is now defined by her mate's prison record—especially if he cycles in and out of the criminal justice system.

Hazel, for example, tried to remain loyal, cared for the children, and continued to be dedicated as a partner, as evidenced through frequent visits with the children to the prison. However, her spouse challenged her level of commitment to their relationship. She indicated that, at times (while incarcerated), he became suspicious of her activities when she was not at home to answer the phone. She recalled, he questioned her inordinately, "Hey, why didn't you answer your phone? I was calling!" Hazel said she responded to him by saying, "I was really asleep." She told me that this type of exchange usually ended in a big argument: "it was days that we couldn't get past that point—a point that wore me down." She said, "It would have been nice to have a group of women who would, you know, say 'Hey, we go through that all the time.' ...It would have made it easier."

Forty-percent (40 percent) of the women in my study were in their relationship for a year or more. The other women did not disclose their tenure in their relationships, as it was not an interview question. It is obvious that these women had invested time and emotional capital in their relationships. Indeed, some women in my study suffered from low self-esteem, which led to negative thoughts of not being able to find another relationship. Chaney (2011) found that women who partner with an incarcerated man tend to feel loneliness and sadness that may reinforce the need to remain in these relationships. As a result, an ostracized woman may feel that her interpersonal relationship options are limited to her relationship with an incarcerated partner.

ROLE STRAIN

Successful relationships are generally reciprocal and have elements of trust. This tends to be the case whether the relationship is interpersonal, spiritual, or contractual. People want to believe that those toward whom they place their loyalty will in turn treat them with reciprocal devotion. Research indicates that when there is an imbalance, it may lead to role strain (Katz & Piotrkowski, 1983). Role strain describes how women may become overloaded because of the numerous expectations of filling multiple roles, can lead to exhaustion (Katz & Piotrkowski, 1993). These researchers studied the degree to which role strain affects the African American women's family, children, and job. The findings suggest that having an absent husband compounds the woman's distress as she augments her new role (Katz & Piotrkowski, 1983). In the current study, some women faced challenges of finding new ways to balance their responsibilities related to their jobs and familial relationships while maintaining a romantic relationship.

Discussion

In this chapter, we examined how women learned to improvise to find ways to show commitment and affection toward their incarcerated loved one. Finding ways to express emotions to the loved ones helps overcome the physical constraints of prison. We also discussed psychological and social conditions that align with Symbolic Imprisonment, Grief and Coping Theory. Specifically, through Hazel's story, we learned that her devotion to her children and her incarcerated husband are priorities in her life. However, it is also apparent that her commitment to travel to the prison almost every weekend with her children is challenging, requiring both planning and sacrifice.

COPING AND INTERVENTION

In reflection, Hazel appeared to suffer a great deal of survivor's guilt associated with her mate's incarceration. As such, she may have felt guilty because she was able to live freely outside of prison and go about without restriction. Her sense of freedom may have felt unjustified and her guilt of not doing things differently may have led to her thoughts of trying to punish herself or restrict herself. As she indicated, "The street got more control over him than I did." It appears that Hazel felt that it was her responsibility to control her mate. She also remained loyal to him for 10 years while he incarcerated. She discussed the importance of managing his career and guiding his job search. Each of these efforts indicates that she took part ownership of his problem. The danger in doing so is, when he fails, she may feel failure and responsibility as well.

In a study conducted in New York state, Brink (2003), a female chaplain, described her romantic relationship with a prisoner. Prior to her relationship, the chaplain volunteered in the secure medical unit of a prison facility. Brink later became the wife of a prisoner whom she met at the facility. Brink's (2003) description of feelings paralleled with women in this study. She indicated feeling:

• criminalized;
• as if she were serving a sentence with her mate;

• stigmatized even though she had worked in the criminal justice facilities, and
• that her dignity was tied to the prisoner, her husband.

Brink (2003) indicated that she felt that a support group (e.g., See Box 4.1) was one of the most effective means of support. Her husband died five months later, which added to her grief.

**Box 4.1. Psycho-Educational Grief Classes
(Hart-Johnson [2016])**

In my work as a human services practitioner, I facilitated a seven-week course where women with incarcerated mates learn to focus on:

(1) raising awareness of underlying grief and loss;
(2) acknowledging and working through the pain, and
(3) finding ways to live with the incarceration of a loved one through incorporating the absent person into daily life and especially during holidays.

This work aligns well with Worden's (2009) prescribed *Tasks of Mourning* activities for grievers. During my classes I instruct women to engage in facilitated letter writing. As a homework assignment from class, I invite the women to write three letters over a seven-week period. A significant number of the women have underlying pent-up anger and other emotions that they are never able to show because the feel that they must remain strong for their husbands. In essence, these bottled-up emotions are released as narratives in the three separate letters. (These letters are *symbolic* and should *never* be sent to the addressee.)

• *Nemesis:* This letter is to a person with whom the writer is angry or disappointed. The purpose of the letter is to allow the women the freedom to express their frustration.
• *Letter to Significant Other:* The second letter is a letter to the significant other. I tell the women that they should be 100 percent honest, to take their time, and to write as much as they want when completing this homework assignment. What generally happens is the women have the opportunity to release unacknowledged anger and pain toward their significant other. The release of these pent-up feelings allows women to acknowledge the grief and begin to find ways to manage their loss. This step is consistent with Worden's (2009) Task 1, accept the reality of the loss, and Task 2, process the pain of grief.
• *Letter to Self:* The last letter is to the woman herself. When writing this letter, she is guided to be specific and honest about her feelings. She is encouraged to offer herself forgiveness for any wrongs.
• *Other Losses:* Finally, if there are other losses that have occurred and are unresolved, she is encouraged to write a letter to that individual as well. These letters acknowledge loss and express its associated pain.

Worden (2009) posited that the next natural step after Task 1 & 2 is to begin to design a world in which the griever can operate without the absent person.

QUESTIONS TO PONDER

1. What activities and/or intervention strategies would you recommend for clients who have symptoms or reactions consistent with survivor's guilt?

2. How can women balance their need to maintain strong relationship bonds while also developing healthy boundaries for themselves and their children?

3. What recommendations would you provide to women who are trying to find ways to overcome the constraints of geographic distance of remote prisons?

4. How might women maintain the emotional health of a relationship while dealing with the physical restrictions of prison?

5. What is Kenneth Doka's meaning behind his reference to: *Invasion of the Body Snatchers*?

PART II

The Theory of SIG-C

5

SIG-C and Codependency

In this chapter, I explain Symbolic Imprisonment, Grief and Coping Theory (SIG-C). To explain the SIG-C model (Figure 5.1), I use Poppy's story and weave together major concepts and emotional responses explored in Chapter 1 through 4. In previous chapters, we have found that there are many events that can disrupt a person's life and cause one to feel a loss of control. The incarceration of a spouse can create highs and lows experienced during the *incarceration continuum* (from the time of arrest through release depicted in Figure 5.2.). As shown in Figure 5.2., when life disruptions and crises includes financial decisions or choosing between necessities for oneself and children, a woman's *priorities* can become skewed. This is especially true if she feels forced to choose between a decision such as paying the rent or mortgage and using money for her mate's bail. She may opt to take care of her mate through his controlling influence. Depending on how tightly knit she is within her social or family circle, she may not have someone to speak with to help her work through the dilemma. In fact, she may have already *withdrawn* from her social network because she may be overwhelmed from the stigma and exposure of her mate's crime. I refer to this phenomenon as "exposure fatigue." The term *exposure fatigue* explains how a woman might react when her spouse commits a heinous crime and she feels shame and guilt stemming from continuous coverage of the event through television and other forms of media. Without the support of family and friends or a formal support network, the woman may begin to make *irrational decisions* if she is left on her own to figure it out. In extreme cases women, have even become complicit in committing a crime or even lying for her mate in court. This scenario is partially demonstrated through Poppy's case study.

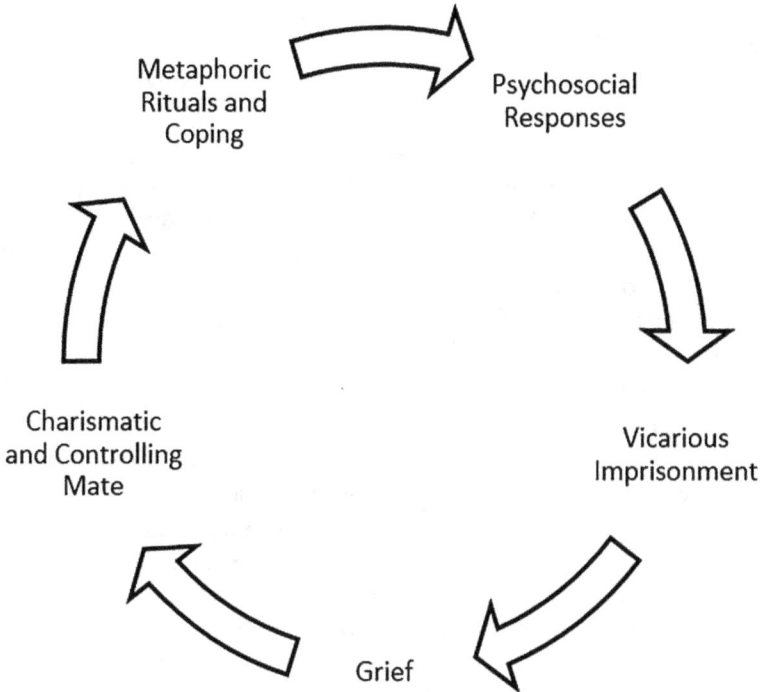

Metaphoric Rituals and Coping

Psychosocial Responses

Charismatic and Controlling Mate

Vicarious Imprisonment

Grief

Figure 5.1. SIG-C processes.

Case Study: Poppy

Poppy is a 48-year-old African American woman. She is dedicated to her relationship with her mate even though they have suffered several breakups. When I interviewed Poppy, I could hear the heaviness in her voice as she described her grief. She said her feeling of being completely alone felt similar to how she felt when her father died—she could not shake the deep sense of loss associated with her boyfriend, James, going to prison. Poppy expressed that these feelings were both "real" and "debilitating." For more than ten years, she remembered the shock of his arrest as if it were fresh pain. She still cries, a lot, today. During his initial incarceration, Poppy said she funded his canteen (prison commissary account), provided his clothing, and attended to his needs. James, she said, made her feel beautiful and valued. He understood her, she said, like no one else.

Poppy said she spent her days waiting for his letters and, especially, his collect phone calls. She knew better than to leave her home when anticipating a call. Her unavailability would upset him and it might take weeks to repair the damage. At times, James could be brutal on the phone, she noted, calling her derogatory names and assaulting her character because of what she referred to as his "trust issues." If she threatened to leave him, his romanticism would lure her back in the relationship. She found herself carrying his photo and playing his favorite songs on her playlist, to feel close to him. At times, she became overwhelmed with hopelessness and with sadness, especially if they lost touch because a violation resulted in his transfer/sentence to the SHU (the segregation housing unit) or to another prison. Shame or stigma complicated her feelings of not having a normal relationship.

Eventually, Poppy began punishing herself by staying indoors for long periods, only leaving the house for obligatory reasons, such as going to work. She had decided she would no longer enjoy her personal freedom if James could not. She cut herself off from her social networks and friends.

I interviewed Poppy during the time when James was on parole. During that period, he had an affair with another woman. He eventually pleaded to Poppy for their relationship to be reconciled after he learned that he violated parole and would be returning to prison and serving a 17-year sentence. Poppy indicated during our interview that anticipating his return to prison was the reason for her extreme sadness.

What Does SIG-C Really Mean?

Poppy's story conveys themes similar to those identified in other women's interview transcripts covered in previous chapters. Poppy's story highlights several aspects of the set of behaviors under the umbrella or model, *Symbolic Imprisonment, Grief and Coping (SIG-C) Theory*. Teasing out the specific themes, we find five main sub-areas or categories of behavior occurring in the research subjects. As a recap of the previous chapters, this theory includes:

Symbolic Imprisonment, Grief and Coping Theory (SIG-C):

- Vicarious Imprisonment
- Psychosocial Responses to Loss
- Charismatic and Controlling Mate Encounters
- Grief Akin to Losing a Loved one by Death
- Metaphoric Rituals and Coping, and

Using SIG-C as a lens, we can compare and interpret Poppy's isolation as a state of *Vicarious Imprisonment*. Her isolation may be a conscious response from a lack of social support from family or friends. Her life as described feels unpredictable and she feels cheated from a future that she felt she deserved. *Why me?* is a question that women in her predicament commonly ask—as if life rudely targeted them for crisis. Examining Poppy's story further, we learn that she is also subject to a power differential in her relationship. In other words, James is controlling, verbally abusive, and demanding, and Poppy feels compelled to be submissive to his demands.

One might think that Poppy is influenced by her social environment. Her behavior, value system, and expectations appear to be influenced by her social networks and inner circles. However, during the interview, I learned that she is very dependent on James for companionship and lacks close friends to balance out that dependency.

Through her trauma, Poppy has learned to suppress her feelings, hide her relationship, and adjust to a volatile relationship with James. He fills the void of her abandonment (e.g., family and social networks). In her community, she may feel embarrassed because she does not have a "normal" relationship, but, rather, one generally frowned upon by the public, and she is viewed as guilty by association. Each of these conditions evolves from her *Psychosocial Responses to Loss.*

Although Poppy is ashamed of her relationship, her current identity appears to be defined by her success or failure as James' girlfriend. Even when Poppy threatened to leave him, she believed that James was in control and ultimately had the last say in the matter. Through manipulation, James was able to influence Poppy's thoughts and, in some cases, control her behavior. James' influence is identified in the SIG-C model as *Charismatic and Controlling [Mate] Encounters.* This element describes how men may be romantic and wonderful at times, cruel and chauvinistic at others. In essence, James is controlling Poppy's freedom from his prison cell.

Grief is another component of SIG-C exhibited in my interview with Poppy. Her "deep sense of loss" is descriptive of dreams not realized: a longing for a normal relationship. Her life is incomplete and she longs to be self-actualized, but she does not know how. She recognizes that her relationship lacks the element of mutual respect. Poppy may have equated James' infidelity with her own negative self-appraisal, or, said differently, she may think that she is not good enough for him. This type of evaluation may adversely affect her self-confidence and self-esteem. These negative thoughts create a cycle of self-doubt and self-criticism. Her feeling of being *stuck* may compound her grief.

Poppy's *psychosocial* reactions and emotional conditions are a bit complex. She feels incapable of walking away from the relationship, given that she has no support system. This theme of being drawn in to stay in the relationship is consistent throughout this text. Poppy doubts her ability to form new, healthy relationships. Her coping strategies include clinging to James for companionship and reassurance. In summary, this reinforcing cycle of Poppy's reactions include: emotional responses such as feeling stigmatized, victimized, abandoned, and exhibiting self-defeating behaviors (*Psychosocial Responses*); social withdrawal and self-punishment (*Vicarious Imprisonment*); grieving the loss of a life not realized and the loss of James' physical presence (*Grief*), and at times, feeling manipulated and charmed (*Charismatic and Controlling Encounters*). Finally, her method of enduring these challenges was through communication and interaction with James (*Metaphoric Rituals and Coping*). Each theme is each illustrated in Figure 5.1.

THE CYCLE OF SIG-C
AND THE POWER OF CHOICE

The complexities and emotions related to SIG-C are intrinsic to Poppy's story. A supportive social environment could help Poppy to adjust and obtain affirmation from others that her responses to her situation are

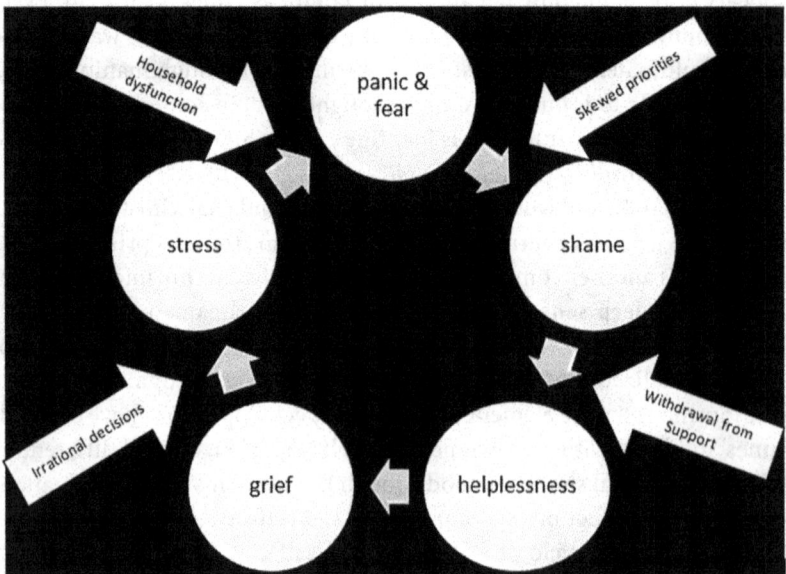

Figure 5.2. Emotional cycle of a mate's incarceration

sufficient and that relationships typically have hardships. In contrast, a lack of support and exclusion may convey the message that she does not fit established norms, and further, her relationship is socially unacceptable. Poppy must come to recognize her own strength and exercise her power of personal choice. Before examining coping strategies, I offer insights on women's experiences during the continuum of arrest through release phases of incarceration (See Figure 5.3).

THE EMOTIONAL CYCLE
OF A MATE'S INCARCERATION

The adverse impacts of incarceration begin long before the absent mate begins serving his prison sentence. The psychosocial impacts include family and social disruptions. This emotional cycle can become overwhelming for the woman who is on the outside. Using Poppy to illustrate, the *incarceration continuum* (Figure 5.2), we learned that Poppy experienced *crisis* during the time of James' arrest. She experienced both *panic and fear* (Figure 5.2). Poppy was not alone with this feeling. The overwhelming majority of women in this study also experienced crisis, followed by a sense of panic and anxiety. Following these intense feelings, women also experience the *shame* associated with a mate's incarceration

Whether Lotus, Hazel, Willow, or others, these women each felt shame. Some women felt they must lie about the arrest and incarceration to save face. Although the feeling of *helplessness* is not linear, generally, when combined with fear, shame, and feeling overwhelmed, women begin to feel as though they have no power in the situation.

As a common practice, women mobilize support for their mate. They seek out resources to support their husbands or boyfriends, often putting aside their own needs and feelings as they try to navigate the criminal justice system on behalf of their loved ones. They may find attorneys or draft legal briefs. Women have contacted the media or engaged family members to support their loved ones. When their efforts fail, *grief* ensues, and *stress* is a common occurrence. In the theoretical model, these emotions are properties of the construct, *Psychosocial Responses to Loss*.

Manifestations of this emotional cycle are *household dysfunction, skewed priorities, withdrawal from support networks, and irrational decision-making* (as noted in Figure 5.2). When women are not thinking clearly, they may make choices that result in a breakdown of the family system. This is one of the reasons that a support network is critical and instrumental to women's recovery from crisis. Codependency is another phenomenon, mentioned earlier, that is also worthy of highlighting when exploring Poppy's relationship.

SELF-BLAME AND
SELF-DEFEATING BEHAVIORS

Poppy is in a codependent relationship. Her husband has a drug problem and a pattern of re-offending. Women in codependent relationships experience the addict's behavior projected on them as being the supporter or enabler. This creates an imbalance and imposes the burden of addiction on the supporter. The supporter becomes a victim in the cycle of the addicted person's enslaved habits. This cycle results in the supporter feeling as though he or she is responsible to "fix" what is broken, as illustrated through both Lotus' and Poppy's story.

Through the vicious cycle of trying to fix what is broken, Poppy engages in self-blame, which in turn becomes self-defeating and a toxic ingredient in the codependent relationship.

One characteristic that makes Poppy's outlook rather bleak is that she has no strong support system. Therefore, her alternative is to continue to remain in the relationship because it is familiar, even though her mate mistreats her. She stated:

> He wasn't really sincere. I didn't back completely off, but I am already in love. [I thought to myself], "I have been giving you my *all* for the last six years." Then I had to do the right thing for myself and back away, but I still got hurt. It is a vicious cycle. I tried to stop dealing with those things. A week or two later, he comes back and he wants to know about my attitude. The person you broke bread with ... now you going back to prison for 17... calling and asking for me and that you need your friend back. The last time I opened the door, he put a gun in my face.
>
> I went through this with someone [I] love. I really haven't accepted this situation. It is a process for me right now. I really need to get myself together. I was really fucked over for no apparent reason. [He] used me because he was able to use me.

Recall that Hazel's experience with her beau was different from Poppy's experience; both, however, are in a codependent relationship. Hewitt, Coak, and Smale (2004) indicated that it is difficult to define a codependent relationship because of its complex nature. These relationships tend to be prevalent among drug- or alcohol-dependent individuals. Generally, relationship bonds between dependent and codependent persons are unbalanced. The dependent person may become hostile, manipulative, and even abusive (Wright & Wright, 1999). I would suggest that having one's life centered around the issues of a mate's incarceration and meeting the demands of being at home to answer the phone, cater to the incarcerated mate's needs, as Poppy did, is consistent with a codependent relationship.

The topic of codependency needs more exploration in the literature. Yet, this notion brings about a need for a robust discussion on relationships where reciprocity is lacking. One might say that incarcerated men may not have the ability to reciprocate a woman's needs while incapacitated by prison. This topic certainly bears exploration. It is realistic to assume that negative encounters between parents may have a spillover effect on children.

Themes and Insights

FAMILY SYSTEMS SHAPED BY INCARCERATION

Codependency and incarceration can influence the family system. Groom (1991) corroborates the notion that codependent behavior can extend to the entire family, whereby the focus becomes the addicted person's wants, needs, and demands. If children are involved, they may become a secondary focus for the parents; the members of the co-dependent relationship lose sight of family priorities and, consequently, the children may miss out on proper nurturing, affection, and possibly the formation of secure attachments. This can be especially troubling to children when there are indicators of loss and separation even before the incarceration of a parent. According to Ackerman, Kashy, Donnellan, and Conger (2011), a *functional* family unit is fundamental to a child's development of healthy social networks and personal well-being.

During family chaos associated with a parent's imprisonment, both parents may appear to be unavailable to the child or children. Therefore, it is reasonable to assume that a child may suffer. For instance, one parent may have demanding and addictive behaviors and the other may be psychologically preoccupied and emotionally unavailable, unable to care for the emotional needs of the children.

Based on the family system theory, when there is disruption to the family system, members of the household tend to struggle to regain normalcy to restore equilibrium within the household (The Bowen Center for Study of the Family, 2016). To do so, they may also find themselves even changing roles to compensate for a family member's absence. They also may try to cover up or conceal public humiliation and public embarrassment caused by a family member's incarceration.

The nature of codependent relationships involves one's self-identity towards another, and the individual becomes deeply enmeshed with his or her partner's growth. From the view of individuals outside of the family unit, it may appear to be a dysfunctional relationship. On the inside, family members may feel a great deal of pain and suffering, especially when a family member's behavior has shaped and defined family member identities. I have found through this research that when the loved one is no longer there (is incarcerated), as odd as it may seem, the family members may feel loss and abandonment, similar to Stockholm Syndrome, where a person develops a relationship with his or her captor. This parallel is tightly coupled with the concept of *Symbolic Imprisonment*. To recover, the members must figure out who they are as well as what their new role will be. The danger associated with negative societal or even familial attitudes towards the codependent person can result in exacerbating this condition. Affected people tend to turn their insecurities inward and indulge in self-loathing and blame. When others slight them or ostracize them, it reinforces their own personal narratives of being "broken."

It is clear that not all women will experience a relationship with a dominating boyfriend like James. Some men are the opposite of James, where their protective qualities are the norm rather than exhibiting restrictive or jealous assertions of power. Different family configurations may also influence how women respond to their loved one's incarceration, especially if the woman has children. In the next chapter, the family dynamic as it relates to incarceration of a significant loved one is explored through the lens: *Psychosocial Responses to Loss.*

Discussion

In this chapter, we examined Poppy's exposure to stressful conditions from a crisis associated with her mate's incarceration. In her vulnerability, she was susceptible to emotions reinforced by her mate's manipulation. We examined the entire set of processes of Symbolic Imprisonment, Grief and Coping Theory, as realized in her story. These thematic constructs are apparent in each of the women's stories. As a review, in this section, we covered the following constructs:

1. **Psychosocial Responses to Loss:** Women exposed to the effects of the incarceration continuum may experience a cycle of emotions leading to skewed priorities, withdrawal, irrational decisions, and family dysfunction.

2. **Charismatic and Controlling Encounters:** Women in a vulnerable state are susceptible to manipulation by the incarcerated loved one and can be at risk for codependent relationships.

3. **Vicarious Imprisonment:** The state of withdrawal reinforced by shame is the state of *Vicarious Imprisonment*. This construct represents the behavior of feeling criminalized and is nested under the larger whole, Symbolic Imprisonment, Grief and Coping Theory. In this chapter, we also see repeat themes of women remaining in relationships because they are committed and sometimes, *stuck*.

4. **Grief:** A consistent theme found in each of the women's interviews is resultant grief. Their expressions of this emotion tended to vary. Women

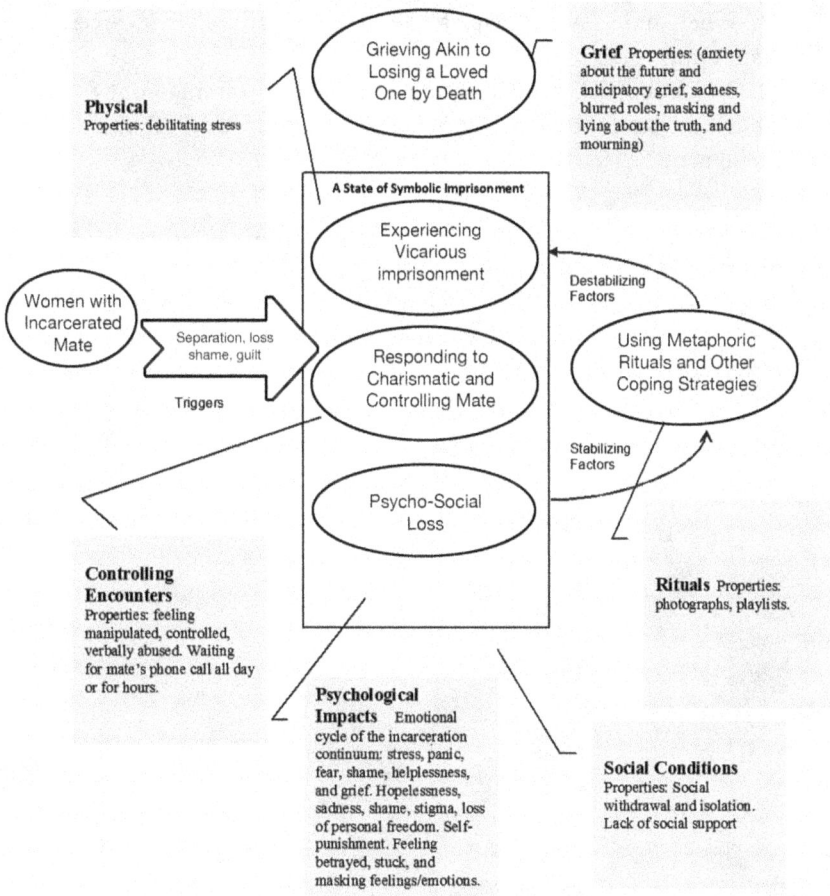

Figure 5.3. SIG-C model: Poppy.

grieved the life that they felt would never be their future(s). They also grieved the separation from their mate. Women also experienced grief during their mate's arrest. During this early period, they began grieving with anticipation of what would be lost after their mate's sentencing.

The theoretical model in Figure 5.3 reflects Symbolic Imprisonment, Grief and Coping (SIG-C) as aligned with Poppy's story.

Questions to Ponder

1. What resources would you recommend for clients such as Poppy?

2. How might a human services practitioner provide expertise in the area of family systems?

3. What strategies can help affected women endure the incarceration continuum?

4. The full SIG-C model is displayed below. Examine Poppy's story through the lens of this theory. What parts of the model require further development?

6

"Down to ride"

Sometimes, to preserve human dignity and respect, people rationalize the qualities of their relationships, telling themselves stories—then, believing them. Some women in this study felt compelled to tell me their mate was smart or intelligent. They needed to justify the relationship. Laura Fishman calls this process, "Accommodating to Male Criminality" (Fishman, 1990, p.51). This rationale for women justifies the relationship and is exhibited as preserving their dignity of being in the relationship:

• Explaining how they partner with these men, regardless of the crimes committed;

• Merging their stories with their husband/boyfriend as a singular, ill-fated set of circumstances—leaving both victim to a corrupt criminal justice system.

Case Study: Sage

I was petrified of this guy that I met in a T-Mobile store. But, his conversation.... I was like, "Mmm, let me find out what this guy is about." His, vocabulary is [such, that], you would never be able to put it with his outside appearance. He doesn't look like he's intelligent at all. He looks like he's airhead, you know, a hood rat off the street. He looks like a statistic. That's exactly what he looks like. He fits in. At first, he had dreads and tattoos everywhere, so he really didn't look like a smart guy. But he's really smart. So, that really like pulled me, reeled me in quickly.

Sage's boyfriend was her love, someone she could talk to, and someone who understood her "like no other person." Sage recalled the day of her boyfriend's arrest, a day that changed her life as she previously knew it. She indicated that he called her just before arriving to school. Sage reflected:

[He said] "you know, I love you and I'm getting ready to, um, lay down for a while [go underground/lay low]." And I was like, "What?" And, he was like, "I can't really talk to you too much about, what's going on. I just need you to know that and I need you to be on my side. If anything happens, I need to know you are going to be *down to ride* [stay loyal]." And I said, "Of course." And then I go to call the phone back like two hours later, because he said he's going to call me back. And I go to call the phone and the phone was shut off. So, I'm like "okay ... that's weird." It wasn't like him, the service was disconnected or anything like, that, it was the phone was going straight to voicemail. So, maybe a week later, I got a phone call from his mother saying that, um, he is locked up and he was getting ready to go to the hearing to find out if he was going to get a bail or not, a bond. And, then, when she called me back two days after that, she was told, they weren't going to release him and he was looking at doing fifteen years to twenty-five years, and I was like, "Whoa. Okay. Where do I go from [here]?"

Sage and her boyfriend formed a pact. She told him that she would support him while incarcerated. The shock of his arrest may have been one of the most significant life-changing events that she experienced. At one point, she was in denial. As she indicated, she called his phone with expectations that he would answer. It must have been devastating to learn that he would be facing 15 to 25 years in prison.

At times, an incarcerated loved one brings together family members who do not know each other, but learn of each other through a common crisis and difficulty. Sage shared what it was like to interact with his family:

I never really dealt with Miss [mother-in-law], um, I'm just starting to warm up to her really because she doesn't know me, I don't know her. She only knows what her son tells her, but seeing as though he got locked up, when I was so young and I, I haven't even experienced yet; I'm still a baby. I was completely just shocked. It was just a sad, I was, not even sad, more so depressed, that this guy, that I'm madly in love [and he is] really incarcerated. Like, he's not in jail; he's not coming home in two weeks.

Here is evidence of Sage's denial. She is struggling with fathoming that her boyfriend is going to remain in prison for a long while. In her reasoning, she clearly makes the distinction between a jail sentence and a prison sentence. If sentenced to jail, he would at least be in the D.C. vicinity. However, a prison sentence meant both an out-of-state sentence and a longer incarceration.

I was telling to myself [he], is going to find some way to get his self out of this mess. He got himself into this mess. So, he's going to find some way to get out. I was also lying to myself, making myself believe that he really wasn't in jail. He was just avoiding me. You know, lying about his location. Not picking up the phone to call me. I was really lying to myself. To keep myself from going crazy although I knew the truth. I really told myself a lot of lies just to make believe, "Oh, he's going to knock on the door tomorrow and everything's just going to be back to, how things were."

Box 6.1. Nasir Jones (Nas):
Time Is Illmatic

During this *Time Is Illmatic,* documentary, when the theme song played, Q-tip, a fellow rap artist, explained that the meaning behind these lyrics convey a strong message about the Black community. He stated, this song is about "keeping people's head up in locked-up situations." This song details African American men's incarceration as well as how women in these relationships are expected to ensure that they stick by their man while he is in the system [prison] or doing his bid [serving prison sentence]. Q-tip further stated:

> *"Not only do you [criminal justice system] incarcerate them [Black men] in a physical sense, but you emasculate them. There's this thing that we say in the hood 'Yo, she's a good bit*h, she going to bid with you, she not f*#king around, she's galvanizing all your people, making sure you get visits, she's holding you down"* (Frame 57:44).

He added that when a woman is Black, living in a dysfunctional society where jobs are few and that the prison system "destroys union ... promise and hope" (Frame 59:56).

Twenty-five years is a long time to remain loyal to anyone. "*Being down to ride,*" is code for standing by your man during his incarceration, or *doing a bid.* The urban sub-cultural expectation and *de facto* school of thought is that when a man goes to prison, his woman is supposed to support him. Nasir (Nas) Jones conveyed this notion though the lyrics of a rap song, discussed in Box 6.1.

Popular hip-hop or rap music often tells a story of how individuals view their lives and their communities. Nasir Jones's documentary focuses on how a significant number of his friends are serving time and describes how, while doing so, life is continuing without them. The notion that the non-incarcerated women must galvanize friends, family, and other modes of support as the conduit on the outside of prison is a reality that each of the women in this sample understood and obliged, even if they were on the verge of ending their relationships. Finally, the song implies that women should keep their heads up, serve time along with their mate [e.g., *Vicarious Imprisonment*], and ensure that family and friends on the outside do not forget the inmate. This burden and responsibility may also explain why women such as Lotus did not leave their husband or mate once they became incarcerated.

TIME STOLEN: IN LIMBO

While loyalty may be an expectation held by incarcerated men, as for Sage, 15–25 years is a long time to support her boyfriend. The grief over losing a relationship during youth can be quite devastating (Martin, 2002). Some researchers have found that this grief is just as intense as a loss through death (as discussed in Chapter 9). When Sage stated that she became involved with someone else, it was not only a coping mechanism, it appeared that she was also trying to justify how he qualified as her other boyfriend at the time of the interview:

> Before he went to jail, he was my boyfriend. Then, when he got in jail, he was still my boyfriend. Then we broke up. Then we got back together. Then, three years went by, he didn't hear from me, and so, of course, I had met this [other] guy, fell in love, got married, blah. Then I talked to him right before I was getting ready to have the baby. And then I told him right after having the baby, because we weren't together, I told him I had the baby. And my husband told me that he wanted to get a divorce in the delivery room and I don't know what I did wrong. And then he was just like, so we just need to be together. And then from April fifth now we have been together.

Sage felt betrayed by her husband by marriage. She indicated that she did not know "what she did wrong" to cause the divorce, an indicator that she had a tendency to self-blame in certain situations. Perhaps that is why she rekindled her original relationship with her incarcerated boyfriend.

Sage's situation primes additional discussion for the benefits of *Vicarious Imprisonment* when having an incarcerated boyfriend or husband.

VICARIOUS IMPRISONMENT (VI)

Vicarious Imprisonment (VI) is an aspect of the model SIG-C that describes both emotional and physical self-imposed confinement. Mothers may impose these restrictions on their children as well, thereby incorporating them in the state of *Vicarious Imprisonment* or restricted confinement. In my research study, women described what the term *VI* includes:

- Debilitating stress, fear, anger, and overwhelming sadness associated with their significant other's incarceration
- Depression and extreme bouts with sadness
- A withdrawal from family and social networks
- Reduced attendance at social events and activities

One woman in the study shared, "I feel like a prisoner in my own mind." Another woman indicated, "I restrict myself; I do it a lot," and another shared, "If he was in pain, then I was in pain." The most common themes and characteristics related to VI and reported by women included:

- Shame and disgrace
- Having a strong sense of guilt

- Taking part in strict regimens and controlled behaviors
- Exacerbated and perpetual grief
- Confinement that includes purposely creating uncomfortable living arrangements for self
- Identifying with feeling criminal, even though no crime has been committed, and
- Wanting to emulate the mate's state of incarceration (reduced food intake, restricting television, no sex, and reduced social interactions).

Notably, I found no other scientific research that described the above conditions of *Vicarious Imprisonment*. However, women indicate that when men begin to serve their sentences, the women on the outside may feel sentenced, as well. However, I believe that SIG-C, in its totality, more appropriately describes the broad range of emotional responses by women that may occur during this type of crisis. An interpretation of *Vicarious Imprisonment* or *VI* behavior is that women emulate their mate's confinement as a defense mechanism, an extenuation of grief, and at times, as self-punishment.

This condition is concerning when women are vulnerable and possibly at weak points in their lives. Helping professionals may offer support, assisting women to understand where their self-sabotaging behaviors originate. It may also be helpful to understand their feelings of guilt. Practitioners may be able to help women to focus on the positive aspects of their lives, such as their ability to work and to support the family. Women may also learn how to develop stronger self-esteem, where the perhaps dependent conditional approval of others and outsider evaluations does not cause them to lose perspective of who they are.

Women who did not experience *VI* were self-described as having resilience, self-efficacy, and a low tolerance for anything related to the criminal justice system. These women used words to describe their own characteristics, such as: "independent," "strong," "in control," "faithful," and "hopeful." Inversely, those whose behaviors were consistent with *VI* expressed self-doubt, low self-esteem, or indicated that they did not feel confident at the time of their mate's incarceration. They self-identified with terms such as: "helplessness," "doubt," "controlled," "manipulated," "criminalized," and "shunned."

Shaming and Social Isolation—Characteristic of Vicarious Imprisonment

Finally, shame may operate as a catalyst to women's need for social isolation. Women who socially withdrew and confined themselves to restricted behavior indicated it was intentional. I do not proclaim that social isolation, in itself, is problematic or even pathological. It is possible that this state of isolation is necessary to recover and adjust. What I do suggest is that social withdrawal for an extended time may be cause for concern, especially if a woman's quality of life and her health suffer. Extreme levels of avoidance may be a sign that the woman is having a hard time coming to terms with the situation. Rose's stress, as conveyed below may exacerbate other existing emotional conditions as detailed here:

> I guess I could say, I'm [an] emotional person. And everyone is sad for me. I [would] just rather be by myself [than] to deal with … my own issues. I'd rather not keep talking about it [to others], going over it and over it. So, I don't really involve people with my emotional aspects of the situation.
>
> … I can't really think of nothing that was good; like I said, I was going through so many different things at that time. So, I can't think about anything as good. And, I mean 5 days a week … it [was] a bad situation within itself.

Although the majority (80 percent) of the women in this study convey the extreme state of *VI*, as I examined other women's interview transcripts and subsequent themes, it became apparent that there are exceptions, examples which show that some women may actually benefit from isolation. Therefore, the state of *VI* is not completely adverse. For example, *VI* can help to:

- Resolve the guilt and shame.
- Provide time to meditate and contemplate new goals and recover from shock.
- Serve as protection from harsh critics and judgment from others.

The above forms of protection may help women to avoid another commonality of having an incarcerated mate: "victim blaming." This term is explained in Sage's remarks, below, where she conveys that her friends have placed conditions on their friendship concerning all discussion specific to her incarcerated mate. In other words, her friends are tired of hearing about her problems with her incarcerated boyfriend:

> I really can't get it together. I'm very emotional. I'm not really focused. When I'm at work, I'm not focused. When I'm out with friends, I am not focused. I am focused on paying attention to taking care of him. I'm thinking about everything. It was just like a[n] overload. Sometimes I get overwhelmed and I get sick—I vomit.
>
> I really feel like I'm crazy sometimes because I never experienced this before. It is a human being we're talking about here. I don't really have anybody to talk to. When I talk to people, they [are] like, I don't want to hear that. I just shut down and get into my own world—where I'm just sick.

At a time when Sage needed her friends the most, they left her to work through her pain, alone. She is distraught and stressed to the point of sickness—"I vomit," she said, when speaking of her anxiety-induced sate. Indirectly, her friends appear to infer that they do not want to deal with this messy part of Sage's life or blame her for her perils, known as "victim blaming." Perhaps, her friends are intentionally withholding empathy and support. It is also possible that her friends do not know what to say or how to address her situation.

Themes and Insights

Victim Blaming

Discussing a person's incarceration or arrest may be uncomfortable for family members or friends. Surprisingly, I found that, in general, women did not want to have a discussion, per se; they simply wanted someone to listen to them, not solve their problems. As noted, an empathetic listener may help the woman draw upon her personal resources to regain a sense of inner control.

Unfortunately, some people have no sympathy for wives of offenders. Victim blaming generally refers to blaming a person victimized by crime, as if he or she caused the crime. In a way, it makes the victim feel inadequate from not preventing the situation. By labeling or stigmatizing the victim, it establishes that the victim is *different* and creates a *"them versus us"* mentality. Sometimes, stigma and victim blaming are accomplished indirectly. For example, the use of passive rather than active words to describe a woman's relationship with an incarcerated husband might include these variations:

- John is incarcerated
- Mary's husband, John, is incarcerated
- Mary is a prison wife

In the first bullet, the burden and emphasis points to John's incarceration. Therefore, an insinuation is that John bears the responsibility of his incarceration. In the second bullet, the emphasis is on Mary, subtly suggesting that it is her burden and choice to be in a situation with an offender. The third bullet also places the emphasis on Mary. In the last occurrence, Mary chooses to be a prison wife. These slights may be inadvertent, subtle, and commonly used phrases of victim blamers.

There is a myth that women who partner with offenders are themselves criminals. This myth validates the narratives of these victimizers and judgmental people. In contrast to this myth, I found that, in two cases (10 percent), women indicated that their first interaction with the criminal justice system was during their husband's arrest.

Finally, victimized women fit the risk pattern of ending their marriages or relationships because of external pressure by friends or relatives. At the very least, outside influences, friends, family and extended family, and those in the community may cause these women to question why they are in the relationship at all.

WHY ARE WOMEN
IN THESE RELATIONSHIPS?

People may ask why women are in these types of relationships that come with so much emotional baggage and stigma. We can only conjecture the true answer. Inward-directed feelings such as guilt and shame may manifest as self-blame and as a direct result, from a lack of control over a problem such as women in the study experienced concerning their boyfriend or husband's incarceration. Typically, women who have low self-worth or low self-esteem desperately need to be loved and will try to sustain their relationships at all costs. It is possible that women with low self-esteem are the primary targets of men who are seeking out a partner to help sustain them during their incarceration. An example from Rose:

> My dad wasn't in the house. So, it was just me, my sister, and my mom. So, no; this man shall be something—he said he loved me. Even though I know in my heart the part he was out doing other stuff. Do you know what I'm saying?—cheating and all that stuff. I mean, self-esteem. I just didn't love myself. I really did not love myself for even taking myself through that [prison experience with my mate].

From the example above, it is clear that Rose experienced betrayal; she also indicated that she did not love herself. In her vulnerable state, Rose is a prime candidate, vulnerable to control and manipulation. Rose's profile also fits the criteria for women whom I identified as high-risk for grief. These women may be:

- Clinging and dependent
- Ambivalent about the relationship
- Alone, with no close family or support network
- From a family or cultural background where she is frowned upon for disclosing her problems

These characteristics tend to align with the reactions included under the rubric of what I have termed: *Charismatic and Controlling Mate Encounters,* outlined in Chapter 8.

Discussion

In this chapter, we learned about the *de facto* commitment and expectations for women to remain faithful to incarcerated mates. This does not necessarily mean that the woman will remain faithful to the relationship for the entire time of the mate's imprisonment. However, it does suggest that there is a creed that operates at a substrate level that I have not found reported in the literature, but is certainly in evidence in certain subcultures.

Additionally, a woman's need for loyalty may cause her to feel as though she is stuck, in limbo, or feel as though her life is on hold, as described by the women below:

Jazmine: "Like I've stuck it out."
Mansi: "Sometimes, you know, I'm stuck in the house, so you...."
Willow: "I'm so stuck in [the] depression...."
Rosemary: "Now, with my husband, we lost five years of the time—five years; we can't go back."

Women may have felt stuck; however, most remained loyal and committed to maintaining their family and supporting their husband or boyfriends. *Vicarious Imprisonment* appears to be a powerful reinforcing cycle that shows how women have a propensity to stay in the relationship even when they themselves are free. As Lotus indicated: "While he was in prison, we were in prison, we should have [been] free."

In this chapter, we also examined how Sage expressed intermittent loyalty to her partner. We also learned about women "doing their bid" or serving a *Vicarious Incarceration* along with their mates. This characteristic is also associated with properties such as social isolation and withdrawal.

Women also gained benefits from a mate's incarceration. For example, their relationships offered support in lieu of disapproval by family and friends of their relationships. We learned how women experience stigma and victim blaming. Finally, we covered themes that help us to understand why women stay in relationships with a confined person. The sections below highlight aspects of the SIG-C model as constructs and supporting properties, and/or triggers.

1. **Psychosocial Responses to Loss:** Some women felt that their lives were placed on hold. To preserve their dignity and respect, they sometimes embellished the truth; at other times, they felt they were compelled to lie. Stress and sadness were also prevalent in Sage's case example. Sage was torn between allegiance to a non-incarcerated man and loyalty to the incarcerated man.

2. **Charismatic and Controlling Encounters:** In this chapter, both men manipulated Sage: Her non-incarcerated husband mistreated her, and her incarcerated mate kept her in the relationship through his charm.

3. **Vicarious Imprisonment:** Sage demonstrates the state of *Vicarious Imprisonment* through her expressed desire to place her life on hold for 15 or 20 years. She exhibits both physical confinement and psychological constraints. Shame and social isolation from her friends reinforce her need to hide or to withdraw.

4. **Grief:** Again, grief is prevalent as an underpinning to *Symbolic Imprisonment*.

5. **Metaphoric Rituals and Coping:** Sage used her affair to cope.

6. **Shame, stigma, loyalty, and loneliness, as triggers:** Women tended to be prone to social withdrawal resulting from stigma, their loyalty to their mate, and as a form of *Vicarious Imprisonment*.

QUESTIONS TO PONDER

1. How would you approach a discussion regarding a woman being "down to ride"? Would you encourage the relationship if the mate were facing 15 to 25 years' incarceration, as was Sage's boyfriend?

2. If a woman is married to a person facing life in prison, how, if at all, would your answer to item number one change?

3. What intervention strategies would you offer Sage?

4. How could Sage increase her support network?

5. How could Sage address here isolation?

7

Charismatic
and Controlling Mate—
A Jekyll-and-Hyde Situation

In this study, among the women interviewed, two types of self-image are prominent: women who are self-confident and those who lack self-confidence (according to their own accounts). Women such as Ivy had a high degree of self-confidence. This feature, likely, offsets manipulation by others, specifically her mate.

Case Study: Ivy

Ivy is a 50-year-old African American woman. Ivy's relationship with her incarcerated mate is complicated. Having a family eases the pain of her relationship, strained by her loved one's imprisonment. He is her "secret." Even though she now is married to someone else, she says that she never stopped loving her beau. They still talk, she says, about twice a week. They can talk about any topic. She still feels deep love and respect for his intelligence as well. She met him in high school. He was brilliant, she said. She loved him deeply, but he began to sell drugs. It was too easy back then to become "a runner" and "sling" drugs on the street. He first started selling marijuana and then started selling crack. The laws were changing back then. She recalled President Clinton was in office during the 1990s, and there was a get tough on crime movement and legislation that caused young men, especially Black men, to end up in prison for long sentences. Her boyfriend was one who was caught up in the system.

Ivy wanted more out of life. She wanted college. She had dreams of doing well and helping segments of the populations like her then-boyfriend, who was caught up in the whole drug scene.

Now, she reflects, if he had not gotten involved in the drug scene, she would have married him. Although Ivy is loyal to her husband, she admitted that she cheated when her incarcerated beau came home from prison. He has, since then, become incarcerated again. However, she explained that she was not really cheating. They have been together in spirit for so long. She will always love him, and she emphasizes ... however, her family and current marriage are good. Her children are doing well in school. Her husband acts responsibly. Life is good, but she still misses the part of her life that never stood a chance against the drugs and the street. Therefore, now, she simply enjoys her weekly phone calls and looks forward to discussing a wide range of topics with him. She is a good mother, a family woman and a good wife, with a secret. She reflected on how her attitude has changed over the years. When asked about her feelings towards the treatment of family by society and even the penal system:

> All of those people [affected by incarceration] have different stories. They have families and love lines [sic]. You know, at that point, in the past, I didn't think of this life. But now I know it hurts me. It hurts me that they're just putting people away and not understanding the consequences that they have on almost everyone—not just one person that's been there for him, but the whole family.

THE MATE'S CHARISMA

Based on the stories of the women interviewed, their husbands or boyfriends were not all saints. However, to save face, women rationalized and, at times, constructed counter-narratives that tended to reflect their husband or boyfriend in a more positive light. For example, a husband may have been described as a drug dealer, but the wife may have emphasized his role as a "breadwinner," "a smart man," and a "caring father."

Impression management was important for these women. In other words, it seemed that they wanted me to believe their partner was a "good man," worthy of their relationship investment. During the interviews, I never got the impression that women lied to me. The more positive stories I concluded were an important justification for these women. Some women invested tremendous resources in the relationship. For example, women learned how to become legal advocates for their husbands, investing personal resources and time. To sacrifice so much energy, the man must be worthy; otherwise, she may look foolish and gullible.

Some women inferred that their husbands were victims of an unfair criminal justice system. Perhaps he was racially profiled or railroaded. Although I did not ask the details of their husbands' offenses, women wanted me to know that they were in a relationship with a decent person.

"He is a manipulator"

As suggested earlier in this text, some of the women in the study recognized that their incarcerated loved one was both manipulative and charming. However, it appears that this phenomenon can also have a bit of collusion. For example, some women indicated that, at times, they were coaxed into doing things that they did not want to do and that their engagement in the activity was immoral.

> Indigo: "He blamed me for not following him to Canada and for not listening to him, or he started blaming me—I'm like, 'Look, I've always had my job. I've always worked for my kids. I've gone to every basketball, football [game], and choir rehearsals and violin [practice].' But he blamed me, so that was the start of being broke. He put me down. I was afraid. It was round two—but I was down, for my husband."

Vulnerability appeared to be another common theme, especially apparent in the descriptions of how women felt at the time of their husband's or boyfriend's arrest and incarceration. What was apparent for a few of the women (20 percent) is that the arrest and subsequent incarceration occurred during a time when their self-confidence was in question.

> Lotus: "I was not feeling confident, looking for a relief. Until you know that there is going to be hope, it stays the same. That is the only way to shed the layer of bad skin."

Wives and girlfriends of offenders described their partner's behavior by a variety of terms, including deceptive, smart, romantic, conniving, loyal, and charming. I describe this mixture of reactions to these men, as *Charismatic and Controlling Encounters* in the SIG-C theoretical model.

This phenomenon not only describes how women were attracted to the men, but it also helps us to understand why women may have remained in relationships that were deemed questionable or a bad influence on them by others.

This element of SIG-C is one that also helps us to understand how the reinforcing cycle of *Symbolic Imprisonment* does not necessarily go away once the inmate returns home. Lotus, shared her thoughts about the time when her husband was temporarily released on bond:

The aftermath of his incarceration conveyed that things were lying underneath. After he came home, and he became more comfortable with being released, he said, 'You did nothing for me.' I was not expecting the aftermath after making that sacrifice for him. Anger was very prevalent. It came back—old things started to surface. [He said] 'You haven't done shit for me!' Prior to him going in the system, I was ready to divorce him. He was desperate. I stayed, instead.

[He's a] chameleon—[it's] trickery. They change their behavior to fit the circumstances.

Women sometimes feel exploited by their mate's narcissism. At times, some women expressed, almost in a joking manner, that their mate focused on his own demands for the things he needed and wanted. The women were expected to "jump" to meet their imprisoned mate's demands. Vulnerable women tended to be the most affected by this behavior exhibited by some of their partners.

The interaction between women and the inmate spouse often occurred through telephone calls, in-person visits, and through letters. While confined, men showed their most sensitive side and presented their appearances of love. Through these forms of communication, these men revealed rarely disclosed emotions to their wives and children, as shown through Violet's reflection, followed by an interviewee named Mansi:

Violet: He doesn't show his emotions too much, but it's, like, since he's been in jail, all his emotions are poured out in that letter—and for him to hold on to that letter, like you know, it's really something. I don't know if it's just something different, because they never got a letter from him before. It's just something that they [the children] want to hold on to because they know that they know how he feels— but they know that they're probably never going to get another letter with all the emotion and all the feelings in it. It's just like holding on to something—like that he's just there.

Mansi: I mean, it's like this different religion and it is chasing me. It just really taught me so much … as meditation—it is amazing for me. I feel like I said, I feel closer to him than I ever have before and I feel like he's closer to me because I am able to express myself in ways that I wasn't in the past.

Violet and Mansi share insightful and telling accounts. From their excerpts, we learn that for some women and children, this is the first time that they have been able to tap into the emotions and "feelings" of their incarcerated loved one. We also learn that there is a fear that this may be their last chance to do so. As Violet stated, "they're probably never going to get another letter with all that emotion…." The letter writing shown above demonstrates the power of written letters and expressions as a means to convey deep feelings.

Sage shared through her example how little control women have over communication. She spoke about how the telephone operator cut her off during the last 30 seconds of their conversation before she could complete her thoughts. This experience may be a reminder to women that they no longer have complete control over their communication with their mates. At the very least, this may cause frustration.

Finally, Mansi shared how she felt so much closer to her husband. Perhaps her mate's incarceration is in some ways beneficial. This may be one area that helping professionals can explore together with the client in reframing the crisis in a manner that reveals at least one of the benefits of this type of crisis.

A significant portion of the women interviewed (70 percent), also felt that it was their responsibility to help solve the problem of their mate's incarceration. At times, women indicated that their mate made them feel empty and filled with distrust. Willow also provides her perception:

> I know it's in the past, but trust is a factor—[it is easier] to lie and [know] the relationship is not growing because [he is] incarcerated. It isn't just okay, now you are incarcerated! I'm just going to trust you? When you come home, we realize this can't be [a] happy relationship. Remember, before you were incarcerated, you have to be somewhat of a liar to be cheating. So, you've been incarcerated—don't make believe you're hiding. So, I'm feeling a little empty because I'm just still trying to figure out: Will you be willing to be with me when you come home and away from the cops? So, it was very topsy-turvy.

From Willow's excerpt, we detect her distrust, her disappointment, as she recalls her mate's lies and cheating behavior. She also acknowledges that he must have been deceptive before being locked up. Clearly, there are trust issues and she seems to believe that one of the reasons that he is so loyal at present is because he is locked up. She asked, are you "willing to be with me when you come home and away from the cops?" This element of doubt is strong and revealing in the phenomenon, *Charismatic and Controlling Encounters.* This element of SIG-C is worthy of a study in itself. Future research may provide insight into how strong and significant this factor is in maintaining relationships between the woman and the incarcerated man.

Themes and Insights

LOW SELF-IMAGE
AND MATE'S DEPENDENCY

It was apparent that some incarcerated men used women's empathy as another means of controlling their behavior and gaining their loyalty.

This truth is hard to accept. Some men take advantage of women whom they perceive as weak, or vulnerable, or who have a low self-image. It is also plausible that women who feel unlovable may receive an emotional pay-off from being in a relationship with an incarcerated man. Their relationship may offer the women an opportunity to nurture and support the man and in return feel needed. The woman who lives on the outside of the prison walls may feel a sense of empowerment and the ability to regain control over a situation where she otherwise may have felt helpless.

In this study, women reported that the roles of supporter and caregiver were important to their mate's existence—their mate depended on them. They become the conduit of communication to the outside world and, by fiat, a bridge to other people and resources. These women also reported assisting in maintaining the prison commissary or canteen and contributing to the inmate's phone card. This role may also be reinforcing to the women and this situation provides them with a sense of importance.

As documented earlier, a few of the women openly expressed self-confidence and feeling less than worthy; yet, these women drew upon internal strength to support their mate during his incarceration. All of the women (100 percent) had a strong sense of loyalty that superseded their need to display any personal emotions, especially while in their mate's presence during prison visitation. It appeared as if they wanted to shield and protect their mate from their own vulnerability, sadness, and distress as a display of their sacrifice and loyalty. This type of allegiance and support is shown in the following narratives:

> Olive: "it means not having him to hold me at night and to tell me everything ok, to not be able to be there for him when he needs me and hurting him and his pride for him to depend on me for his needs because he doesn't have it and it means more time in between us getting married."
>
> Jazmine: "Um, I think that, through it all, he knows, like, I'm gonna be there, no matter what. Like, I … I've stuck it out. We've come through all kinds of hard times, tests, and trials and, um, I mean, I think that I am the backbone to the family, and I think that he recognizes that on a daily basis because of all that we've come through."
>
> Poppy: "When he was gone, I always made sure that he had money. I am 48 years old. [Just] think where I could have been. I have grown daughters who told me—don't blame yourself. It is him, not you. What a loss. I have cried a many days and night. I feel so betrayed.

I needed him to be back. Boy ... tried to stop [him from] dealing with those things [drugs]."

Through the narratives of Olive, Jazmine and Poppy, we learn that each of these women acquired a sense of personal empowerment and pride in being able to meet their mate's needs, given his dependency. This sense of loyalty is not necessarily good or bad. These women clearly received satisfaction through providing support and being the "backbone." On the other hand, Poppy conveyed that her relationship resulted in missed opportunities in life. She reflected, at the age of 48, her regret at not being able to control her boyfriend's drug habits; yet, she was unable to walk away. As she indicated, "I needed him to be back"; even though he put a gun in her face, she still was drawn to him.

It is possible that the charismatic behavior and the romance articulated through letters and phone calls from the imprisoned men fill a void and help to provide the love that these women seek.

Discussion

In summary, *Charismatic and Controlling Encounters,* refer to women's reactions and interpersonal relationships with mainly their significant others. Simply put, vulnerable people are sometimes at risk for manipulation. At the extreme level, we saw examples of a mate trying to engage his wife or girlfriend in nefarious acts. Women appeared to have low self-confidence on one hand, but showed strength and nurturance on the other. Women also felt the need to hide their weaknesses and fragility most of the time, especially during prison visitations.

Although women in this study may have exhibited low self-esteem, they may also have gained a sense of power or, perhaps, control over their incarcerated mate in their nurturing role. Additionally, by masking their emotions, they demonstrated to their partner that they could remain strong under stressful circumstances, and, as a reward, had their behaviors appreciated by the men.

Finally, women who cling to men due to their mate's insecurities, the imprisoned status, as well as physical and emotional deficiencies, may become detached from their own social networks while fulfilling the primary role as caregiver. This makes women who fit this profile prime candidates for manipulation. However, as a trade-off, they may rationalize that it is better to have a relationship than to be lonely.

In this chapter, I have explored what I describe as the Jekyll-and-Hyde behavior of a mate who may be thought of as both charming and manipulative. This characteristic, described as Charismatic and Controlling Encounters in the theoretical model, SIG-C. A woman's low self-image and manipulation by her mate could be reinforcing phenomena that perpetuate the ongoing cycle of *Vicarious Imprisonment*.

QUESTIONS TO PONDER

1. How would you address a client who describes herself as devoted to her mate, but you suspect manipulation?

2. How would you establish goal setting with your client?

3. What intervention would you use for self-image and self-esteem building with your client?

4. How, if at all, would you work with your client, specific to her establishing informal support networks?

PART III

Grief, Coping and Ritual

8

Grief: "It's like death"

"Like, I'm grieving over someone [who] died—You know, he's right there; he is alive. But that's how I feel, sometimes. I do feel like, in essence, he is gone. Not like dead. But I do feel that he's gone. He's not there.... I can't roll over to him and touch him. I can't get up in the morning and say goodbye to him, or say good morning, you know. He's not there..."—Sage

"Like I'm grieving over someone who died"

In this chapter, we move from in-depth case studies to select quotes and focus on grief, coping, and ritual used to help women manage their loss. Feelings of sadness and incompleteness, and grief are often the manifestation of women's loss. These women often drew upon their emotional reserves during times of crisis and came up empty. They expressed a profound sense of grief when explaining what it feels like to have a significant other imprisoned.

When the term "grief" is used, generally what comes to mind is permanent loss—or grief from loss because of someone's death. Permanent loss usually generates an outpouring of support from family, friends, and even sympathy from strangers.

However, in cases where the absent person is both alive and incarcerated, the sympathy, support, and outpouring of kindness may not be as forthcoming, if at all. Over half of the women (55 percent), in this study related their experiences of non-death loss, of grief, as having intensity similar to death-related loss. To them, there was minimal difference—in either case, the "physical body is missing." Each of the women indicated that they felt some variation of grief over the incarceration of their mate; the data was consistent with typical expressions of grief. One woman shared, "I feel guilty; sometimes I think that if he were at least dead, we could just move on and get over this grieving."

Grief Work Is a Process

Grief tends to have a lingering presence. In fact, sometimes the family makes decisions, solves dilemmas, and engages in problem solving as if the absent person is still there. Their grief does not necessarily end. Some women indicated that they experience elevated grief and anxiety when their husband or boyfriend filed an appeal to augment his incarceration. They find that they are hopeful, only to be let down. Each cycle of legal challenge may raise unrealistic expectations and yield disappointment. This continuous cycle of appeals, legal filings, and ongoing court appearances prevents women with an incarcerated mate from emotional healing and recovery; this is due to the continuing external focus and ongoing stress.

Grief work takes time. It is realistic to assume that as women adjust and, perhaps, open up to the possibility of new friendships, they may go back into the cycle of grief when other, associated crises occur, such as when their husband or boyfriend is in segregation or transferred to another prison, or reaches out for additional assistance.

The Nature of Loss

Many individuals can adjust to the upheavals of relationships, including separation due to incarceration, without having to seek out professional help and intervention. Those who have support networks in place may find that it is easier to overcome loss if someone is available to listen or provide support.

The nature of loss generates emotional reactions such as sadness due to the absence of an individual or the inability to provide or receive affection. Kenneth Doka explained that separation and even breakups in relationships can result in intensified grief (Doka, 2002). He provides several applicable themes:

- Broken heart (let down, disappointed, and unrequited love);
- Unrecognized grief—discounted by the public;
- Unsanctioned relationship (prisoners are not condoned as an ideal mate for relationship bond);
- A lack of social support.

As illustrated here and thematically in earlier chapters, each of these conditions may elicit disenfranchised grief and add to the person's inability to recover from the loss.

Compromised Quality of Life and Disenfranchised Grief

Kenneth Doka provides a theoretical framework to understand the disenfranchised grief of the affected women akin to those in my study. Doka's (2002) disenfranchised grief theory describes a state of grief where the affected person feels unsupported, ostracized, and at times stigmatized in their grief experiences. This form of grief entails conditions that prevent the individuals from moving through their grief; they feel and often are told that the object or conditions for their grief are unworthy since their loss is not accepted by others as having recognized worth. Although this type of loss, as described, is a non-finite loss, it does not depreciate the amount of pain and suffering a person may feel. Members of society may infer that this type of grief breaks the traditional rules of grieving. Commonly held thoughts may manifest in expressed family and community member reactions, including telling the person:

- You are grieving over a criminal; you are better off without him.
- You should not talk about his incarceration; you make people feel uncomfortable with that type of discussion.
- You should find someone else. The children do not need that type of father to pattern their lives after.
- Okay, it has been a couple of months, you need to get over this man and move on. Life waits for no one.

The aforementioned statements are just a few of the types of insensitive statements that family and friends might convey to a woman who has an incarcerated partner. As indicated, families are unique in their configurations and, generally, they have established norms and expectations. Even if people on the outside are judgmental, this is their family. Negative societal responses may further justify family members' negative views of the women's relationships. The woman also may blame herself for making poor choices in a relationship. The concern here is not to validate or invalidate relationship choices, but rather to determine how best to support a woman's well-being without passing judgment.

Non-Finite Grief: A Number of Emotions

Non-finite loss may excite varied emotions. Both finite and non-finite loss may be socially acceptable, depending on the context. With finite loss, it is customary to hold a ceremony celebrating the life of a loved one and memorialize their death through ritual. Ceremonial gatherings tend to bring together support networks and offer a display of acceptance for the absent person, condoning that the individual relationship is meaningful and accepted.

Women who experience non-finite grief may suffer intense grief and not know that one can mourn the loss through separation of a living loved one. Therefore, it is important to sensitize helping professionals to the wide array of losses that fall outside the general context of grief. Additionally, the grief modalities should be developed for women with incarcerated mates.

Grief can become overwhelming and all-consuming for some individuals who experience significant loss. In general, when people experience a finite loss such as death, their support network of family and friends may rally to help the person regain normalcy. However, in the case where there is an absent spouse or boyfriend who has been convicted of a crime and sent to prison, the support network may not be as forthcoming; people may hold and offer negative opinions of the crime and the person incarcerated.

Consequently, the affected person, Jazmine, for example, is left to her own devices to recover. However, as we have learned through Jazmine's story, she may begin to question herself and express self-defeating behaviors due to her own toxic thoughts and negative self-talk.

Women with an incarcerated mate may feel disenfranchised, unable to express grief and hurt, disappointment, and feelings of loss associated with the absence of her loved one. This lack of free expression is compounded by other environmental factors that may weigh on her, such as the perceived responsibility of funding the canteen or prison accounts for her husband or mate—even though she has limited financial means. Her grief may become intermingled with anger because of perceived limited options. The more these issues go unaddressed, the greater the risk for a compromised quality of life.

Grief and Guilt

Grief and guilt can coexist with stress and resultant anxiety or, separately, with varying degrees of intensity. For example, when we reflect on Willow's experiences, she also had to contend with the grief and guilt. When Willow's son became incarcerated, she already felt the emotional and financial strains of having an incarcerated boyfriend. This scenario ushered in a combination of confusion and blurred roles. Willow finds herself in a predicament of having to choose whom to support.

The recommended goal here for helping professionals is to facilitate a discussion with Willow about her goals and desires to move towards personal well-being. It may become apparent that there is a need to address her grief, as well. As noted earlier, Willow spent so much time focusing outward, on the situations with her son and boyfriend, that she has not assessed her own grief and personal disenfranchised status.

Kenneth Doka (1999), author and thanatologist, discovered the concept of disenfranchised grief theory in his work nearly two decades ago. Doka described a type of grief that leaves the affected person feeling denied the right to express and to experience the mourning related to a loss that society deems as abnormal (e.g., an incarcerated individual).

Disenfranchised Grief and Vicarious Imprisonment

Social norms stipulate that people who offend are criminals; those who love and are connected to and grieve the loss of offenders may subsequently feel disenfranchised. Grief that is not deemed worthy of social support may remain buried and hidden, among the marginalized (Doka, 2002). These feelings of masked grief may also reinforce social isolation, the feelings of *Vicarious Imprisonment*. Recall that this state of VI is nested under the entirety of the set of behaviors entitled *Symbolic Imprisonment, Grief and Coping Theory*. Grief is a prominent feature of this theory and can exist without the women feeling vicariously imprisoned. However, when these two phenomena are experienced together, it is likely that the grief is intensified.

From the women's stories, we learned that enfranchising women grievers is a first step toward healing. Second, we learned about the importance of both informal and formal support.

A few of the women (30 percent), expressed concerns that irrevocable change might occur in the family dynamic via a family member's incarceration. Further, they feared that the family would never return to the same level of unity. Therefore, it is especially important to ensure that family members help each other and their affected children to meet these challenges.

We discussed children's reactions to incarceration in earlier chapters.

Children, at times, may act out when they are confused (Wildeman, 2010). This behavior may be the result of family stress. Young boys have displayed uncharacteristic behaviors in school (see Wildeman, 2010); adolescents may engage in inappropriate behavior. When children experience shock and trauma, it is advisable for parents or caregivers to check in regularly to ensure that they are not struggling with adjustment issues. In this case, I recommend professional consultation.

As a general recommendation, during family disruption due to incarceration of a significant member of the family, the entire unit may need to work on key areas to survive crisis and function effectively. A few suggestions include:

- Find ways to rebuild trust through gradual or incremental steps.
- Recognize that the family is not to blame for the circumstances.
- Learn to reframe the meaning of the dilemma or crisis to one that draws upon the internal fortitude and strength of the family unit.
- Allow the unity and love within the family system to create cohesive bonds that withstand social stigma and being ostracized.
- Seek support from outside services if needed, to help stabilize and ensure the emotional, financial, and social balance within the family system.
- Develop or evolve into new roles as adjustment to the absence of the incarcerated loved one and progress towards stability with new focus.

In summary, rebuilding a family relationship may require deliberate effort, especially if family members feel deceived or betrayed by the incarcerated member. Family members may, however, express anger and be unwilling to repair the broken bonds. One woman indicated that she was "really angry" at her husband for breaking what she termed their "contract." She felt they were a team and that he had violated the conditions of their partnership by going to prison. She indicated that it took months to reestablish trust and the belief that they would make it again as a team. Through this example, we learn that emotional repair is not easy. However, it can be accomplished through incremental steps if trust grounds the relationship and it is considered worthy of repair.

Complicated Grief

Grief may become complicated when the griever does not work through his or her grief. It can manifest as a psychological state whereby the griever remains in limbo and has not recovered from the loss.

In contrast to death-related losses, when grief is complicated, clinical intervention may be necessary (Worden, 2002). Complicated grief is acute and prolonged (see, Diagnostic and Statistical Manual of Mental Disorders—V). Social losses may include a person feeling ostracized and abandoned by support networks. Researchers have suggested that women are prone to experience an accumulation of loss and stressors that co-occur when their significant other goes to prison (Perry, Pullen, & Oser, 2012). This is evidenced in Iris' statement:

> The separation and loss for me, is like, you have nobody to talk to when you're there with the person for so long, and then they're gone. It's like, okay: Who do you talk to? Who can listen? Who will agree with you? So, you feel a little alone. Someday[s] you could feel lost and someday[s], it is like, you know, it's like losing my love to talk [with]. This is exactly the ancient type of thing—If I were to talk to someone today, you know, my mind [would be] different. [Now, it's me] being cared for by me. I would think different [if I had someone]. It's ... only the isolation left there for you.

Loneliness and heartbreak are obvious feelings conveyed in Iris's statement. The reasons that heartbroken women may experience intensified grief are two-fold. First, they may feel abandoned and, second, they may feel vilified by society. A lack of support, as experienced by over half of the women (55 percent) in this study, may translate into a genuine feeling of desertion.

Compounded Emotions and Grief (Psychological Reactions to Loss)

It bears repeating here that women who experience separation and loss because of a loved one's incarceration may exhibit a variety of responses: depression, anger, fear, numbness, separation anxiety, sleep disorders, and other problems. While interviewing women for this study, I found that they rarely compartmentalized their feelings related to the effects on them of incarceration.

If I asked about anything good that may come out of the event, they shared the good but quickly returned to the ill effects, of loss, and grief. Through their stories, I learned that their grief was complex and intense. Throughout all of their sadness and grieving, however, they were somehow able to mask these feelings when needed:

> Iris: I didn't know where to start. I was so used to him doing everything. I was spoiled. I looked at my kids and that makes me feel worse. I

can compare that pain to the one I felt when I lost my mom. Sorry, but that is how I feel—then, not knowing where to start—I could only cry. I didn't want to leave the house. I was indoors for 3 months—just going out when I didn't have a choice. I still have a long way ahead. I still have to experience a lot, but so far, I focus on continuing our plans, my studies, look after my kids and be there for him. I [am] staying busy and making sense of this time…. I'm planning on doing [this] while dealing with all this up and downs and roller coaster of emotions that I constantly feel.

Iris' association and references to "having a long way ahead," and "making sense of this time" seem to parallel the state of her mate's incarceration. It is common knowledge that inmates are told to "do their bid" (serve their sentence) one day at a time, focusing on the future. Iris remains busy to pass the time and her behaviors are consistent with the phenomenon, *Vicarious Imprisonment*, the construct under the broader auspices of Symbolic Imprisonment, Grief and Coping Theory.

My findings show that half of the women (50 percent) felt that their grief was debilitating. Jazmine recalled:

Jazmine: "Definitely, um, [I felt] helplessness and also [had] a constant awareness of how much of a struggle I had ahead of me."

Like Iris, one woman described how she was able to force herself to move beyond the state of debilitation by focusing on her responsibility and caring for her daughter's needs. This helped her to move beyond the paralysis of her own grief. She said, "I was in robotic mode—in a fog: you got to do it. A child is depending on you—all the things to take care of on the outside … you don't want to do it. You have to do it," she said.

Foreshadowing Death

Sage indicated that, prior to her mate's arrest, she experienced a foreboding sense of grief, and she felt that separation or even death of her mate was imminent:

I have [had] several dreams of him being dead. He wasn't even supposed to make it to jail. Somebody was supposed to kill him before he even got there. And as, like I said, it is by God's grace the he made it, you know. But [I know] there is a difference and I'm just like, I've been stressing. I can show you my hair. I have bald spots everywhere, because right now I am physically stressed…. It's just really stressful. It's really stressful.

During her interview, Sage acknowledged that she knew the difference between death-related losses and her experience, yet her rich description conveys that her grief was just as valid, as if, to her, there was little difference. From the examples of the women interviewed, we learn that their grief was at times debilitating, compounded, prolonged, and, possibly, complicated.

Themes and Insights

PSYCHOLOGICAL IMPACTS OF GRIEF AND ISOLATION

The psychological impact of having a partner in prison is not limited to women with children. Women who do not have children may not necessarily have less stress than those who do. However, in this study, in ninety percent of cases (90 percent), the women indicated that having children helped them to focus on parental responsibilities rather than on their loneliness. Some single women suffered sadness and depression, as evidenced in the words of Sage:

> When your significant other gets incarcerated [it] is not just, like, okay, [and] your days just move on. It really takes a toll on your life. I'm not comfortable, um, and like I said.... I do feel depressed ... [I] was just a sad, I was, not even sad, more so depressed, that this guy, [who] I'm madly in love with is really incarcerated. It took a toll on me. Like I said, I went through the, uh, depression. I lost weight. I gained weight. I was sick. I didn't want to eat. I don't have friends. I didn't want to talk to nobody. I couldn't go out, to mingle. I was uncomfortable. I didn't feel secure. I felt like I really needed him to be around. And I felt like I wasn't able to enjoy myself....

Sage's story provides rich insights into her state of mind. We learn how her grief-led depression may manifest as self-imposed social isolation and feelings of insecurity. Her reactions are similar to other women (90 percent) in the study, who expressed a constellation of physical, psychological, and emotional responses. Sage described not eating, feeling depressed, and most importantly, not having friends she could count on for support and advice. In Sage's mind, she was cut off from the outside world—and treated as "different." *For Sage, it is all or nothing.* If she cannot enjoy her relationship with the man she loves, she will dissociate from others.

Again, we see a manifestation of behavior that captures the true nature of *Vicarious Imprisonment.* This combined set of behaviors helps to explain women's need not only to hide from others, but also to isolate from support networks that may ultimately help reduce emotional crisis.

What makes *Vicarious Imprisonment (VI)* so troubling is that we don't know if it is damaging for women to experience this state of self-made punishment for lengthy periods. Further, we do not fully know the long-term implications of *VI* on the women's psychological disposition. This state of *Vicarious Imprisonment* is especially concerning if the affected women are predisposed to psychological disorders.

Peony used both medicine and alcohol to cope with her problems and ongoing depression during the absence of her imprisoned loved one:

> Peony: "I've had to talk to therapists, then, take depression pills. At this point, I got to scratch my heart out. I take medication ordinarily, anyway. Sometimes, I get into those moods that I just want to maybe sleep it away, and I would drink, but now I'm still waking up with the same problems as I'd go and get all drunk. I'd be at home. I don't be out in [the] streets."

Peony's example—isolation and coping—illustrates how psychological challenges may manifest as problems such as drinking, along with exacerbated depressive symptoms. My conjecture is not given as a mental health assessment counselor, but rather a gentle warning to loved ones and others that women may resort to self-medicating behaviors that may put them at risk. Therefore, when these types of concerns arise, as an intervention, it is wise to consult with helping professionals.

SOCIAL LOSSES, GRIEF AND INTERVENTION

Women and their families may experience social loss in a number of ways. Social stigma and subsequent challenges are prominent themes in the stories of the women whom I interviewed and appear to trigger the stress-related reactions and aspects of SIG-C. Social loss also may include a decline in social status. In other words, some women may feel singled out as "different" and somehow tainted by their mate's incarceration. For example, during prison visits, women (55 percent) felt singled out and humiliated by the interrogation methods employed by corrections personnel during security checks. Some women experienced police dog searchers, where the dogs sniffed them in private areas—an experience that was embarrassing and dehumanizing—while others in the prison visiting area watched.

Other women conveyed that corrections officers stereotyped them as potential carriers of contraband (e.g., drugs and/or other illegal items). One woman reported having to remove metal bobby pins from her hairpiece to prove that she did not have any weapons stored. By the time she was able to pass through the sensitive metal detector, the hairpiece was fully disassembled from her head; she held it in her hand and then placed it to the tray for inspection.

> Azalea: "It was so scary. I was so scared. I was petrified and knowing I had to drive that long distance [to the prison]. I have only 3 times to [get] through the metal detector. I have [body] piercings, of course, and my hair was all done up. I had a lot of bobby pins, so I was thinking [after the second rejection], oh my God. I'm not going to get through. I'm not going to be able to see him—mind you, I haven't seen him in six years."

As with two other women, Azalea later told me during the interview that she had lost her hair from the stress of the whole ordeal of her husband's incarceration. Obviously, this exposure left her feeling humiliated and her secret about her alopecia condition (i.e., hair loss), exposed. This and other experiences convey the need for policymakers to consider how to treat women in a more humane manner. Specifically:

• Punitive visitation practices can intimidate women (and children) resulting in fear, embarrassment, and signify that these women are "bad" for attempting to see an incarcerated mate or family member.
• Stereotyping women because of how they look (e.g., Azalea's body piercing), possibly feeds into the context of social stigma, reinforcing the notion that women who partner with inmates are inherently criminals.
• Social exclusion may perpetuate women's grief, and the underlying social devaluation of the woman, as demonstrated through dehumanizing treatment, and may reinforce the woman's negative self-appraisal and confirm that she is unworthy of respect.

Prison policy modifications could minimize emotional harm to vulnerable people. This could be accomplished while balancing the need for public safety and security. Advocacy groups may also draw attention to this matter as a means of intervention It is reasonable to understand why women may be less willing to visit prisons and expose their children to these conditions. Not all prison facilities are the same. However, these facilities are generally located in remote areas, at long distances from urban areas and where public transportation is rarely an option. To experience these problems with the fear that a visit may be in jeopardy is just one more trigger of stress and a barrier to maintaining a relationship.

There is ample research that indicates that both family support and stable relationships help to contribute to family reunification as well as reduce recidivism. Therefore, it would appear to be beneficial to make the conditions of prison visitation more humane.

Discussion

In summary, in this chapter we learned that women and their families may face psychological and social challenges that cause dysfunction and chaos within the family system. Due to financial strains, women may struggle to manage priorities of the family while grieving, and ostracized by other family members and the community. These challenges are not limited to mothers. Single women have stress and psychological reactions with similar if not greater intensity. The emotional and financial demands on the affected woman underscore the need for social support from family, friends, and, possibly, the intervention of helping professionals.

From an outsider's perspective, an affective woman may appear to be fine, simply wanting privacy, rather than to disclose the nature of her boyfriend or husband's incarceration. In actuality, she may need help and support but not know how to reach out for assistance as she masks and hides her true pain. Therefore, helping professional will need to build trusting relationships to get to a level of elf-disclosure that reveals what she is feeling.

In this chapter, we read about women in this study who experienced non-finite and disenfranchised grief. Their grief at times may be compared to experiencing the death of a loved one. Women expressed grief complicated in nature and, for some, compounded. Combined with the complexities of mourning a loss, women also endured psychological impacts as well as social loss.

Questions to Ponder

1. The absence of formal support systems tailored for this unique population appears to be problematic. How would you imagine starting a support group in your local area?

2. What approach to intervention would you consider most appropriate when working with this population of grieving clients (person-centered, motivational interviewing, and cognitive-based therapy)?

3. If a client presented problems relating to depression, would it be necessary to understand the nature of her relationship with her incarcerated mate? If so, please explain.

9

Coping: God, Sex and Rituals

"I love him unconditionally, regardless of his past and his darkness. I remind him of his good heart and soul and encourage him to open up to me. I am him—his sounding board when he gets angry or frustrated, his cheerleader when he is down and out.

"I am his light and beauty in a world that is mostly dark and ugly. I help him find the goodness in all that appears bad"—Lilly

Coping Through Ritual

Women who participated in this study found ways to make meaning of their experiences and to cope with their grief and loss. For some, the use of photographs, music, and charms and crafts served as symbols holding deep and profound meaning. Symbolic objects and keepsakes can be a representation of comfort and a way to refocus attention to the comfort it provides rather than reflecting on the distress of separation and loss (Norton & Francesca, 2014).

It was kind of hard for me to visit. Sometimes, I had to ask friends to take me. It was extremely hard because I was homeless. I had no place to stay. So, it was just *me and him*. So, when he got locked up, it was horrible.... I was homeless on the street by myself. I had no one. I started drinking and stuff ... like this is happening to me here—trying to numb the pain. It was just a bad situation.... I mean [my] self-esteem—I just didn't love myself. I was just angry all the time. I was unhappy—unhappy with the situation. He was gone. I was always fighting with myself. Do you know what I'm saying? I just don't understand why I can't keep myself away from this person.—Lilly

For Lilly, coping with her state of homelessness while also dealing with the loss of her husband led her to drink alcohol and to find other ways of numbing her pain. Anger is also a common response to loss and grief and may be a way to cope. Here, Lilly indicated that she was angry because of her loss of control and feelings of abandonment. She was left to figure out how to find shelter as well as how to maintain her relationship with her imprisoned mate.

My study found that coping through symbols and ritualistic practice provides value in a variety of ways. Jazmine, in her response, offers insight:

> I tell you what, there were times when I would actually wear his shirts and read the cards over and over again. Also, I think that it made me kind of closer to my children because I have all sons and I never want to see them in that position.... I would go as far as to have them sleep in [my] room with me, just so I know that they're all right—I don't know, it's like being closer to the kids is being closer to him, as well.... Because, you know, it was just, I don't know, I felt the need to hold on to what I had left, even though he was not there, and maybe hold onto them even closer.

Rituals, routine and symbolic proxy, provide comfort and substitution for the absent person. Over half of the women (55 percent), whom I interviewed, used proxies that might include a place setting for the absent person on an important holiday that has significance to the family. The affected woman might keep a place setting for the absent loved one at her dinner table to represent his presence. One woman carried a drivers' license belonging to her husband everywhere she went as a source of comfort. Some of these quotes, previously shared, are apropos here:

> "I just had a picture in my house."
>
> "I've been looking at his picture.... It's just.... It's just that...."
>
> "I have it [picture] in my purse, like it's [eases the pain] by taking it with me, to see how he is facing and how we look [together]. So, I've been looking at his picture."
>
> "He makes something.... So, I mean I would get his picture and I think about [our]love; the good times, when we stayed at the white sand beach-, that's why I carry his wallet with me. Well, now, after he moved from [the jail] to federal.... Federal is all about the money now. So, you have to always put money in their pocket. So, now, while money is tight, it's strict ... and I had to stretch it."
>
> "I had a lot of things, like pictures. He had sent me cards. I still have those. One time, he got a picture painted, picture of me and him. I still have that. Me and him never—even though there's a communication gap, right, we never lost complete communication. So, I still have a lot of things from when—he's in prison and then when—before he went to prison, he would [*sic*] on the hall monitor and try to do a lot things then, no one there, okay; it may come a time that he do have to do some time in prison. So, I have another set symbolic thing. To our relationship..."

For the women in this study, rituals provided several valuable functions:

- Create an outlet for grief and other pent-up emotions.
- Allow for engagement in fantasy as relief.
- Help to bridge the gap between physical absence by creating a proxy.
- Honor the sacredness of the relationship.
- Allow for severance of the relationship by symbolically breaking the ties, and
- Provide helpless women with direct control over the process.

As noted earlier, Sage described her vivid recollection of the last time she touched her boyfriend and inhaled the scent of his body. In her mind, she associated the smell with Ivory soap. To relive that moment, to hang on to his scent, she purchased the Ivory detergent and washed her bedding and clothing. Here, we see also that she integrates her son in the experience. Her use of the five senses is remarkable in that she was able to recreate an image and smell, as well as replicate her mate's physical body scent to soothe both herself and her son.

Other women described how phone calls and letters were instrumental in their survival. These coping mechanisms help to bridge the gap between an in-person visit, or even a video visit. Some women used the prison e-mail system (Corlink) to stay connected. Two examples:

Lotus: "I would just read the letters constantly over again and see if I missed something.... What I did to cope, is, I see another letter.... The letters are definitely, um, special to me, as well those words.... So, just those little things. He can say something and I'll be.... I have to read it, like, six times."

Rosemary: "He would send me things home. He would send me all types of crafts and artwork and I would just post it up around the house, and it was always something that was unique. A cross that was handmade to a flower that was made out of paper towels. A vase that was made out of glass. It was—CD's with our face on it and songs that he had hand-picked. It was all kinds of things that just always kept me—he always reminded me of the love that he had for me."

Rosemary's reflection ties to what I refer to as *Charismatic and Controlling Encounters* (see Chapter 7). I found that the men in these relationships tended to be both romantic and controlling, and used various techniques to maintain the relationship in lieu of their actual physical presence. They extended gifts, letters, and trinkets to solidify their bonds. As Rosemary indicated, these things *"always kept me."*

Finally, some women described placing pictures of their mate in their homes, at work, in their cars, in their purse, and in other prominent places. However, when asked who the person was by a co-worker or stranger, they might lie about his identity. Insiders were privy to the truth. This conundrum likely left the women feeling ashamed of their behaviors and what they considered "lies" about their relationship. However, in at least one case, a woman justified having to tell untruths, as described, below:

> Olive: "So, I just told them: 'That's my friend [in the picture] and I do what I do to help him out.' I felt guilty for that, but I think that's probably when I felt the most grieving and the most alone and the most conflicted about it. Does that make sense?"

From Olive's description, we can discern that she felt it was easier to avoid the truth rather than to explain her boyfriend's whereabouts, and possibly leave her openly vulnerable to criticism.

Coping Through Faith, Sex and Familial Support

> "I really, really, really, believe in the Lord Jesus Christ as my savior."—Tulip

Women used a number of ways to cope with their stress, related to their boyfriend or husband's incarceration. These coping strategies included drawing upon their spiritual or religious faith. As one woman declared, "I have good days and I have bad days, but I know that all things are possible through Christ, who strengthens me, and that is my game face." At least one woman indicated that her faith was tested: "I used to just pray to God and ask, 'Why can't I have what I wanted?'"

Blossom compensated by finding a substitute partner:

> When he first was incarcerated, I didn't want to be bothered or hang out. I didn't want to talk much on the phone [to anyone]. It took a month or two to completely accept he was gone and go back to my normal routine. We came to an understanding that, while he was gone, I could date ... it took forever for me to do. When I finally had intercourse, I felt empty and guilty afterwards—like I had a void and no matter how much sex I had, it wasn't being filled. I later realized I didn't want to date. I didn't want a sex-buddy or boyfriend. I just wanted to be held and have a shoulder to lean on.

Some women found that family and friends provided critical support as they sought ways to cope. Formal support such as self-help or psycho-educational support groups and tailored counseling are options women in the study indicated they wished were more available. However, it is unclear if any of the women in my study sought out this type of service:

> Jazmine: "I'd like to see counseling—or a support group. Somewhere to go where somebody understands what I am going through and just the fact of knowing, I'm not going through this alone. Just someone to say, 'Hey I'm going through this,' or 'I've been through that,' and you would know that everything is going to be fine."

Because these women are likely to be sensitive to stigma and, possibly, the judgment of others, identifying an effective means of unobtrusive support for these women could provide needed relief.

Raising awareness among family members, clergy, and others who are in a position to provide gentle, effective, unobtrusive support could be a critical form of intervention to help women to learn to cope during crisis. I also acknowledge rituals as a valuable and purposeful function, not to be discounted for their effectiveness. Rituals appear to be a means of acknowledging and coming to terms with loss. These symbolic forms of honoring the living yet absent hold meaning. Women who use these practices should not be judged as odd, or unorthodox, or pathological, but rather as able to have developed acceptable coping strategies.

Family Ghost

The idea of an incarcerated loved one's presence symbolically looming over or embodied in the family as if he or she is present in daily life is not new. In a study of death-row inmates, Long (2011) found that the phenomenon, *family ghost,* serves as a means of substitution, and a reminder that the family remains locked into the experience with the inmate. The family integrates into the decisions and life events of the inmates, sometimes virtually placing their own lives on hold, in limbo. In the example, Long (2011) provided, the family, too, experiences the fears, worries, hopes, and anticipatory dreams of the inmate.

The individuals in this study who are related to non-death row inmates can experience the same phenomenon. Women such as Sage engaged in ritual(s). Learning how the lives of women are enmeshed with the life of the inmate, as evidenced by the opening passage of this chapter, led me to ask for clarification about whose role the participant was describing. The blending of roles becomes apparent.

These ideas about a family ghost are not new to therapists and helping professionals. Professionals sometimes use an "empty chair" to facilitate client therapy—to release anger, frustration, unresolved communication with a deceased person, and, other emotions. This practice also offers a safe manner in which to voice concerns to the missing loved one without him or her being present.

The "empty chair" technique was used in experimental research to help clients process grief and loss. Shane Harberstroh, Assistant Professor in the Department of Counseling and Educational Psychology at the University of Texas, San Antonio, suggested that clients using this technique found a way to restore interpersonal healing (Haberstroh, 2005).

Empty Chair Technique:

• Person speaks to the empty chair as if the chair represents a living person;

• Communication is one way and directed to the chair that represents the absent person;

• The client/person imagines that the chair is able to hear her and she is free to release the emotions that she desires to express in person, but is unable to do so.

Family Ghost and
Metaphoric Rituals and Coping

• Person speaks to object as if the object is a representation of a living person;

• Communication is one way and directed towards the object as if the affection can be transferred and reciprocated;

• The woman imagines that she is able to touch, smell, and speak to the absent person and release her desires and express herself without criticism or shame.

Presented above, the "empty chair" technique offers a means to achieve transformation through a release of pent-up emotions. By doing so, women who have been burying years of repressed feelings are able to express love, hurt, anger, and other emotions within a safe environment. This exercise also allows the woman to have a voice in matters where she is often otherwise silent.

Themes and Insights

THE POWER OF SYMBOLIC RITUAL

Sometimes physical symbols give us something tangible to hold on to—to see—to feel when the real world does not hold meaning and our assumptive world is altered. Maryland Barnes, a grief advocate who frequented a Lutheran hospital to engage with people suffering immense grief, drew strength and even courage from a symbolic representation of faith, focusing on a bracelet (Barnes, 2014). During her work, she shared how symbols and mementos could aid when a loved one is transitioning from life to death. Barnes found that families who witness the death of a loved one are often plagued with painful memories that tend to create an emotional loop in their minds. The last moments of a loved one's life are, then, constantly replayed. Rather than to focus on the last moments, Barnes found that by focusing on symbols, such as a blanket or an object that represented comfort rather than the pain, family members were able to use such objects in a soothing manner.

A similar process held significance in this study. Women refocused their attention on objects that held fond meaning; for example:

- Music
- Photographs
- Husband's driver's license
- Mate's clothing (especially his shirts)
- Jewelry (his wedding ring, neckless)
- Visiting places where they used to go, and
- Embracing his hobbies or habits.

Each of these symbols may help to ease the pain of witnessing and reliving the arrest, the image of a handcuffed loved one, the image of an incapacitated person behind Plexiglas, and other unpleasantries.

Discussion

Here, rituals and symbols are used to give comfort and aid healing. I discussed how symbols, keepsakes, revisiting locations that evoke pleasant memories, and even how the ritual of wearing a mate's clothing may serve as a source of comfort and a means of coping with loneliness. While symbols and symbolic acts aid in coping, they may, however, also serve to reinforce isolation and withdrawal. A healthy lifestyle and interaction with others may counter the need for social isolation.

QUESTIONS TO PONDER

1. What are two cultural example(s) of ritualistic practices of other cultures which you think compare with the construct, metaphoric ritual and coping strategies?

2. As a practitioner, what is your role when working with a client who uses rituals to cope?

3. Name three examples of how symbols used in your own life were reminders of a fond or even serious event in your life.

PART IV

Cultural Sensitivity
and Intervention Challenges

10

Cultural Awareness

As society begins to grapple with helping families affected by incarceration, cultural competence will certainly play a role in providing effective intervention. Culture can shape a person's worldview and dictate how people interpret and respond to their hardships. The differences between people are more than slight nuances in the color of their skin. These variations can partially explain how two people can experience the same or similar life event, with different outcomes.

As you have read in previous chapters, the women in this book come from a variety of backgrounds. Their shared stories and their belief systems may be similar to or different from your own worldview. This section explores areas specific to African American women that may foster multicultural awareness for the practitioner, advocate, or others who are working with this population of women. Multicultural awareness can help you to understand the unique challenges faced by women of this demographic.

Therefore, insights included here are nuances about the structure and variations in the Black family. To illustrate, I share one story of a biracial relationship through Violet's narrative. This narrative may seem insignificant, but it may provide helping professionals with insights specific to the perceived challenges of personal identity when a woman is struggling with her own racial identity and has biracial children who have a Black father. While this configuration may seem insignificant to others, when a mother visits a prison with a biracial child and the mother looks White, women such as Violet have indicated they are treated differently and even sometimes harassed. This makes family configuration and makeup important to understand.

I found this situation to be yet one more issue that prison visitation highlights. Issues regarding image is an important discussion to help frame how and why African American women have cultural issues to contend with, not just the issue of stigma and shame associated with an incarcerated mate. I wrap up this section with questions and recommendations for the helping profession.

Biracial Struggles

CASE STUDY: VIOLET

Violet is 45 years old, and she has begun to question her self-worth and identity. She questions her race and evaluates how people treat her and view her relationship with her incarcerated mate. Her father is White; her mother is Black. She could pass for either. Her incarcerated husband is an African American man. Violet said:

> My dad was raised by the KKK [Klu-Klux-Klan]. When he met [my husband], it was just like, you know, he was just another man to him. He was the man that was taking care of his daughter. You know I'm a daddy's girl—and for my husband to come in being a black man and say, hey 'I'm in love with your daughter' and one day I'm going to marry her [is a big deal]. He's, like, all right, as long as you do right by her. I really did not expect that coming from—you know a KKK-raised man. And you know, my mom loves him to death.
>
> [My husband], at any given minute stop [*sic*] what he was doing and do something for my parents. My dad had a stroke once. They live in an old farm house, so the original steps, they're, like, really narrow and go straight up. My husband went upstairs, and put my dad on his back and carried him down and out to the ambulance. Right there, my dad said he just gained even more respect for him.... People just cling to him, like a moth to a light.

It is unclear how being in a multi-racial relationship, with the added stigma of having an incarcerated husband, may have affected the quality of their relationship, if at all. Violet shared that she and her husband have multiple children, also biracial and all girls, who adore their dad.

Violet's biracial status is not uncommon. Almost seven percent of all births in the United States are biracial children (Miller, 2015). Identity affecting a biracial couple is not prevalent in the literature. Violet and her husband have been together, off and on, for more 22 years.

Things are complicated now. Violet and her husband separated for a brief period. During that time, he got someone else pregnant. Now, her children have a little brother whom they do not know very well because of the conflict between Violet and the girlfriend. As close neighbors, the tension has escalated and the situation, as she describes it, is "in her face." This hurts Violet deeply. As she reflected on her separation from her husband, she said:

When the baby was born, you know, the baby's mom started being aggressive [with] me because [my husband and I] were still friends; then he took the baby away from my daughter one day.

After that, he wouldn't even let her visit the baby—after that. I mean, it's just, that we were friends on that level, but we weren't as close as we had always been, you know. I could still call him about a flat [tire], and he'd come and help me. Or, you know, early mornings when he was going hunting, he'd call me for me to wish him luck. I loved him much more than that and I hated to see him with other women or just with the one he was with—But as long as he was happy—the only thing I ever wanted was for him to be happy.

At the time of Violet's interview, her husband was not seeing the other woman, as far as she knew. While incarcerated, he was dependent on Violet to send money to his account for buying snacks and toiletries. He depended on her to bring his children to the prison. This bothered her greatly, but she said she learned to get over it because of the children's need to be with their daddy.

When I see the look on my kids' face, when they actually look at their dad or they start talking to him ... just that little twinkle in their eye—to see how happy they get when they see their daddy [makes me happy]. You know, Christmases and birthdays, you do everything just to make them happy and to watch them smile; but that minute when they look at their daddy and they get, they just get tickled pink. "Oh daddy, daddy's here! Daddy!, Daddy!" You get so mad when you know you punish them and they don't want to listen to being unholy [sic], but one word out of daddy's mouth and all the kids straighten up. I don't know if it's that tone or that demeanor, but Daddy's just always had that keen [sic], that knack. They looked at daddy one time and you know he's the king. Daddy don't do nothing wrong to them—Jus [sic] to see them smile when they see their daddy.

Violet shared the importance of family events, how specific outings helped to establish strong bonds and ties with extended family and how her husband needed this sense of unity:

Family ... you know going to his family barbecues. He enjoys hanging out with his family. To see him, you know, happy, you know—going to the family reunions— I'm there on his arm. He makes sure that I'm mingling and, you know, everyone's getting along—and it's usually pretty much all the time.... We used to go sit on the side of the road under a bridge and go fishing and be just as happy and content.

Violet said that her husband is currently in a work release program where he can now leave the prison. Before that, the children would visit him. Violet does not know for sure, but she said she feels that their biracial status may influence the way that the corrections officers treat them. She finds it difficult watching her children interact with their father in the prison setting. She noted that these visits were extremely stressful on their children: "[w]hen they see daddy, they want to run and jump on him and hug him … they can't grasp that fact that there's a glass right there in the middle of them and they can't get to him."

Violet's children love their father unconditionally. A father's prison sentence is hard on the mother and can be even more difficult for the children. Children may not understand why there is a need for a Plexiglas partition or other barriers to separate them. Although safety and security in the penal system is an ultimate goal of the corrections system, children's needs to have physical contact with their incarcerated parent remains. These physical restrictions encountered when making visits to a prison are just a few of the barriers that families must overcome. In addition to administrative hurdles, Washington, D.C., prisoner families may need to plan for an out-of-state visit. This can be expensive, as described in an earlier chapter.

INTERRACIAL WOMEN, CHILDREN AND THE PRISON VISIT

Even after getting to the prison, the visit itself can be confusing for the children. I asked Violet what the visitation experience was like for the family. Her response was:

> Sometimes it depends on the guards, and sometimes like [Daughter #1] and [Daughter #2] can go at the same time, but if there's different guards, then they have to be one at a time. There is a certain amount of visitation time, so you have to split it up like everybody will get, like, 5 minutes a piece; if [Daughter #3] wouldn't stand there longer and take [Daughter #1's] spot, I'd give her my spot just so they can spend more time with him. And on family night there can only be one adult and then the kids, so, like, me and my sister-in-law went one night and she hadn't to see him the time before, I let her take my spot so her and the kids went and visit. I just stayed and waited in the line.

It appeared Violet was challenged to juggle which child got to see their dad first. This may seem like a small task, but imagine having to choose on behalf of children who are waiting to see their father during a visit, and who must visit, one at a time. Imagine having to explain to the children why they cannot all go in the visiting area to see their dad at the same time. Sometimes, Violet said, the guards treated her fairly; other times, she wondered why they were hard on her.

As noted, prison policy is generally specific to the jurisdiction. There are schools of thought that argue that the highest priority of a prison is to maintain safety and security. It might be beneficial for penologists to examine how these goals can be met while also ensuring that visitors, including the children are treated unfairly.

As helping professionals, you will find that it is difficult to gather data specific to incarceration and the family through normal federal reporting channels. Family and relationship statistics are not typically captured as a part of federal inmate reporting. Therefore, we are left to estimate the holistic impact of inmate incarceration on the lives of the African American woman and her family, using pheripheral data. We can start by looking at common statistics associated with Black woman and relationship pairing:

• According to the U.S. Census Bureau's *America's Families Living Arrangements*, issued in 2013, 94% of African American women have a Black husband.

• Eighty-percent (80%) of African American women partner within their own ethnic group.

• Approximately 43% of African Americans are married and almost half of these households have children under 18 years of age (Vespa, Lewis, & Kreider, 2013).

To further investigate, DeVuono-Powell, Schweidler, Walters, and Zohrabi (2015) provide that:

• One in 28 children in America has a parent in jail.

• Two (2) out of three (3) families struggle to maintain basic household needs while the father is incarcerated.

• Seventy percent (70%) of families are supporting children who are living at home and are under 18 years of age.

• African American families share the same reactions to a family member's loss/incarceration do other racial and ethnic groups.

• Contemporary literature conveys that destabilizing a family through involuntary separation can have deleterious and economically devastating effects on families (National Research Council, 2014).

Themes and Insights

African American Women and Family Structures

We have learned through the stories of women such as Aster, Lotus, Sage, Violet, and others described in this book, that African American families have multiple family configurations. In this text, a family is described as: individuals who share a family dwelling, or live outside of the household, and/or maintain significant ties.

These members may or may not include kin or those who are not blood relations (fictive kin). These complex networks of family configurations present several challenges when seeking to understand the impacts of incarceration on the *Black family.*

What we have not discussed is whether family configurations, which include variations of racial composition, affect how the woman and her family contend with the same issues. We briefly explore this dynamic of race through the profile and interracial family composition as detailed in Violet's narrative.

BLACK WOMEN AND SELF-IMAGE

"Telling stories is ... empowering for people and helps to create and inspire a vision of a better future. It helps individuals and collectives to reclaim their history, to understand and appreciate their strengths, resilience, and resistance, to overcome their silence and shame, and to build community."—Nelson and Prilleltensky (2005)

Learning about African American women and their culture requires a look at how they are perceived by others as well as how they view themselves. Throughout this book, we have examined African American women's lives in the context of their mate's incarceration. Over past decades, both qualitative or quantitative researchers have analyzed how a mate's incarceration affects African American women's sexual risks of HIV; the educational achievement or the longevity of their heterosexual relationships (e.g., Harman, Smith, & Egan, 2007; Mechoulan, 2011; Mahoney, Bien, & Comfort, 2011; Woods-Giscombé & Black, 2010, p. 115, respectively). Mechoulan (2011) even studied how black men's incarceration affects the possibility of matriculation of young black women in higher education (p.1). Each of these insights is meaningful and helps us to understand this cultural group of women.

Ethnographers have made tremendous progress in studying this cultural group of women (e.g., Brown, 2006; Prince, 2008). However, they live their lives in a far more complex world than just their relationships.

I now turn our focus to an examination of how African American women are a part of the broader context of challenges that occur at the micro and macro levels. Issues such as negative stereotypes of women play into the micro and macro level of social issues.

To understand characterizations of Black women, researchers have used a number of approaches. For example, scholars have conducted studies using limited viewpoints such as *the strong black woman* phenomenon (Davis, 2015) or *the needy black woman* perspective (Monahan, J. L., Strule's, I., & Givens, S. B., 2005). The former label conveys that Black women are thought to be hardened, independent, and resilient and do not need social support from others (*see* Woods-Giscombe & Black, 2010, p. 115). This stereotype generalizes and categorizes these women as resilient. Hence, instead of seeking support, women may dismiss their own needs for social support or intervention.

Polarizing labels, such as *the needy Black woman* are damaging to African American women, even when reflected in the academic literature. This label may further perpetuate the use of negative images in overt or covert ways. Hence, through this lens of *neediness*, the characterization of the Black woman' is that of a drama queen recorded in popular media, where the depiction is the image of her reliance on public entitlements or social services, also known as welfare. These images ultimately can cause the public to look upon African American women unfavorably. The important connection here, is if Black women are characterized as flawed, then how does this affect the piling-on of additional negative stigma and stereotypes because she partners with an offender?

These images and labels tend to show up in various forms in the media. For instance, an article authored by Katherine Boo, a Pulitzer Prize-winning journalist, in part, focused on gender gap issues confronting Black men and women as they seek to acquire employment. In this excerpt, Boo (2003) offers her opinion on the *welfare to work* policy as a framework to discuss Black workers who commute to work:

> It may be the greatest policy achievement in recent history: over the past decade significant numbers of formerly welfare-dependent black women have successfully entered the work force—But what about black men?" …The U8 [bus], which serves the easternmost corner of Washington, D.C., is what's known in public-transport parlance as a circuit bus. Its African-American riders are among the most isolated of the urban poor: those who not only can't afford private transportation, but can't afford to live near efficient versions of the public kind. These men and women rely instead on buses that wend from one remote housing project to another, collecting riders who are eventually deposited at some central location from which they can take subways or straight-line buses to where the jobs are.… Every weekday at dawn the U8 offers its passengers the predictable dystopian ghetto vista: a drug-treatment clinic, its parking lot aligned with spent needles; a minimart with a sign on its doors begging, PLEASE!!! No ski masks allowed! [Boo, 2003, p. 107]

This excerpt shows how newspaper journalists working in the public sphere have the power to shape public opinion about Black women. The reality is that non-researchers and non-students rarely pick up academic or professional journals (which are based on empirical research) to glean an understanding about the cultural aspects of other ethnic groups. In contrast, a large number people may read a magazine article such as the one written by Boo (2003). Popular media—television, the Internet and social media, and the print media—share the responsibility to truthfully characterize Black women.

In her research study of 134 White males, Slatton's (2009) interview questions were designed to understand what terms come to mind when these men think of Black women. Typical responses were: "I have yet to meet a black woman who is well proportioned and has a good personality," "fat," "sloppy," "ghetto" (p. 134–136). These labels distort the uniqueness of Black women through an assignment of negative descriptors and connotations.

In contrast, through their self-defined labels, these wives, girlfriends, and mothers consider themselves *the core of the Black family*—the matriarchs. If she is not strong, in appearance and reality, her family system, too, can become frail and weakened.

American history of politics, public opinion, and racial attitudes has been shaped largely by White men (Krysan, 2000). Research informs us that when surveyed, these men have been found to hold negative opinions of "Black women" in general. White men still dominate positions of power in fortune 500 companies, in politics, and in the media. Therefore, their opinions seem to have economic, social, and even psychological implications for African American women.

NEGATIVE IMAGES OF AFRICAN AMERICAN WOMEN

Image of Self: The Superwoman

"Myths and negative caricatures of the African American female can tarnish her image and reduce public empathy, support, and tolerance of her relationship with an incarcerated man."—Hart-Johnson

"I think that I am the backbone to the Family"—Lotus

The implications of a mate's incarceration on women who head households may also be unique. These women conveyed that at times they were expected to be *superwomen*. It was evident from women's interviews that over 50 percent of the study participants strive to keep their family unit connected, despite the financial, psychological, and societal difficulties associated with having a loved one in prison.

From an outsider's perspective, African American women may appear as though nothing upsets their strong constitution. However, as with any other group of women who grieve and suffer loss, these women need support. The findings in this book confirm this assertion.

The title, "matriarch of the family" comes with an expectation that the affected women will conquer the challenges and overcome the stresses of daily life, bouncing back with resounding resilience, no matter how tragic the event. Based on interview responses, this expectation is unfair and unjust for these women, who also are at high risk for experiencing overlapping losses, and grief, and emotional pain associated with the incarceration of a loved one

The aforementioned scenarios exemplify why support systems are beneficial to women affected by the numerous problems associated with incarceration of a loved one. Support systems may help these women to make better decisions that ultimately contribute to the family's well-being.

Discussion

In this chapter, we read about how issues of culture may impact a person's prison visitation experience. We also found that women may struggle with their own identities as a matter of personal importance. These reflections and questions may also merge with thoughts of self-worth, especially if others are insulting and judgmental about their relationships. We also learned through Violet's experience that families have different configurations. It appeared that she struggled with the new addition to the family, now that her husband had a new baby outside of their relationship. This appeared to be awkward and even hurtful to Violet.

QUESTIONS TO PONDER

1. As a helping professional, when you reflect on Violet's situation with her husband and children, what do you believe is a priority focus for the family system?

2. What recommendations could you offer Violet to help her children cope when visiting the prison environment?

3. What intervention would you recommend for Violet and why?

11

Intervention

In this chapter, I call out specific examples of why the *elements* of SIG-C may be challenging to identify (For example, grief is hard to identify if a person is masking her feelings and pretending to be fine). I focus my discussion for the helping profession. I consider helping professionals to include practitioners, such as mental health counselors, members of the clergy, professional coaches, and others in a position to provide formal support on an individual or group level to women affected by their mate's incarceration.

As practitioners, when women's informal support networks fail, you may be sought as a solution. As with the previous sections, the next chapters include quotes and interpretations; in addition, each section includes recommendations. Ultimately, as professionals in your field of expertise, you make the final call regarding the best interests of your client. You may also find that using an integrative approach (combined modalities) is effective as an intervention strategy.

My philosophy and orientation is person-centered theory. This orientation is non-directive, and its principles are rooted in the work of the American psychologist and the founder of client-centered therapy, Carl Rogers, who pioneered empirically-based insight on this intervention modality (Rogers, 1951). This method is ingrained in the following concepts (Rogers, 2004):

1. Clients have the capacity to become autonomous, self-directing, and may emancipate from their oppressive circumstances;

2. The helping professional is a facilitator and an equal partner, while the client is the subject matter expert of her life;

3. The facilitator treats the client with unconditional trust and the belief that she has the potential to solve her own problems—she just needs the capacity to understand the gap between her current state and ideal state; she can develop the steps toward change and growth.

Identifying SIG-C in Women May Be Challenging

A significant challenge helping professionals may face in identifying the elements of SIG-C is that affected women often learn to mask and hide their emotion(s) and predicaments. These women may bury their feelings, rationalizing that their own emotions as secondary in comparison to those of the confined significant other. This theme is repeated throughout the book and is significant in understanding the importance that women place on the value of their relationships. It also details the stress women face when stifling their emotions:

> Violet: I was thinking about how much I missed him and I was really thinking that when I went in there [the visiting room], you know, I was emotional. I was going through menopause, you know—women with menopause cry at the drop of a needle. I was like—you know, he is going through enough. I know he is emotional. I hope I can just hold it together when I go back there and not cry because I know he don't want to see me cry. I don't want to see him cry. So, you know, I was just thinking about, you know, if I miss him that bad, imagine how bad he misses me and the kids…. It was just one whole big, you know, emotional crying mess. He knew that I wanted to cry, but I just started smiling. He's like—I never thought I'd miss your face.

RECOMMENDATIONS
TO HELPING PROFESSIONALS

The goal of the helping professional is to establish a trusting relationship with the client and provide the conditions of a safe environment where women such as Violet can talk freely about their feelings. During a meeting or session, the helping professional might facilitate a discussion using empathetic listening and provide nonjudgmental feedback.

Through the facilitator's approach, from a person-centered perspective and a genuine and authentic approach to building the relationship, he or she and the woman will explore feelings that are obvious to her as well as those feelings that are below the surface (Miller, 2002). The helping professions should collaborate to examine what might be preventing her from actualizing her complete and whole sense of self. Further, the helping professional can navigate through what may be causing her distorted view of and expectations of herself. The women should learn that it is natural to have feelings of sadness and fear. You can help her to explore ways to express true emotions without being compelled to force a smile or mask these feelings (Miller, 2002).

Eventually, through a trusting relationship with a supportive, helping professional, women like Violet will come to realize that they have the capacity to be in control of their decisions and choices. During the process of facilitating change, the helping professional may challenge the woman to explore what she believes are viable options for her problems. Ultimately, it is the woman herself, not the facilitator, who will choose here, based on her value system and situation, not others.' The following recommendations are offered, using Violet as an example:

• The role of the helping professional in this relationship is to establish an egalitarian relationship, but prevent codependency.

• This safe environment of unconditional positive regard will include the practitioner's requirement to put aside all preconceived notions about prison, offenders, and other associations to the criminal justice system that might bias the relationship.

• Helping professionals may assist women like Violet in discovery of their positive qualities. In Violet's case, she is nurturing, supportive, kind, and loving. The helping professional can provide a trusting climate where she will feel safe to explore things that she may not ever have acknowledged or discovered about herself. This discovery can lead to her using positive qualities as applicable to achieve personal satisfaction. For example, she may learn to become nurturing, supportive, kind, and loving towards herself.

• Violet's incongruent view of herself reflects her desire to meet the expectations of others. There is also a mismatch between who she thinks she should be and her current reality. In essence, she feels as though she is *failing herself.* The change within can occur when she begins to understand her feelings more and establish a true connection with herself, rather than to focus continuously on external sources of validation and acceptance.

Recognizing Hidden or Covert Shame— The Example of Dahlia

When I interviewed Dahlia, I could sense that something was going on, but I couldn't quite pinpoint what it was. She was willing to be interviewed, but she was guarded and she wanted me to know that she no longer had feelings for the man with whom she had at one time been in a relationship, prior to his incarceration. I learned that their relationship had continued for several years before his incarceration. She said the two had a daughter together. However, she was adamant that she no longer considered them a "couple." She expressed no feelings of grief or sadness because of their separation. Later, upon reflection and when she became comfortable with the interview, she shared: "I wasn't as close to him at the time; in fact, I wasn't dealing with him. He molested the young daughter of some woman he was messing with … we were shocked for a while, but that is the kind of stuff that ole' family would do." After hearing Dahlia's story, I realized why she felt such a strong need to distance herself.

RECOMMENDATIONS
TO HELPING PROFESSIONALS

Although some women may use the terms "guilt" and "shame" interchangeably, in reflection of this study, it appears that shame is related more to how they feel about their relationship, and how their partnership is viewed within their social circles. Again, we see an overreliance on external validation.

• Helping professionals may guide women similar to Dahlia to realize that they are not inherently flawed. Facilitators can help these women discover their desire for personal growth, development, and self-actualization. Through this partnership, the client can express her feelings and the facilitator will paraphrase his or her understanding of those emotions. For example: "You sound really angry at your ex-husband, Dahlia." This technique may offer women validation of their feelings and an opportunity to recognize and work through their true feelings.

• The goal of working with women like Dahlia will be to facilitate the discovery of how to ensure that her feelings are congruent with her values and belief system. Without this true understanding, she may bury her anger and disown any feelings of loss and betrayal. She may also be inclined to shy away from establishing future relationships, based on her lack of trust.

• It is possible that Dahlia places high value on how she is viewed in relation to her estranged husband. To her, it is important not to affiliate with a sex offender. Helping professionals can help women work through understanding their role in relationships and facilitate the process of coming to terms with understanding that they are responsible for themselves and are not the source of blame for their husband's choices.

• Facilitators can help women explore feelings of shame. They should come to realize that they can only take responsibility for their own life and actions.

Triggers of SIG-C: Guilt and Shame

As I listened to the women, it became evident that guilt and shame not only coexist, but that these two ingredients also became triggers to reinforcement of their social withdrawal, otherwise referred to as *Vicarious Imprisonment*. It is possible that shame did not always originate from external sources but rather from internal networks such as friends and family, who may have frowned upon the relationship or judged the partnership. In some cases, the men in the relationship were already estranged from the women's friends and family before the man's incarceration.

> Violet: "I really don't think that I would have been able to come through the situation because there are some things you just can't discuss with other people because you don't know, um, how they're going to take it—you don't want them repeating it."

Women indicated that, at times, their feelings of shame contributed to a reoccurring self-appraisal or self-evaluation, and concern about how they themselves and their families would be publicly viewed, even scrutinized. The shroud of guilt is a prominent feature of the SIG-C model that conveys women's responses to the disruptions of their relationships. As such, shame should be examined from the perspective that some of the women feel as though they do not conform to the standards established by society, or even by their families.

Their shame is likely a result from not meeting external expectation(s). This failure to meet expectations may lead women to make irrational choices and seek out alternative methods to solve their combined feelings of guilt, shame, and grief. Their guilt may also be a result of their inability to resolve the problems surrounding the incarceration of their husband or boyfriend.

Women also may have a combined physical and psychological reaction to their circumstances:

> Olive: "I felt grief when he called to tell me he was sentenced to three years in prison when we expected way less. I felt like I lost my significant other, like someone took a part of me. I cried as if I was told a close family member had died, because that's what the pain felt like."

Hazel: "it was a sick feeling and when I [left] him, I would get migraines… Physically, I was wearing myself down. I was breaking myself down."

In cases similar to Hazel's, women may seek out a medical practitioner rather than the support of a helping professional in the counseling or mental health field. They may also seek out pastoral counseling or advice. However, the concern here is that the symptoms are being treated rather than the root cause. This is why it is so important to understand SIG-C in its entirety and to learn how to recognize how it may show up.

Women may self-assess and second-guess their worth and value in their relationship. They may scrutinize their worthiness in the relationship, and this evaluation may cascade to self-criticism of how they deal with *all* relationships. Using unrealistic measurements to live up to, they may struggle in this cycle of mismatched expectations versus what is realistic.

Acacia: "I was sitting back and thinking, before I went back [in the prison visiting area] to see him, and I was like, you know, [he's] going to be a very different man. You know, I don't know, I've never been introduced to this single life, you know. You know, a medicated young man—what if, you know, his feelings about me change when he's straight and sober? Cause, you know, when a man is drunk, you can look like, Beyoncé and when you're straight and sober, you're going to look like Barney Rubble or somebody you know. I feel like just the emotion in itself is—you know, he's going to be sober."

Here we see, with Acacia also, what could be interpreted as a discrepancy in a woman's ultimate ideals and image of herself, and reality. It may be unrealistic to try to compare oneself to a celebrity such as Beyoncé. This incongruence between their reality (what is) and what they feel they should be, shows up as anxiety. This causes incongruence and leaves these women fearful, vulnerable, and anxious. Below are a few recommendations that may assist in the change process.

Recommendations
for Helping Professionals

- Empathetic listening is one of the most effective micro skills that can be used to understand the women's perspective. These women must be understood from their worldview—without judgment. They are unique and a product of their fears and personal beliefs. Although the facilitator or helping professional may be tempted to solve the problem for the client—you must refrain. The relationship should be founded upon the belief that these women possess the resources within; they just need to acknowledge and tap into that source.

• The nature of your interpersonal communication with the client is to interpret, not judge the client's response. Your role will be to repeat through paraphrasing that you understand the client. This will assist with trust building and establishing a safe environment. As the helping practitioner, you will seek to understand the underlying meaning of the woman's self-appraisal. You will help her to navigate her emotions and feelings in the effort for her to recognize these feelings, triggers, and, ultimately, do the work to increase her self-awareness

• It is important to understand the woman's perceptions, through her words, and actions—all combined, this leads to a better understanding of what she is feeling. This becomes your road map as a facilitator, as you guide her through the exploration of her emotions.

• In all cases, the helping professionals' perceptions related to the woman's boyfriend or husband's incarceration, or any disclosure, must be bracketed or set aside. You, as the facilitator, should have unconditional positive regard and trust that she knows what is best for her at any given time; she just needs to be provided with the right and safe conditions to explore the alternatives.

• Finally, under these conditions, women may also learn techniques to live up to their full potential by gaining self-awareness and to move from the state of incongruence to congruence. Through this intervention, women may learn to discover that they have multiple choices that are "safe" and self-satisfying.

Crisis Points

Women with an incarcerated loved one may experience crisis points. These crisis points may trigger the phenomena that I termed in the SIG-C model as *Vicarious Imprisonment,* as well as *Psychosocial Responses* to loss. I consider crisis points to be a period that individuals go through when experiencing life events that are traumatic *and* which can be defined as a point of no return. In the context of this book, a crisis point is referred to as: a critical moment where the affected person realizes that things may become worse, or even, at times, better, but never be the same.

Not all crisis points are bad. Some crises cause women to dig deep, draw upon their personal internal resources to overcome their predicament and find ways to develop new and skills. Other crisis points, however, may deplete a person's resources to the point where they may feel debilitated or overwhelmed.

RECOMMENDATIONS
TO HELPING PROFESSIONALS

From a person-centered philosophy, reduced anxiety and less self-doubt may occur when the affected women's beliefs and expectations of themselves are in alignment with their confidence and self-efficacy (congruence) [Rogers, 1951]. When women believe that they are helpless and lack control, they doubt their abilities and, therefore, their perception is out of kilter with their internal strength (incongruence). Helping professionals should provide a safe environment in which they can facilitate processes to help women navigate their personal choices. These steps will help affected women recognize and live up to their true potential. One objective is to increase the woman's feeling of wholeness (rather than to "fix" her self-doubt and anxiety). Changes will likely occur naturally once the client reaches a state of self-actualization to her higher potential.

At times, the affected women rebound quickly from some of the properties associated with SIG-C (e.g., stigma, shame, guilt, and grief); at other times, they appear to be helpless and overwhelmed. Such dynamics can occur when women are exposed to multiple losses, such as the incarceration of another family member, financial loss, or a death of a loved one, especially if these events occur in close proximity. In this case, the woman may feel in turmoil and, as stated earlier, conflicted in deciding how to move forward. She may also be confused about her roles and responsibility.

Additionally, the woman may feel "stuck," as with Lotus, who expressed her panic and felt helpless, as if she had no power over her situation. Lotus must learn how to trust her ability to make the right choices under duress or pressure. She must learn that she does have the ability to discern between good and bad choices. By taking small steps and achieving incremental success, Lotus can move toward regaining confidence as well as move towards congruence.

The Strains of Prison Visitation

As noted earlier, for some women, the experience of prison visitation may be stressful and a reminder of how little control they have over their relationships. The penal system rules and regulations often serve to remind them of how fractured their lives are. One woman revealed, "They make you open your mouth and lift your tongue, to make sure there are no drugs." Another woman said:

Rosemary: "Uh, actually going through the process of, you know, being searched and everything comes back to me. Almost feeling like a criminal myself for a small window of time and then—it's all that brokenness passing through [security] and to actually see his face and knowing that I had to be strong, even though I felt very vulnerable and I wanted to break down. I could not do it there. I had to prepare myself mentally to encourage him to be strong. Um—and that this, too, shall pass. Like, I just had to put on my face of strength—like, we will come through this."

Hazel: "Everytime I would go see him, I would get butterflies in my stomach. …Can't function—he was all I thought about."

FAMILY VISITATION VERSUS PRISON SAFETY

Family visitation can be challenging and stressful for both the mothers and their children, who may drive long distances to see the incarcerated loved one. Boudin (2013) completed a 50-state survey of prison visitation policies and found the following relevant observations that affect the family visitation experience:

• Every state requires preapproved clearance for visitation. In other words, the inmate must add family members to the visitation list. The approval process may take weeks for processing.

• At least 31 states have limitations on the number of visitors the inmate may have. If an inmate has a large number of children, rotating these children on the list may be difficult.

• Pennsylvania is the most liberal of the 50 states with visitor allowance.

• Some states stipulate that family members cannot be on more than one inmate list. This means that if a father and brother are in the same facility, then the family must choose whose list they will choose.

• Some states only allow updates to visitation lists twice a year (i.e., North Carolina).

• Some states require an application process to remain on a list.

• Former felons may not be able to visit at all. This means that if a wife has a felony, she may not be able to visit her husband; a child may not be able to visit his or her father, and so forth.

RECOMMENDATIONS
TO HELPING PROFESSIONALS

• Helping professional should understand women might perceive prison visits as a direct assault to their dignity. Feeling degraded and treated harshly is a common reaction and helping professionals should refrain from dismissing or rationalizing their feelings and fears. Women may simply need acknowledgement that their reactions are normal responses to often harsh and sterile conditions. Helping professionals may provide benefit to these women by offering empathy, genuineness, and acceptance. Given such assistance, the women can better choose to respond to the environmental conditions of the prison, on their own terms.

• Through acceptance of her feelings and a nonjudgmental environment, the client may realize that her feelings are a genuine response to a stressful environment. This may allow her to be less judgmental, herself, of her reactions to the prison setting (or to internalize the rules and regulations as a personal attack). She may then be able to think through ways in which she can make choices that help her to move towards actualizing tendencies, rather than those which cause her to feel weak and afraid.

Familial and Other Support Networks

The women who informed this study indicated that factors such as their spiritual or religious faith and family support are stabilizers and buffers to most elements of *VI: Vicarious Imprisonment*; these support networks, however, are not always available, or they can dissipate over time after an initial crisis.

Lotus: "Well, there was a lot [of support] in the beginning, um, when he first got incarcerated. Everybody wanted to know what happened. And um, eventually there were about 3 of them [family members] who I could speak with. And, you know, it's almost like the rest, kind of shunned you."

From the excerpts above, we learn that support can be beneficial, yet fleeting. Helping professionals can facilitate a discussion about women forming new support groups when a woman finds herself increasingly isolated and/or alone.

RECOMMENDATIONS
TO HELPING PROFESSIONALS

• When these women practice self-awareness, they learn that their progress towards change is not reliant on external support, but rather that they themselves are the best engineers for their progress and well-being. This may help women to accept responsibility for their own actions and make choices that conform to their own needs rather than be driven by the opinion of others.

• Social and mental health practitioners may incorporate multiple strategies to help affected women. Through self-awareness, women can learn that they are human, and humans are fallible. No one individual makes perfect decisions all the time nor does anyone have a perfect life. When women learn that they themselves have the ability to take incremental steps towards self-help and making decisions, they will develop confidence in their problem-solving abilities and, most importantly, move from the cloak of shame and disgrace to a state of acceptance that is the whole self.

• Finally, as a helping professional, you may serve as surrogate support for friendless women. Therefore, it is important to facilitate the growth process with emphasis on her personal choices to avoid a developing dependency. Active listening helps the practitioner to understand the client's concerns and worldview. No practitioner can understand a client completely, due to the complexity of human nature (Miller, 2002). The effective use of paraphrasing, listening to the client, rather than directing her, will provide the climate for her to discover alternative approaches to working through her problems.

In summary, women who experience the array of emotions defined in SIG-C may be prone to hiding their shame and will exhibit a constellation of *Psychosocial Responses to Loss*. They may feel traumatized and shocked from the circumstances surrounding the arrest and incarceration of their loved one. Helping professionals are in a position to provide safe and non-judgmental formal support. The helping professional's office may provide a confidential and safe space. The helping professional who uses a person-centered approach and expresses unconditional high regard may positively assist these women on their journey to live up to their full potential to self-actualize under the right tutelage, climate, and intervention (Rogers, 1951).

It is my hope that the insights, self-help strategies, and recommendations that are offered for overcoming grief may be useful for practitioners and helping professionals. I also hope that the affected women are encouraged to become advocates for their own causes and can themselves help to effect social change for a better world for themselves and their children.

12

Poverty, Health
and Social Consequences

"Poor people, especially poor people of color, face a far greater
risk of being fined, arrested, and even incarcerated for minor
offenses than other Americans."—Dolan, & Carr, 2015

The collateral impacts of incarceration tend to impact multiple areas
of affected women's lives, including their health, social interactions and
economic status. This section provides helping professionals with additional considerations to ponder when developing effective interventions
with clients. The linkage between poverty and incarceration are covered,
followed by a discussion on Black women's health.

Poverty and Incarceration

Families who already are prone to the adverse impacts of living at or
below the poverty level in urban areas can be deeply impacted by the
incarceration of a significant family member. In my study, the economic
status of women and their living conditions ranged from economically
strained and homeless to financially stable and upper-middle-class. Prior
to their mate's incareration, 70 percent of the women in this study indicated that they had some form of employment or a fixed source of income.
However, it appears that the impacts of separation and loss seem to know
no social or economic boundaries.

There appears to be an intersection between poverty and incarceration. High incarceration rates tend to manifest as structural inequality,
mostly affecting those living in poverty (Berman, 2010; Nkansah-
Amankra, Agbanu, & Miller, 2013). According to the 2013 U.S. Census,

25.8 percent of African Americans lived at the poverty level (Macartne, Bishaw, & Fontenot, 2013).

When examining poverty levels across 43 states, African American poverty levels remained constant at a 20 percent rate for most states, and higher for Wisconsin, which hovered at 35 percent. While there is no confirmed causal relationship, when examing states such as Wisconsin's high percentage of poverty to its incarceration rates, according to the Prison Policy Institute, this jurisdiction's incarceration rates appeared extremely high [incarceration rates for Blacks was 4,042 per 100,000 compared to 416 White people per 100,000 residents (Sakala, 2014)].

I repeat, here, that there is no master list that aggregates the ill effects of how the phenomenon ofpoverty and rate of incarcerationll come together and adversely affect the lives of Black women, families, and children. People who are poor are, seemingly, with no civic voice to fight these perils. These ill effects may not stop at paternal incarceration.

Research suggests that a parent's incarceration may influence intra-generational incarceration cycles (Siegel & Welsh, 2012). These adverse consequences are not pervasive just because African Americans are somehow deeply flawed and prison-bound. These issues appear to be integrated into a set of policy-driven, political, and even legal forces that trickle down to affect African American people and threaten their family system. If unaddressed, it is likely that the damage can be far-reaching and long lasting.

Black Women and Health

It is also unclear, from the paucity of the literature to date, what number of women are affected on a physical level and are exposed to health risks due to loss and separation from their incarcerated mate. To address this uncertainty, researchers recently have turned their focus to how incarceration has affected the physical health of women. The focus of recent study has been on the sexual health of the African American woman, not her holistic well-being when the mate is incarcerated.

BLACK WOMEN AND HIV RISK WITH INCARCERATED PARTNERS

Women who partner with incarcerated men face a risk of contracting sexually transmitted diseases. This risk may be especially concerning for women who partner with men who cycle in and out of prison as repeat offenders (Frost, Freillch, & Clear, 2009). Research shows that men generally have unprotected sex with their mate within the first 72 hours of their return home (Mahoney, Bien, & Comfort, 2013). It is possible that women are not aware of the risks involved when sleeping with a man who has not been tested for HIV. The Mahoney et al. study highlighted that there are multiple risks for concern among this population. They may:

1. Have sexual relations with multiple partners;
2. Find it confusing to understand prison HIV testing policy (thinking that all men are tested and, therefore, not HIV positive) and
3. Believe that men are monogamous while in prison because most prisons are not co-ed facilities.

These risks are concerning on several fronts. First, if the non-incarcerated partner is coping through multiple partner relationships and having unprotected sex, then the risk increases if the incarcerated partner is also doing the same. It would appear in this case that both partners become high-risk. The second issue is concerned with whether women understand the prison policy related to HIV testing. Prison policy is confusing for many people. It is recommended, to enhance a person's understanding of the risks, that both partners be afforded orientation as a part of the process of incarceration. There is certainly a need to explore how effective these prevention programs are and how well the consumers of the educational literature understand the content.

Finally, the last item speaks to the complexities of accepting that incarcerated men are at high risk of HIV infection—which may be too overwhelming for women to consider, thus creating an element of denial. Generally, men of color have been found to have lower access to health care (Woods, Lanza, Dyson, & Gordon, 2013). Incarcerated men are at 6 times greater risk of HIV infection than non-incarcerated persons (Harman, Smith, & Egan, 2007). Washington, D.C., has one of the highest HIV rates in the nation.

Female-Led Households and Quality of Life

How female-led households affect the overall structure of the family system is not always obvious or apparent. It is challenging to understand how this phenomenon inextricably ties to women's quality of life. However, research informs us that there are health consequences associated with having an incarcerated mate. Examples are given, below.

• One study indicated that women in these partnerships are exposed to greater health risks such as hepatitis, HIV, or other diseases associated with incarcerated populations (Mahoney, Bien, & Comfort, 2013).

• Another suggested that paternal incarceration has been shown to have a correlation to child homelessness (Wildeman, 2014), child and adolescent behavioral and mental health issues (Wildeman, 2010).

Each of these adverse consequences has linkages to the African American woman. Somehow, as researchers, practitioners, helping professionals, we must answer the call about how to provide solutions to this complex social problem.

Mahoney, Bien, and Comfort (2013) suggested that, given the diaspora of incarcerated men in the African American community, there is a lack of available partners for females to develop lasting and meaningful relationships. Consequently, narrowed options for partnership may result in an increased HIV risk (Mahoney, et al., 2013). As a result, the family structure is potentially weakened, and the woman's health compromised. Moreover, women who have sexual relationships with incarcerated or recently incarcerated men were found to be at higher risk for HIV infection (Davey-Rothwell, Villarroel, Grieb, & Latkin, 2012; Reznick, Comfort, McCartney, and Neilands (2011). This finding was due partly to the high HIV rate in U.S. prisons, which are especially high-risk, in part, because the distribution of condoms is largely banned in U.S. prisons. Additionally, these authors found that there was a perception held by some women that incarcerated men are more faithful in prison (Harman, Smith, & Egan, 2007).

Extending the line of research on women's health risks, Mahoney, Bien, and Comfort (2013) found that there were women who covertly engaged in sexual relationships with multiple partners (while in a relationship with an offender). This behavior placed them at a higher risk of HIV than monogamous individuals (Mahoney, et al., 2013). Women used in the sample for this quantitative study were exposed to an evidence-based intervention program that provided education on HIV prevention, domestic violence, and other information for empowerment. Sixty percent of the women in the sample were recruited from a drug treatment plan. Women in relationships with offenders rarely receive interventions and social services programs designed to meet their needs because they simply are not able to access them, for one reason or another (Mahoney et al., 2013).

Lee and Wildman (2013) studied other health-related risks; for example, they studied the association between a family member's cardiovascular disease, the negative impacts, and the correlation of an incarcerated loved one. The findings were exceptionally disturbing for women.

Data obtained from the National Survey of American Life comprised a cross-section survey of African Americans and Caucasians. High-risk conditions, such as diabetes, obesity, heart conditions, and stroke were assessed. Women with incarcerated significant others were found to have a 95 percent greater chance of high-risk, health-related conditions than those who did not. In addition, if they were obese, the likelihood increased, as with poor health. Lee and Wildeman (2013) found that the majority of African American women in the sample were disadvantaged at the outset. While the literature offered a partial picture of how women may be at greater health risk when in relationships with incarcerated men, it appeared that additional findings from my study could offer a more representative view of this group of women.

Health scientists have suggested that there is a connection between a person's well-being and their culture (Thurston & Vissandjee, 2005). Thurston et al. studied the intersection between cultural aspects of migrant workers' employment experiences and their well-being; there is a similarity between this population of immigrant workers and women who partner with incarcerated men. For instance, both populations have displayed nomadic patterns when having to move out of necessity. Women with incarcerated mates have been known to move from town to town to be near prisons and their loved ones to reduce the stress of being separated and having the children separated from their father.

One woman in my study was contemplating moving out of state to be in a town near her mate to reduce the stress of being separated. As she considered the pros and cons of renting out of state, she indicated:

> I live with my parents right now and I would absolutely not live with my parents if he wasn't doing time—that because there was a time I would visit twice a month and it's six hours away—gas and motels and then to see him in there at the prison and everything and see myself with him all that stuff. It's probably coming out to— it's not the same, possibly even a little bit more than I'd be paying to rent an apartment in [state removed] near him.

Although, there is no clear understanding of how stress from moving out of town compares with the stress of reduced communication and contact, it is understandable that uprooting and moving to a new town could introduce several challenges. The stress from finding a new job, meeting new people, developing a new support network and other situations involving the children may be overwhelming. Children who move from town to town because of military parents experience stress which may translate as a concern for the parent. Stress has been known to exacerbate pre-existing health conditions as well. Therefore, preventative care becomes a fundamental goal and a protective factor.

The Center for Disease Control suggests that there is a natural link between education and health literacy and healthy living (Center for Disease Control, 2015). Health-literate women may be able to stave off some of the stresses resulting from the ill effects of incarceration, the risk of exacerbating preconditions such as high blood pressure, diabetes, anxiety, and depression. Education not only increases the possibility of Black women rising to the middleclass, it may also be tied to disease prevention and exhibiting behaviors that contribute to higher quality of life. This may mean not only using strategies to prevent ill health but also having the insights and efficacy to employ stress reduction techniques.

Culture plays a critical role in Black women's health. To understand the system of culturally specific health habits for African American women, it is wise to first integrate the importance of the symbology of family values; for example, having meals as a unit and with extended family. Second, it is important to understand if good dietary behaviors are consistent with the ability to obtain the foods that contribute to nutritional meals.

The symbolic importance of having meals together as a form of bonding and support within the Black family may be seen most prominently in the church setting. African Americans traditionally serve food during church gatherings such as revivals, funerals, weddings, and recreational gatherings. Robinson et al. (2015) indicated that the linkage between faith-based institutions and health-targeted interventions are a natural pairing. While the church may provide support to health interventions by integrating spiritual components to nutrition programs designed to reduce stress, thwarting the risk of diabetes and heart disease, there are still health risks that can add to the burden of having an incarcerated loved one. Table 12.1 provides a snapshot of some health-related data for Black women.

Although Table 12.1 provides only a brief outlook on Black women's health, these issues are concerning, especially if the involuntary separation of a loved one exacerbates any current health issues. These issues are not contained, as they cascade to any children involved, affect productivity in the workplace, and may add to medical costs. HIV is another risk that appears to be of concern when women collaborate with imprisoned men.

Table 12.1. Black Women's Health

- African American women face a 4.7% chance of having a stroke, with a slim chance of survival 1 year post-stroke occurrence, compared to other women if the stroke type was ischemic (Go et. al., 2013; Quereshi, Suri, Zhou, & Divani, 2006).
- Almost 45% of African American women suffer from hypertension.
- Approximately 1,700 Black women die each year from breast cancer.
- Black women are 19 times more likely to contract a STD.
- Teen births have dropped for women whose ages are between 15 and 19 (7% drop between 2011 and 2012).
- Depression is common when Black women live in neighborhoods with high concentrations of incarceration and low levels of education attainment (Wildemna, Snittiker, Turney, 2012).
- Approximately 8 million Black women receive some form of health insurance (Guerra, 2013).

Race, Class and Public Attitudes

Public attitude can play a critical role in reducing the negative impacts of mass incarceration through becoming more sensitive and tolerant, given the stigma associated with criminal offenses.

Providing equal treatment of diverse groups and respecting the difference in ideologies can go a long way towards empowerment. Nelson and Prilleltensky (2005) referred to a psycho-political climate. This term nicely captures the nexus in a society of psychological and politically influenced public attitudes. These beliefs can generate both positive and negative reactions to social issues such as the imprisonment of loved ones.

Informed citizens can help reduce the ill effects of incarceration on children and families through advocating and using their political capital to assist the most vulnerable families, helping them to rise out of hardship, poverty, and perils not created on their accord. This support may empower the affected individuals to advocate for themselves as they strive to make social change by influencing leaders, legislators, and others to make change that moves from status quo toward transformation.

The intersection between race and class and positive public attitudes could improve social and political conditions for downtrodden people. Nelson and Prilletensky (2005) argued that marginalized populations often contend with oppression, power and empowerment issues, and consequently become victims.

Table 12.2 contains a generalized overview of demographics for African American women. This table also provides an outlook of their social and political status. Although Black women have become widely

**Table 12.2. Demographics of Black Women:
Social and Political Status Indicators**

- **Population:** Black women account for 13% of the United States' population (Guerra, 2013).
- **Households:** These women were more likely to be heads of household (29%) and bear the costs of maintaining the family unit (U.S. Department of Labor, 2016).
- **Marital Status:** 26% are currently married; almost half of the population has never been married (48%).
- **Arrest Rate:** 9% of these women were stopped by police but not arrested.
- **Marital Ethnic Group:** The majority of these women are married to Black men (94%).
- **Births:** Those who gave birth while married were 33%.
- **Divorce:** Divorce among Black women was at 13%.
- **Religion:** 83% were affiliated with some domination of religion.
- **Spirituality:** 19% attended church at least once a week.
- **Politics:** During 2012, 53% indicated that they were of democratic political affiliation. While, 1% were self-described as strong Republicans.
- **Public Office:** Two out of 73 women are serving in political office across the states (Guerra, 2013).

integrated in vocations that reflect growing acceptance of diverse roles, there is still opportunity for other groups to be more tolerant. For example, Black women are not widely featured in prominent positions in mainstream media, politics, entertainment, fashion, religion, and other areas which would indicate social acceptance. Their legacy of being treated as inferior still has a bearing on their status and, therefore, is limiting to their obtaining positions of power in society. Finally, the expectation of the ideal female image is in great contrast to how these women are characterized. When adding these negative connotations, coupled with having an incarcerated loved one, the complexities of stigma may be overwhelming.

Conclusion

The absence of research on African American women who partner with incarcerated men undoubtedly diminishes one's understanding of the cascading impacts of this social problem. Moreover, the current lack of research limits our understanding of how this issue may translate into macro-level problems.

A goal of this study was to provide a contribution to the literature through my doctoral research and, thereby, extend the knowledge in the domain of human services and in the field of counseling. This research, among emerging studies, is just a beginning to understanding this social problem.

This book is intentionally written in a tone that broadens the outreach to the women who have endured symptoms consistent with SIG-C, and for their family members and friends, as well. It is my hope that through this book an understanding of women's plights can be learned, and social change will follow.

This discovery and application of SIG-C theory enables the silent voices of affected African American women to be heard through these findings. While this theory is context specific, it has limitations. The limitations include a small sample. Future researchers may wish to explore how to test identified SIG-C variables and determine if these attributes have generalizability or external validity. Research could also further build out the SIG-C model to include newly identified themes and constructs.

Ninety-percent (90 percent) of the women who participated in this project indicated that my interviews with them provided them with their very first opportunity to speak out about what they have experienced. They indicated their interviews provided them with both an outlet, and relief. One woman who was interviewed indicated, "This is the first time someone listened to me without cutting me off or sweeping it under the rug." Her statement suggests the importance of simply listening to those women whose lives may be disrupted, in turmoil, and who may be experiencing emotional pain as a result of their mate's incarceration.

It is my hope also that this is only the first of several studies that will explore the dynamics of SIG-C and that future study will add to, clarify, and broaden this theory.

The Social Consequences: How Did We Get Here?

> We are just beginning to reflect upon the political and cultural meaning of this new institution, upon which it means for America to be a mass imprisoned society—a process of reflection that has begun somewhat late in the day.—David Garland

There is a social consequence to be paid for allowing this experiment of mass incarceration to go largely unaddressed. Restorative and family-focused strategies were largely not on the legislative agenda as a priority until as recent as 2014.

As a researcher reflecting upon the mass incarceration experiement, I belive that America must find a way to respond to issues stemming from mass incarceration which surged during the early 1970s (Nixon's war on drugs that emerged as the trigger for over-incarceration). Now, we must find a way to contend and fix what has resulted in the flow of approximately 11.4 million people who enter and exit America's jails, prisons, and corrections institutions (Bureau of Justice Statistics, 2015). At present, more than 7 million individuals are on some form of parole, probation, or community supervison. Almost 40 percent of those who occupy prison cells are African American men (BJS, 2015).

After the enactment of the *Comprehensive Crime Control Act of 1984*, federal parole was abolished, which mandated that prisoners serve 85 percent of their sentences (GovTrack.us, 2004). Therefore, a large number of inmates are required to serve their sentences for greater lengths of time away from their families. Yet, approximately 95 percent of these prisoners will return home one day. Rehabilitation post-incarceration may be far more challenging than beginning the intervention while the inmate is incarcerated.

The unintended social consequences of four decades of punitive criminal justice policy and draconian sentencing laws resulted in the extended arrest, incarceration, and harsh prison sentences of African American men. Marc Mauer coined the calamity and collateral damage associated with incarceration as "invisible punishment" (Mauer & Chesney-Lind, 2002, p.5). This punishment is an assault on the African American family system. As a result, this racial group is predominately challenged with family system breakdown and left with matrifocal-configured families or female-dominated households.

Mass incarceration of African American men weakens affected families and increases the likelihood of broken homes. This legacy of mass incarceration, if not addressed systematically and nationally, could alter generations to come of the Black family.

Collectively, the combination of disproportionate arrests and sentencing of Black men, the criminalization of Black children, and the lack of formal support systems for Black women, all point to disturbing patterns and concerns for this ethnic group of people. Therefore, this social dilemma should infuse each of us with a moral responsibility to understand how we may offer transformative micro- and macro-level efforts to foster social change as a humane thing to do. Any effort that thwarts the adverse impact of four decades of mass incarceration on Black women and their families is a movement in the right direction.

At the outset of this research, I assumed that by association and through their partnership with imprisoned African American men, this group of women was likely to be affected more than other groups in the United States by the phenomenon of mass incarceration—or what I refer to as a *legacy of mass incarceration.* I base this assumption on the high incarceration rate among the racial group of African American men. I conjectured that when large numbers of imprisoned Black men are missing from communities, it affects the family's future economic possibilities, the family structure, and influences in some manner the cultural group as a whole. Ultimately, I assumed that, at the very least, the African American women who become *de facto* heads of household suffer the most while their husbands or partners served their prison sentences.

Mass Incarceration and African Americans

The implications of this research may go beyond women. I believe that the implications of this phenomenon, SIG-C, may also be extended to impact entire families, and cascade to communities. I base this assumption upon the work of David Garland, the scholar who coined the term, *mass imprisonment,* and who described this phenomenon as one "that has no parallel in the Western world" (Garland, 2001, p. 1). He pointed to African Americans as one of the primary groups affected by America's failed experiment of mass imprisonment. Garland further added that this phenomenon has the potential of achieving "the systematic imprisonment of whole groups within a population" (Garland, 2001, p.1). His ideas have been substantiated. In Black communities today, incarceration is so commonplace that it may affect several generations of a family's lineage—and it has become a common occurrence in a Black male's lifetime. This phenomenon may cross cultural boundaries and gender. Future research in this area will reveal the countervailing consequences and legacy of mass incarceration. In the interim, uncounted numbers of women and their families in these communities may be affected by the diaspora of sons, husbands, fathers, and other male relatives who are incarcerated, as a result.

Monique Tate, a scholar familiar with Symbolic Imprisonment, Grief and Coping Theory, posited that it is possible that the general statistic used to refer to the aggregate 2.5 million Americans incarcerated may need to be expanded exponentially, to include literally millions more who may be *Symbolically Imprisoned* (Personal Communication, May 2015).

Quantifying its impacts on Black women is also difficult because statistics on wives and girlfriends of inmates are rarely, if at all, captured in federal reporting databases. Moreover, few studies focus on the effects of incarceration on this group of women. Of the statistics that are recognized by federal reporting agencies, including that which are reported by the Bureau of Justice Statistics, it can be shown that it is not an unreasonable stretch to assume that African American women are likely to be adversely impacted by one or more of the following conditions as shown in Figure C.1 (Bureau of Justice Statistics, 2013).

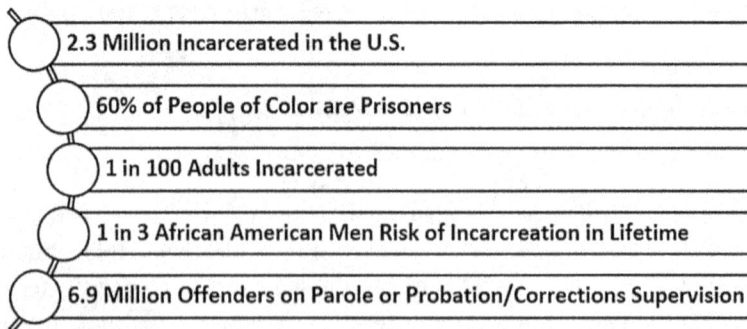

| 2.3 Million Incarcerated in the U.S. |
| 60% of People of Color are Prisoners |
| 1 in 100 Adults Incarcerated |
| 1 in 3 African American Men Risk of Incarceation in Lifetime |
| 6.9 Million Offenders on Parole or Probation/Corrections Supervision |

Figure C.1. National prison/incarceration statistics.

Implications: The Link Between Family and Recidivism

The implications of this research are multifaceted, yet there is much more to be understood about this grounded theory, SIG-C. This research may have natural ties to understanding and combating *recidivism*. Through my discovery of this theory, *Symbolic Imprisonment, Grief and Coping* (SIG-C), I uncovered and explained the [interrelated] cognitive, emotive, and physical responses to loss, specific to a group of women. This becomes particularly important in understanding how families who support returning citizens may remain strong, and intact.

Research tells us that offenders' recidivism rates are reduced when they have strong families to provide a safety net and support (Wildeman, 2012). Therefore, I recommend future research be conducted in this area. Until we conduct more research on SIG-C, and broaden this research area, we may not know the extent to which women and others, such as children, caregivers, and men, are symbolically imprisoned.

How Do We Fix These Problems?

From an African American perspective, one might ask: How do we as a people, who are at times vulnerable and, at times, targeted people, fix our own problems? The answer to this query is challenging. However, a few considerations might be a starting point for consideration:

• Advocating for social change through enhancement of schools that offer high-risk children, especially those in Title 1 schools, targeted intervention strategies to influence high quality education to offset dropout rates;

• Increase opportunities to reduce neighborhood crime through advocating for increased job training leading to employment;

• Develop grass-roots and advocacy groups that focus on empowerment of this cultural group where collective engagement of advocacy work may give rise to attention to critical areas that thwart conditions that breed poverty and crime, such as poor housing, social disorganization, and low social control of neighborhoods.

• Constituents can demand that politicians invest in improving the local infrastructure by attending community town hall meetings and by requesting to provide testimony during community hearings as constituents.

• Women and their families who tend to make up the majority of Black faith-based institutions can learn to galvanize and request church leaders to play a role in work that supports the overall health and well-being of families and communities where they live.

In addition to these socially conscious movements, advocates, lawmakers, and others can advocate to improve family visitation experiences to offset the fracturing of the prisoner's family. While there is a need to balance safety in the prison setting with family comfort, there may be a way to accomplish both strategies.

Risks to the Black Family?

The absence of Black men in the community translates as having a direct impact on African American females:

• Reduces the number of African American males available to participate in the formation or development of intact family systems.

• Adds to the number of African Americans who are least likely to marry (U.S. Census Bureau, 2012).

• Poses risks to the potential of sustaining relationships with longevity and the likelihood of having healthy relationships with children (Dixon, 2014).

• Places the children, especially male children, at risk for developing aggressive behavioral issues (Wildeman, 2010).

• May contribute to relationship strains that lead to future intimate partner violence (Wooden & O'Leary, 2006).

It is safe to assume that incarceration has general implications in addition to limiting the available choices for African American women to form partnerships/relationships that lead to strong healthy family systems (Dixon, 2014). Family systems can have multiple configurations as stated earlier. However, the goal is to improve the social risks of adversely affecting people's well being.

Perhaps the remedy to healing the Black family is to use a multipronged approach that directly counters Black men's risk for arrest and subsequent incarceration. In the context of this discussion, healing the Black family refers to building strong family units regardless of its configuration (single mothers, married couples, cohabitation). Healing means fostering wellbeing so that the family has the highest potential of achieving a life of health, bonding, and actualization.

Familial togetherness, is dependent upon internal and external situations. Obviously, there are social, legal, political issues that occur in the lives of Black people that position them as high risk for fractured families. For example, Black people are a higher risk for false arrest and racial profiling than other ethnic groups. Moreover, iincarceration is an expected life event for (60 percent) of African American men who do not have a high school education (Petitt & Western, 2004).

These statistics vary, depending on the source. The Bureau of Justice Statistics (BJS) suggests that this concern is not merely speculation. During 2003, BJS projected that 1 out of every 3 Black men faces the risk of becoming incarcerated in their lifetime (Bonczar, 2003). This statistic has not veered far from that estimate. At year's end, 2013, 3 percent of African American males were in prison that year (Bureau of Prisons, 2013). Additionally, men from this demographic group who were between 25 and 39 years of age had the highest incarceration rates in the nation. Those who were between the age of 18 and 19 during 2013 were nine times more likely to face incarceration than their White counterparts (BJS, 2013, p.8.). The incarceration rate of this group exceeded all other race and comparable age group incarceration rates during the same decade (BJS, 2013).

These rates are both alarming and disturbing because these absent men account for 3 percent of their racial group and also are absent from mainstream society.

Symbolic Imprisonment, Grief and Coping— A New Theory

Throughout this book, we have learned that *Symbolic Imprisonment, Grief and Coping (SIG-C) Theory* depicts the experiences of African American women who are in a relationship with an incarcerated mate. As described in detail, the phenomenon of *Symbolic Imprisonment* is a psychological and physical state of self-imposed *Vicarious Imprisonment* where the affected person restricts normal activities as if she is on house arrest or home confinement (Hart-Johnson, 2014). This state, generally triggered by guilt, shame, and social stigma, describes how women feel emotionally stuck, or psychologically imprisoned. These impacts, introduced through the lens of what I have coined the full theoretical SIG-C model, also depict how the affected person can oscillate from normal functioning, and at times appear unaffected and during others, have extreme bouts of grief and stress (Hart-Johnson, 2014; Schroebe & Schut, 1999).

Underlying this framework are two theories: disenfranchised grief (Doka, 1999) and the dual process of bereavement (Schroebe & Schut, 1999). Disenfranchised grief holds that there are forms of grief not recognized as worthy of social support and traditional norms of mourning. The dual process model describes how a person can oscillate between normalcy and mourning a loss. Each of these concepts supports the underlying premise of *Symbolic Imprisonment*.

Appendix A.
AARM Example

AARM® Exercise Based on Chapter 1. Lotus: "The Fixer"

Recalling Chapter 1, Lotus is a diligent and committed mother. She also has demonstrated resilience in overcoming childhood abuse. Her love for family and her protective nature is beneficial in ensuring her own children's well-being. Lotus also appears to have strong interpersonal skills that may help to attract supportive relationships. Her strong family support system can be a source of support as she tries to overcome the stresses related to having an incarcerated husband. Ultimately, Lotus seeks to assume control over her life where she can once again have a sense of purpose.

A STRENGTH-BASED ORIENTATION

Strength-based interventions are ideal in helping clients work on identifying short- and long-term goals that enhance quality of life and give a sense of purpose. This approach is preferred to a problem-centered orientation where the helping professional focuses on problem-solving using a directive approach. Rather than focusing on the problem, a strength-based orientation focuses on the strength that each person possesses to establish goal setting, given his or her unique situation, in the spectrum of self-actualization.

In this section, I draw from the work of William Hammond's *Principles of Strength-Based Practice* (Hammond, 2010). Hammond identified key areas that helping professionals should *not* use when working with clients. If you are a helping professional or a woman with an incarcerated mate, avoid:

- Labeling people as "broken";
- Focusing on what is *not* possible, rather than what is possible;
- Using a one-size-fits-all approach, rather than individualized support;
- Identifying what is wrong rather than what is right;

• Evaluating whether or not the problem was successfully solved (Hammond, 2010).

By using a strength-based approach, we do not ignore the problem or the context in which the problem occurs (Hammond, 2010). We capitalize on the strengths of an individual as they move towards personal empowerment and can, ultimately, make the best decisions, based on personal priorities and personal goals. It is important not to enter into a discussion where self-evaluation becomes the norm. These women may already feel guilty and have subjected themselves to self-punishment or feeling less-than, and stigmatized. For example, Mansi felt responsible for her mate's condition: "I look him, it [*sic*] just mainly look at … and I feel like that's my fault and I'm constantly as forgotten, forgive me…."

Women's interviews consistently revealed that they felt guilty *and* responsible for their mate's incarceration. Therefore, intervention should involve women examining boundaries, roles, and responsibilities, using a strength-based approach. By doing so, we may facilitate a focus on the strength and determination that these women have and perhaps help them to use their competencies to establish personal goals for themselves. Using Hammond (2010) the strength-based principles focus include that:

• People are defined by their strengths rather than limitations and have the ability to reach their highest potential and rise above their current adverse circumstances;

• If people hold positive thoughts and beliefs, they can manifest the same;

• The words that we use are powerful. If we say that we are failures, then these words can become self-fulfilling prophesy;

• Believe that change is inevitable and that we can make positive and sustainable change;

• Change and positive growth occurs in the context of genuineness and a trusting relationship. People know when they are not trusted or if the facilitator believes that they are somehow flawed;

• A person's perceptions *are* their reality. Therefore, meet the client where she is; do not try to dominate their story or solve their problem. Allow them the dignity and respect to dictate what is most important to them (Hammond, 2010).

AARM Model® and Strength-Based Approach as Intervention

A facilitator can use the AARM® model along with a strength-based orientation to help the client to:

• provide topics for deeper exploration/discussion;

- feel empowered to change;
- develop a set of self-defined goals and define small steps towards growth and accomplishment that can be celebrated;
- establish reasonable goals;
- focus on personal endeavors rather than fixing others;
- learn to distinguish between influence the personal responsibility of others;
- Facilitate an environment where the client is willing to confront challenges rather than to avoid situations, which cause her to avoid challenges (Hammond, 2010).

SUGGESTED ACTIVITIES

Again, I offer the AARM® model as one method to foster discussion as a tool to help client self-disclosure. This integrated model is a flexible tool for helping professionals or an individual to:

- Help define the worldview;
- Clarify how an individual view herself in the context of the experience;
- Assist in defining role clarity;
- Assist with boundary setting;
- Provide self-assessment of strength as well as responsibilities;
- Serve as a point of discussion and/or an icebreaker.

LOTUS: The AARM® and Circles and Roles®

BACKGROUND

In this example, we again draw upon the content of Lotus' interview to illustrate the use of the AARM® as a communication tool. Lotus is family-oriented, as we learn from her comment, "family is too important." Her self-efficacy, resourcefulness, strong interpersonal skills, and motivation to survive her crisis, all are assets and complementary as a means to improve her quality of life. In Lotus' words, "I've gotten stronger."

Recall, Lotus was concerned about her husband's safety while incarcerated. She was also concerned about her daughter's emotional status. She had begun to withdraw from her support networks, possibly due to the crisis and even shame associated with her husband's confinement. Using the AARM® and *Circles and Roles*® activity, we might apply the following strategy. The helping professional would direct Lotus, or Lotus herself would:

1. In a sentence or two, describe a circumstance that she would like to see more in alignment with her idea of happiness or a problem that she would like to solve.

2. Draw a circle representing the person, place, or things that are in the context of the problem (nouns).

3. Each of these circles would contain labeled spokes that represent roles, conditions self-identity, responsibilities, related to the issue (using verbs and adjectives as descriptors).

An example, statement from Lotus: "I feel frustrated and scared to leave my incarcerated husband and feel obligated to support him even though I am financially strained."

Talking Points for each step might include:

• **Awareness:** *What is going on? (presenting issue, concern, or unmet goal)* Lotus will draw a circle that represents her worldview. She will draw spokes or lines extending out from her circle that represent her role in the situation. She may use any labels she finds appropriate or fitting.

• **Assessment:** *What is my/her perceived role in the situation? Is anyone else involved? (If yes, then draw separate circles and define roles and attributes as labels to represent these individuals).* During this step, Lotus will ponder or discuss perceptions of her roles and responsibility related to each of the labels.

• **Reframe:** *What can I/she do to improve or change the situation to be consistent with my goals? (write this down as measurable and realistic goal statements).*

Lotus may examine one or more of the labels to discern if there were areas, she would like to change. She can examine the pros and cons of her decision.

• **Match Response:** *What will you/she do? (to accomplish the goals/prioritize the incremental steps)*

In this step, Lotus is asked to write down the steps she will take to move towards achieving her goal, as she has envisioned it...

In the diagram that depicts Lotus' circle, she has defined herself as skilled and versatile. Perhaps, she is concerned about financial stability, as well. This perceived responsibility places a tremendous burden on her, given that she feels responsible for "fixing" the family issues. She believes that she has the responsibility of being the glue of the family, while at the same time she fears being alone. To balance her fears of loneliness, Lotus had the ability to establish support networks, given her strong interpersonal skills. She is a woman who is motivated and optimistic, which makes her a great candidate to examine how to move forward from being frustrated and stuck with an alcoholic husband to that which is a life of fulfillment and purpose.

Questions Lotus might answer:

1. What steps will I take to reduce my frustration of being in the relationship with my husband?

2. How can I find ways to address my fear of being alone? Hint: Lotus has great interpersonal skills. She may learn to develop other meaningful relationships while considering how to meet her needs of family.

3. How can my strength and optimism help me to achieve my goals?

4. What are my healthy options to alleviate loneliness?

A facilitated discussion with Lotus may include asking:

1. Lotus, I see that you have listed the word "strong" on your diagram. Would you share a bit about what being strong means to you? (This question is designed to elicit strength, provide recognition of personal strength and wherewithal).

2. Lotus, if you feel comfortable, could you share a bit about how you consider your role as the responsible person for fixing things? Probe: How does that responsibility show up in what you are feeling?

3. Lotus, I see that you have listed the word "optimism." Do you mind sharing how your optimism plays out in the context of your life?

4. As a facilitator, you can ask Lotus which of the labels stand out as most important to work on now. Generally, her answers will lead to goal setting and prioritizing her endeavors.

5. Using a free-hand approach, Lotus will mark items that are incongruent with her identified goal(s). Note that her goals may be fluid and may change with her insights gained from this activity.

6. Note: There is no right or wrong interpretation of her feelings as diagrammed. If she chooses to redraw her circles and roles on a new sheet that represents her desired future state, she can do so.

The above probes/questions can generate a dialogue and gain clarity for Lotus about her role(s), as she perceives herself in the context of her problem. The next steps will be to drill-down and discuss her feelings and perceptions about her daughter and husband. By doing so, we can learn about her feelings of responsibility to each person. She does not share much about her son; we can assume either that she does not want to discuss this relationship or that it may not be a source of distress.

The next step involves assisting Lotus to expand her worldview to include significant others or entities. Based on what we know, she can draw her daughter and husband. We do not know much about her other child, so we will refrain from assumptions. On the same sheet of paper, assume that Lotus drew a circle representing her daughter. This circle helps her to visualize her daughter's role in the perceived state of distress. Perhaps Lotus' drawing looks like Figure A.1.

In Figure A.2, Circle and Roles, is Lotus' depiction of her daughter's perceived roles and actions related to the identified situation. This map may help us to understand her stress related to family. She may also indicate that

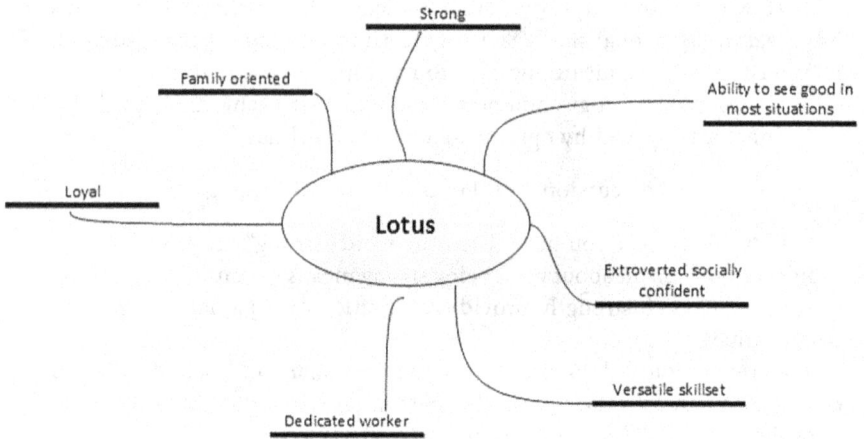

Figure A.1. Circle and Roles: Lotus.

her daughter is vulnerable and she has been "clinging" to Lotus more than usual. This added need for support may also be a source of stress and added burden of expectations. Lotus may not understand why her child is wearing her dad's shirt. She does recognize that her child is afraid for the family and perhaps even losing Lotus to incarceration. Ultimately, Lotus may label a spoke as her daughter missing her father.

The final part of the drawing may include a circle that represents the role of the husband and father of her child/ren (see Figure A.3).

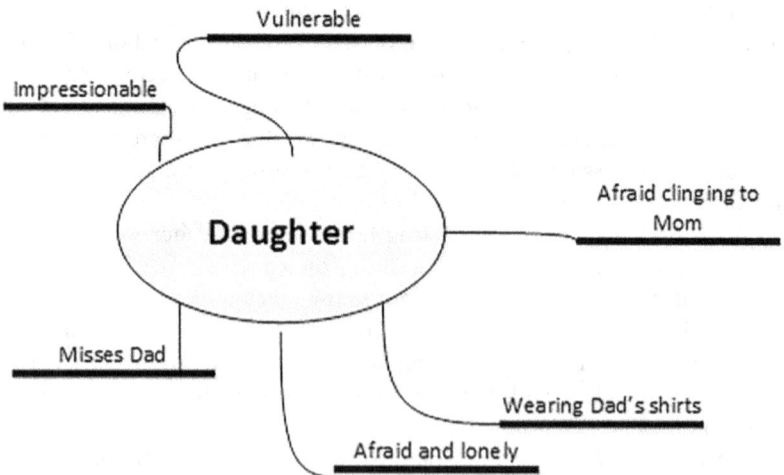

Figure A.2. Circle and Roles: Lotus' daughter.

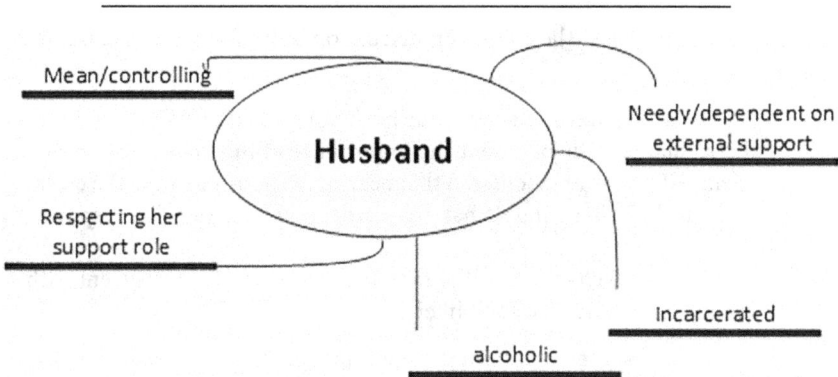

Figure A.3. Circles and Roles: Lotus' husband.

It is possible that Lotus acknowledges that her husband has been mean, even controlling, in the past. It is also possible that she does not feel comfortable sharing that information. Here, for illustration purposes, we imagine that she has. She also acknowledges through her quotes that her husband needs her and is highly dependent on her to take care of his canteen as well as to answer his phone calls. She labels his status as "incarcerated." In role-playing, she also imagines that her husband earnestly respects her support role.

BUILDING AWARENESS

At this point, we have now worked on step one, which is to build *awareness.* We are not problem solving here. We are using the Circles and Roles to understand the context of the source of distress or the challenge that Lotus deems important. We are not addressing grief or other psychological discomforts. Our goal is to encourage Lotus to look at her self-perception with truth and honesty, and with the notion that there is no right or wrong answer.

Now that we have generated a dialogue and raised a level of awareness with Lotus, we will move to the assessment part of the model. At this point, we are asking the question: "How might this picture look if you were to have an ideal outcome?" Lotus can select each label and determine if the label is congruent with her goals, or if it is unrealistic and incongruent with her goals.

As helping professionals, our goal is to facilitate a discussion that helps Lotus to see clearly where her ability and role to change things begins with changing herself through action and goal setting.

For instance, if Lotus selects the circle that says her husband is an alcoholic and further discusses how she needs to get him to Alcoholics Anonymous, then, perhaps, the following discussion will take place, specific to her husband's circle.

1. I see that you have selected your husband's circle as a starting point. Could you share a little bit about the importance of this selection?

2. I can tell from our discussion that bearing responsibility for the entire family might be exhausting. What are your thoughts about this responsibility?

3. If you were to change this diagram in a manner that is consistent with your goal, what would that look like?

Once the discussion provides enough information to create an action plan, it is wise to document the important incremental steps in a manner that is realistic and can be accomplished based on Lotus' ability and personal choice.

Guidance: The facilitator helps Lotus to understand that each individual in her circle, even her child, has the ability to take steps to accomplish their own personal goals.

The final step involves the Matched Response. In this final step, Lotus will be encouraged to take incremental and realistic steps to enable her to celebrate small accomplishments and to build her self-confidence and self-efficacy. For example, she may decide to allow herself an evening out with her daughter so that the two spend time together. This may offer reassurance to her daughter that her mother is spending quality time with her. This may empower her child to have a sense of balance not only in respecting her father but also participating in recreation. Allowing both herself and her daughter to experience an outing also helps to work through the withdrawal and need to isolate as linked to *Symbolic Imprisonment,* as further explained earlier.

There are strategies that helping professionals can use when working with women who struggle with complexities similar to Lotus.' A few intervention options might include goal setting and using emotion-focused treatment. The emotion-focused modality comprises a synthesis of Person-Centered Therapy, Existential Therapy, and Gestalt Theory (see Berman, 2010).

Appendix B.
Research Study
Methodological Framework

Curiosity about the object of knowledge and the willingness and openness to engage in theoretical readings and discussions is fundamental. However, I am not suggesting an over-celebration of theory. To do so would be to reduce theory to a pure verbalism or intellectualism. By the same token, to negate theory for the sake of practice, is to run the risk of losing oneself in the disconnectedness of practice.... In order to achieve this unity, one must have an epistemological curiosity—a curiosity that is often missing in the dialogue as conversation.—Paulo Freire

Symbolic Imprisonment, Grief and Coping Theory

RESEARCH PROBLEM

Studies have indicated that African American women with incarcerated significant others may experience psychological, social, and physical responses to loss, possibly similar to grief. However, at the outset of this study, I found no theoretical model to account for their possible psychosocial and physical distress, potential grief responses, and coping strategies. Therefore, the problem is that helping professionals may not fully understand the impact of separation and loss on the quality of life for affected African American women or know how to support them. The goal of my study was to provide researchers and helping professionals with an understanding of this problem so that possible future targeted and unobtrusive support services could be provided to this affected population.

Beyond a 100-Mile Radius

To understand the nature of separation and loss, and the burden on African American women in this study, and their families, I share the history of the closing of Washington, D.C.'s only prison to ground the reader with this unit of analysis. This content provides an understanding to the geographic challenges, the cost of contact, and other insights.

A survey completed during 2012 showed that over 100 inmates from Washington, D.C., were located as far away as the West Coast (see Table B.1). The rest of the 5,000 or so inmates were serving time at various facilities across the nation. The overwhelming majority—or 90 percent—of the felons sent to prison from the Washington, D.C., area are African American, and an undetermined number—although not all—are from poor families with low levels of education and high unemployment.

Federal Bureau of Prisons Facilities Housing D.C. Prisoners					
Facility	Location/State	No. Inmates	Travel time from DC	Distance (miles)	Public Transportation Examples
FCI Dublin	California	116	43 hrs.	2932	Via San Francisco, Airport 7 hrs. 10 min.
USP McCreary	Kentucky	154	8 hrs. 26 min.	563	Via Pine Knott Lexington, KY
USP Big Sandy	Kentucky	186	7 hrs. 9 min	477	Indirect flight, via Huntington WV. 4 hrs. 35 min.
USP Lee	Virginia	189	6 hrs. 34 min	430	DC to Tri-Cities Regional, TN - Rent a car.
FCI Gilmer	West Virginia	206	4 hrs. 58 min.	278	Flight to Morgantown West VA. Or Car
USP Cannon	Pennsylvania	144	4 hrs. 31 min.	262	Flight and Drive
Rivers Correctional Facility,	NC	770	4 hrs. 45 min	259	Via Norfolk International and Drive 53 miles.
USP Hazelton	West Virginia	289	3 hrs. 51min	233	Flight to Morgantown WV 1 hour, 5 min.
FCI Petersburg	Virginia	204	2 hrs. 48 min.	162	Fly to Norfolk and 4 hrs. train.
FCI Fairton	New Jersey	166	3 hrs. 37 min.	160	Via Newark. 5 hrs. Connecting flights.
FCI Cumberland	Western MD	153	2 hrs. 20 min.	150	Car or public transportation

Table B.1. D.C. felons distance from home jurisdiction (District of Columbia Corrections Information Council [2012]).

Table B.1 depicts examples of the geographic distances of inmates from D.C. This table shows the locations of federal facilities and inmate counts as of 2012. This number changes based on arrest and release of inmates. Two of the facilities located the farthest away are in California, 2,932 miles, and Oregon, 2,647 miles away. To reach these locations generally requires transportation via plane, train, bus, or car.

In addition, visitation is difficult because prisons are typically located in remote areas, requiring multiple modes of transportation. For example, travel by airplane to Federal Corrections Institution (FCI) Petersburg (Virginia), may require a flight into Norfolk, and then travel by car, bus, or taxi to the facility. Most likely, families traveling long distances, of over 6 hours, such as a visit to Rivers Correctional North Carolina or United States Penitentiary (UPS) MacCreary (Kentucky) may require a hotel stay as well.

Travel expenses add up for visiting family members. The nearest facility located near Washington, D.C., is in Cumberland, Maryland, 153 miles away. If family or friends want to visit this destination, ground transportation such as car, bus, or train is required. Transportation such as private prison shuttle service appears to be unreliable. According to a prison-bus-shuttle service owner whom I interviewed for this book, his service from D.C. to Butner, NC requires a minimum number of passengers to make the trip and, ultimately, to be profitable. Tickets range from $100.00 to $125.00 per person. His fee includes the provision of a meal along the way during the 5.5-hour ride. Generally, the bus leaves from a Maryland location. To make the trip, family members must arrange to meet the bus at a specified location outside of D.C. The bus leaves at approximately 2:30 a.m. The operator and owner of the service indicated that there are frequent cancellations due to volatile financial circumstances of the passengers. Even if a family member can afford money for a visit, she is dependent on the bus service option. This can also add to the stress and disappointment encountered by family members.

Table B.1 does not depict the entire population of Washington, D.C., offenders. The table shows a variation of distance away and possible transportation options. Figure B.1. Washington, D.C. Prisoners Census U.S. Locations depicts the spread of prisoners who are located at different federal prisons, nationally. These geographic locations shown in Table B.1 and Figure B.1 emphasize how financial hardships are ongoing challenges associated with maintaining contact via travel. These economic burdens are the hardest for those families already financially stressed. Additionally, those who are not familiar with traveling and associated logistics of hotels, flights, and ground travel may find coordinating transportation to the prisons both stressful and difficult. Peony, a participant in this study lamented,

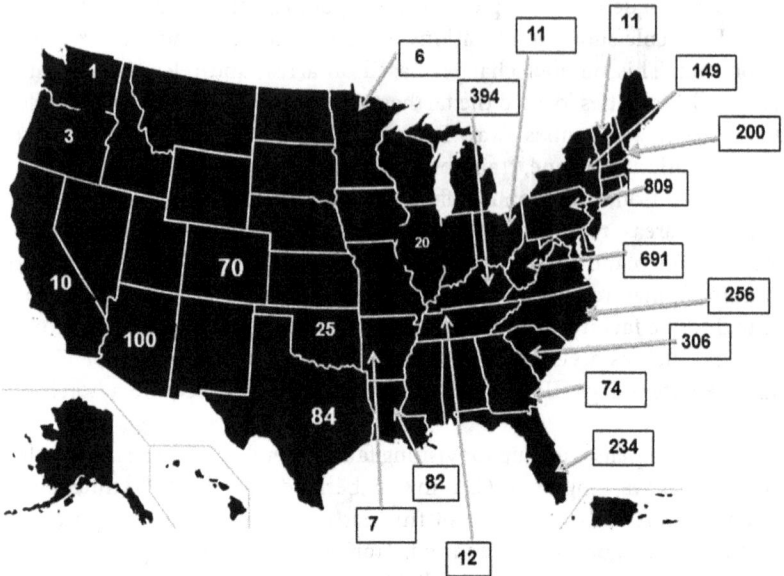

Figure B.1. D.C. prisoners census, U.S. Locations. Not shown are: D.C. 277; Virginia 409; Maryland 144; Massachusetts 35, Indiana 79; Wisconsin 4; Mississippi 10; Minnesota 20, Missouri 41.

This map depicts a point in time where D.C. prisoners were located during 2012. This inmate census includes the following states, followed by total counts: Minnesota 6; Illinois 20; Kentucky 394; Ohio 11; Pennsylvania 809; New York 149; Vermont 11; Maine 200; West Virginia, 691; North Carolina 256; South Carolina 306; Georgia; Florida 234; Alabama; Tennessee 12; Louisiana 82; Oklahoma 25; Texas 84; Colorado 70; Arizona 100; California 107; Oregon 3; Washington 1 (CIC Annual Report June, 29, 2012 Census [2012]).

> I haven't seen him in five years. They shipped him out [to Pennsylvania]. There was no notification about it ... they told me it was for his safety, or whatever. We missed his birthday and I have hard times—holidays, when I'm used to actually seeing him [in person].

Peony's concerns illustrate that even a 2.5-hour distance from D.C. can be a hardship. Figure B.1 shows a United States map depicting the number of inmates from D.C. located across the map. Although the number of inmates varies from day to day because of their releases, during 2012, this map shows 107 inmates in the state of California. Even the state of Florida has 234 inmates. Generally, travel out of state can be costly and driving to another state requires reliable transportation. Another participant, one who was financially able to afford frequent travel stated:

> "[H]otel rooms—from not even the nicest places, like cheap motels are at least a hundred dollars a night. Because it's six hours away, I only go [to the prison] once

a month. I tend to stay all weekend.... I'm usually spending two to three hundred dollars on hotel rooms.

Maintaining contact is a reasonable goal for women who have loved ones serving their time out of state. However, 65 percent of families with incarcerated loved ones also struggle to maintain the minimal needs of the household (Lowery, 2015). Having disposable income may mean the difference in a family's abilities to maintain a relationship. The overwhelming majority of the women in this study expressed their perceived obligation to provide financial support to cover their mate's necessities. These needs ranged from providing funds for toiletries, extra food or snacks, and, surprisingly, to serve as a means of protection. Some of the women in this study indicated that their husbands or boyfriends used finances to barter for phone time or to stave off gang activity.

THE DRUG WAR: WASHINGTON, D.C.

In Washington, D.C, where this study took place, a number of first-time offenders as well as drug kingpins, received life sentences for the use/distribution of crack cocaine or drug-related crime committed (see Horwitz, [2015] and; Hsu & Zauzmer, [2015], respectively). The nation's capital mirrored America's surge in drug arrests and subsequent incarceration rates that took place between 1990 and 2010 (U.S. Department of Justice [DOJ], 2012). In 2010 alone, there were 13 million (state and local) arrests, of which 1.6 million were drug related (DOJ, 2012). As America is currently in the midst of sentencing reform and considering restorative responses to its current opiate epidemic, there are mothers, sisters, grandmothers, and family members who are still suffering the aftermath of a crack cocaine epidemic, (which began in the 1970s and continued at its heaviest rate through 2001).

One woman represented in this study described having to deal with the incarceration of each of her children during that era. She recalled that during the 1990s, it was commonplace to see as many as a thousand individuals from Washington, D.C., arrested on weekends alone in connection with drug busts.

Women who participated in this study were in relationships with men who received prison sentences ranging from a year to life. These men serve their sentences out of state in institutions in the Federal Bureau of Prisons because Washington, D.C., has no local prison.

A significant number of the women (80 percent) who took part in this study described their experiences as a life-altering change that extended far beyond the duration of a mate's prison sentence—life will never be the same for these women. On logical grounds, and through compelling evidence, I have learned through the stories of these women that fear is a cry for help and that self-imposed isolation from their social networks may serve as a protective barrier. Further evidence in this study supports that the African American woman with an incarcerated mate, by association, can be affected emotionally, financially, socially, physically, spiritually, and even politically (Hart-Johnson, 2014). This book engages only part of their stories. However, the personal testimonies presented here often reveal powerful insights.

The Research

This book grew out of research I did for a qualitative grounded theory study. I interviewed a purposefully selected sample of 20 African American women, a small but significant sample for qualitative methodology. My findings resulted in my creation of a theory to explain holistically this phenomenon occurring among the population of Black women with an imprisoned mate: It is called, Sig-C Theory: *Symbolic Imprisonment, Grief, and Coping.*

The results of my findings showed uniformity among these women concerning the psychosocial effects of loss. The main theoretical premise behind SIG-C is that women experience grief, similar to the death of a loved one and the manifestation of this grief combined with shame, stigma, and stress is a state of *Vicarious Imprisonment (also referred to in a broader context in this book as Symbolic Imprisonment).*

This study focused on the affected women living in the United States in the Washington, D.C. (SMSA-standard metropolitan statistical area). Largely ignored in the past, in this book, we now hear the voices of these women. Their silent cries for help are the core essence of *Symbolic Imprisonment, Grief and Coping* (a.k.a. SIG-C) *Theory* and what this book is about.

Building upon the initial work, I extend the content to: provide added perspective on information in the literature; offer analysis of information gained during women's interviews, and provide suggestions to facilitate discussion about possible intervention methods. These recommendations are based on my own fieldwork conducted as a facilitator of psychoeducational support groups for affected women.

Imagine Not Having a Voice

In the United States, almost four decades of arrest and subsequent incarceration of African American men continues to have unaddressed collateral consequences on the families of the incarcerated, including the Black woman (Dyer, Pleck, & McBride, 2012). Being a Black woman in America, compounded with having an incarcerated mate, can also be associated with stigma, shame, and marginalization.

The social problems associated with mass incarceration are complex. The academic literature remains incomplete without providing an understanding of how this labyrinth of social ills affects the mates of the incarcerated and their families. This lack of attention is troubling; when the scientific literature lags, the introduction of programs and support services also is likely to lag. Therefore, uncovering what these women were experiencing is of critical concern for their health and well-being. Further, as the cornerstone of this work, I wanted to inform the public through this exploration: *why they should care.*

The literature, often subsumed with peripheral views of this population, does not lead to conclusive knowledge of the overlapping complexities women face during the incarceration crisis. Researchers Taylor, Gilligan, & Sullivan's (1995) book about Black women and girls captures the essence of how, even as young black girls they are, "not heard in public, or if heard are generally spoken about in third person. These girls have voices, they are perfectly capable of first-person speech, but as they will say repeatedly, nobody listens, nobody cares, nobody asks what they are feeling and thinking" (p.4). This fitting statement also captures the essence of women's concluding thoughts about their treatment as wives and girlfriends of incarcerated men. Throughout different periods of history, disenfranchisement, stigmatization, marginalization, and other forms of societal omission have tended to silence African American women's voices (Houston, 2014). I offer that when one part of society is suffering, the remainder of society is less than whole.

PURPOSE

The purpose of this constructivist grounded theory study was to discover and to build a substantive theory that explains African American women's cognitive and emotional processes associated with separation and loss and to understand their coping strategies. This formulation of midlevel theory provides the basis for future researchers to develop subsequent formal or grand theory. To understand this problem of separation and loss, I interviewed a sample of 20 African American women living in the Washington, D.C., metropolitan (DC, MD, and VA) area. Each of these women was in a relationship with an incarcerated mate.

RESEARCH QUESTIONS

In this study, I referred to grand tour research questions as a consolidation of the research questions, problem, and the central concepts for this study. The primary research questions (RQ) are:

RQ01: What are the processes and theory that explain how African American women perceive their experiences of separation and loss from their incarcerated mate, and what, if any, are their coping strategies?

RQ02: How, if at all, do African American women perceive their current or past experiences of separation and loss from their incarcerated mate as psychological, physical, social, and symbolic loss and potential, resultant grief?

CONCEPTUAL FRAMEWORK

The framework of this study was influenced by concepts derived from the literature and narrowed down to two theories to provide a structured focus on loss and separation. The major building blocks for developing this grounded theory were hinged upon a consolidation of (a) disenfranchised grief [Doka, 2002] and (b) the dual process model for grief (Stroebe & Schutt, 1999).

The concepts of interest specific to disenfranchised grief are: (a) socially unsanctioned loss, (b) hidden grief, (c) circumstances associated with the grief as stigmatized, or negatively judged by others, and (d) grief expressed that does not conform to normal grieving rules and rituals.

NATURE OF THE STUDY

I implemented a grounded theory design for this research study. The grounded theory method enabled me to establish a loose explanatory framework, using the identified tentative concepts (Charmaz, 2006). This approach was best suited because of the paucity of literature and lack of theory for this research topic. I used a combination of Charmaz's (2006) and Strauss and Corbin's (1990) grounded theory methods.

DATA COLLECTION

I performed data collection using qualitative semi-structured, open-ended interview questions. I interviewed 20 African American women who self-identified as having a relationship with a current or previously incarcerated mate. To qualify for the study, the mate must have been currently serving or had previously served greater than a one-year prison sentence. I incorporated other artifacts, as additional data points (elicited materials) and for triangulation. The sample of 20 participants was a large enough qualitative sample to identify emerging common patterns, themes, and concepts. Finally, I chose to use snowball and convenience sampling to recruit individuals who were the subject matter experts for this topic.

DATA ANALYSIS

I used first- and second-cycles of coding, including the use of in vivo coding, which entails respondents' verbatim words, used as codes. The data collection and analysis processes were iterative, in that I repeated periods

of transcription, analysis, interpretation, code creation, property identifi-
cation, theoretical category development, and model building, until the
point of saturation.

LIMITATIONS

There are a few known limitations that should be mentioned. First the
sample was small, (*n=20*). However, this is consistent with qualitative studies. Generally, with a qualitative study the focus to on depth and detail.
Although a small sample is a noted limitation, it is important also to
acknowledge that the purpose of this grounded theory study was to develop
context-specific theory as a foundation for future research. I continued
interviews until I reached the point of theoretical saturation, which means
that no new properties and insights were provided through interviews. This
is the point in which the information was thematic and all of the stories
began to sound similar. Second, I only interviewed African American
women. After conducting this study, I realized that other women outside
of this cultural group likely feel what I described as SIG-C. There is evidence
that this study's design should be applied to other racial compositions, different gender groups, and heterogeneous samples. As noted in Chapter 2,
qualitative samples are intentionally small in order to provide a wide depth
and breadth of participant experiences (Auerbach & Silverstein, 2003). It is
possible that this theory can be extended to other samples to further develop
the basis provided from this study.

Finally, a limitation is that most of the interviews were conducted via
telephone rather than as in-person interviews. Consequently, any non-
verbal reactions and in-person observations could not be recorded.

FUTURE RESEARCH QUESTIONS

Previous chapters highlighted variations of women and their families
in crisis. For example, the social conditions experienced by Aster, Lotus,
and Sage did not occur in an isolated context. Future researchers should
consider:

• Is there a linkage between women's productivity and familial stress
from a mate's incarceration;

• How do vulnerable families remain intact when a significant family
member is incarcerated and sentenced for lengthy sentences (e.g., greater
than five years);

• How can families reduce the cycle of recidivism and prevent intergenerational incarceration?

• How do poor families who live in areas highly concentrated with crime
and incarceration avoid being most susceptible?

The most vulnerable families are likely to be at the greatest risk of suffering the impacts of mass incarceration and social disorganization in their neighborhoods. Social disorganization theory holds: When community health is not held as a high priority by community members, politicians, and lawmakers, the markers for crime are high, and the community will suffer the downstream effects (Harbeck, 2015). This breakdown in social order could involve an inability of community residents to form a collective body that engages in advocacy work to solve its own problems.

Appendix C.
Resources

Organizations

DC Project Connect: This organization Provides support to women with incarcerated mates and mentoring to female returning citizens. www.dcprojectconnect.com

Families of the Incarcerated: http://familiesofincarcerated.org/aboutUs.htm

Riverside, Content from the Mayo Clinic. Codependency Support. http://www.riversideonline.com/health_reference/Behavior-Mental-Health/AN01340.cfm

Websites

Co-Dependents Anonymous: http://www.coda.org

Mental Health America: http://www.mentalhealthamerica.net/go/codependency

Modern/Mom: http://motherhood.modernmom.com/handle-husband-going-jail-8969.html

Social Media Sites

Prison Fellowship: https://www.prisonfellowship.org/resources/training-resources/family/

Prisoner Family Conference: https://www.google.com/?ion=1&espv=2#q=prisoner%20family%20conference

Prisoner's Wives and Girlfriends: http://pwgp.org/

Strong Prison Wives and Families: http://www.strongprisonwives.com/

References

ABC News (2010). *America's 25 most dangerous neighborhoods.* Retrieved from http://abcnews.go.com/Travel/LifeStages/americas-dangerous-neighborhoods-areas-violent-crime/story?id=11803334.

Abrams, D.S., Betrand, M. & Mullainathan, S. (2008). Do Judges vary in their treatment of race? *American Law & Economics Association Papers, January* (2008), 1–46.

Ackerman, R.A., Kashy, D., Donnellan, M., & Conger, R. (2011). Positive-engagement behaviors in observed family interactions: A social relations perspective. *Journal of Family Psychology, 25*(5), 719–730. Doi:10.1037/a0025288.

American Counseling Association (2014). *2014 ACA Code of ethics: As approved by the ACA governing council.* Retrieved from https://www.counseling.org/resources/aca-code-of-ethics.pdf.

American Psychological Association (2012). *Ethnic and racial disparities in education: Psychology's contributions to understanding and reducing disparities.* Retrieved from https://www.apa.org/ed/resources/racial-disparities.pdf.

Barnes, M.D. (2014). Symbols of comfort for a journey of grief. *Illness, Crisis, & Loss, 22*(1), 77–80.

Barrett D, Katsiyannis A, Zhang D. (2010). Predictors of offense severity, adjudication, incarceration, and repeat referrals for juvenile offenders: A multicohort replication study. *Remedial and Special Education [serial online], 31*(4), 261–275. doi:10.1177/0741932509355990.

Bayse, D.J., Allgood, S.M., & Van Wyk, P.H. (1991). Family life education: an effective tool for prisoner rehabilitation. *Family Relations, 40*(1), 254–257. doi:10.2307/585008.

Bell, G.C., Hopson, M.C., Craig, R. & Robinson, N.W. (2014). Exploring black and white accounts of 21st-century racial profiling: Riding and driving while black. *Qualitative Research Reports in Communication, 15*(1): 33–42. Doi: 10.1080/17459435.2014.955590.

Berin, E. (2014, January 31). *D.C. churches and civic groups joined the fight against crack.* Retrieved from http://wamu.org/news/DC-Churches-And-Civic-Groups-Joined-The-Fight-Against-Crack.

Berman, P.S. (2010). *Case conceptualization and treatment planning: Integrating theory with clinical practice* (2nd ed.). Thousand Oaks, CA: Sage, Publishing Inc.

Bermin, E. (2014, January 30). *D.C. residents caught amid crack's bloody turf wars.* Retrieved from http://wamu.org/news/DC-Residents-Caught-Amid-Cracks-Turf-Wars.

Black Demographics (2015). *African American women.* Retrieved from http://blackdemographics.com/black-women-statistics/

Blakey, J.M. (2016). The role of spirituality in helping African American women with histories of trauma and substance abuse heal and recover. *Social Work & Christianity, 43*(1), 40–59.

Boncza, T. (2003). *Prevalence of imprisonment in the U.S. population, 1974–2001.* Washington, D.C.: Washington, D.C.: US Department of Justice.

Boo, K. (2003). *The black gender gap: It may be the greatest policy achievement in recent history: Over the past decade significant numbers of formerly welfare-dependent black women have successfully entered the work force. But what about black men?* (*Welfare & Poverty*). Retrieved from *The Atlantic.* 1, 107, 2003. ISSN: 1072–7825.

Boudin, C. (2013). Prison visitation policies:

191

A fifty-state survey. *Yale Law & Policy Review [serial online]*, *32*, 149–189.

The Bowen Center for Study of the Family (2016). *Emotional cutoff.* Retrieved June 11, 2016, from https://www.thebowencenter. org/theory/eight-concepts/emotional-cutoff/

Bowlby, J. (1980). *Attachment and loss: Sadness and depression. Vol. III.*, London, England: Hogarth Press.

Bowlby, J. (1982). Attachment and loss: Retrospect and prospect. *American Journal of Orthopsychiatry, 52*(4), 664–678. Retrieved from http://www.apa.org/pubs/journals/ort.

Bozarth, J. (2012). 'Nondirectivity' in the theory of Carl R. Rogers: An unprecedented premise. *Person-Centered and Experiential Psychotherapies, 11*(4), 262–276. doi:10.10 80/14779757.2012.740317.

Braithwaite, J. (1989). *Crime, shame, and reintegration.* New York: Cambridge Press.

Braman, D. (2004). *Doing time on the outside.* Ann Arbor: University of Michigan Press.

Brink, J. (2003). "You don't see us doin time." *Contemporary Justice Review, 64*(4), 393–396.

Brown, D.L. (2016, January 28). *A hidden world: Desperation for hundreds of homeless families in D.C. motels.* Retrieved from https://www.washingtonpost.com/local/a-hidden-world-desperation-and-cramped-living-for-homeless-families-in-dc-motels/2016/01/28/279adfda-b4d8-11e5-a76a-0b5145e8679a_story.html.

Brown, E. (2006). Good mother, bad mother: Perception of mothering by rural African-American women who use cocaine. *Journal of Addictions Nursing (Taylor & Francis Ltd)*, *17*(1), 21–31.

Bureau of Justice Statistics (2013). *Prisoners in 2013.* Retrieved from file:///C:/Users/bonni_000/Downloads/p13.pdf.

Bureau of Justice Statistics (2015). *Jail inmates at midyear 2014.* Retrieved from www.ojp. usdoj.gov.

Bureau of Justice Statistics (2015). *U.S. prison population declined one percent in 2014.* Retrieved from http://www.bjs.gov/content/pub/press/p14pr.cfm.

Bureau of Labor Statistics (2010). *Unemployment rates for the 50 largest cities.* Retrieved from http://www.bls.gov/lau/lacilg10.htm.

Buzawa, E. (2007). Victims of domestic violence. In R.C. Davis, A.J. Lurigio, & S. Herman (Eds.), *Victims of crime* (3rd ed. pp. 55–74). Thousand Oaks, CA: Sage Publications, Inc.

Caldwell, C.H. (1996). Predisposing, enabling, and need factors related to patterns of help-seeking among African American women. In: Neighbors, H.W. Jackson, J.S. (eds.). *Mental health in black America.* Thousand Oaks, CA: Sage pp. 146–160.

Carter, S.P. (2007). "Reading all that White crazy stuff": Black young women unpacking whiteness in a high school British literature classroom. *Journal of Classroom Interaction, 41*(2), 42–54.

Cattaneo, L.B., & Goodman, L.A. (2003). Victim-reported risk factors for continued abusive behavior: Assessing the dangerousness of arrested batterers. *Journal of Community Psychology, 31*(4), 349–369. doi:10. 1002/jcop.10056.

Center for American Progress (2015). *The straight facts on women in poverty.* Retrieved from https://www.americanprogress.org/issues/women/report/2008/10/08/5103/the-straight-facts-on-women-in-poverty/

Center for Disease Control (2015). *Education and community support for health literacy.* Retrieved from http://www.cdc.gov/health literacy/education-support/index.html.

Chae D., Drenkard C., Lewis T., & Lim S. (2015). Discrimination and cumulative disease damage among African American women with systemic Lupus Erythematosus. *American Journal of Public Health [serial online]*, *105*(10), 2099–2107. doi:10.21 05/AJPH.2015.302727.

Chui, W.H. (2009). "Pains of imprisonment": Narratives of the women partners and children of the incarcerated. *Child & Family Social Work, 15*(1), 196–205.

Clay, C.M., Ellis, M.A., Griffin, M.L., Amodeo, M., & Fassler, I.R. (2007). Black women and White women: Do perceptions of childhood family environment differ? *Family Process, 46*(2), 243–256.

CollegeBoard (2016). *Trends in higher education.* Retrieved March 12, 2016, from http://trends.collegeboard.org/education-pays/figures-tables/educational-attainment-race-ethnicity-and-gender-1973–2009.

Collett, M. (1989). *The cocaine connection: Drug trafficking and inter–American relations.* New York: Foreign Policy Series. Retrieved from https://web.stanford.edu/class/e297c/poverty_prejudice/paradox/htele.html.

Comfort, M., Reznick, O.G., Binson, D.,

Darbes, L.A., & Neilands (2011). Sexual HIV risk among male parolees and their female partners: The relate project. *Journal of Health Disparities Research and Practice,* 7(6), 26–53.

Congress.gov (2015). *S.502—Smarter Sentencing Act of 2015.* Retrieved from https://www.congress.gov/bill/114th-congress/senate-bill/502.

Corrections Information Council (CIC) (n.d.). *About the Corrections Information Council.* Retrieved from http://cic.dc.gov/page/about-cic.

Corrections Information Council (2014). *Inspection Report USP Lewisburg.* Retrieved from http://cic.dc.gov/sites/default/files/dc/sites/cic/publication/attachments/Final%20USP%20Lewisburg%20Report%2011.5.15.pdf.

Course on Miracles International (2007). *A Course in miracles.* China: Barnes & Nobel, Inc., by arrangement with A Course in Miracles International.

Curtis, R. (2003). Crack, cocaine, heroin: Drug eras in Williamsburg, Brooklyn, 1960–2000. *Addiction Research & Theory,* 11(1), 47–63. doi:10.1080/1606635021000042761.

Daire, A., Jacobson, L., & Carlson, R. (2016). Emotional stocks and bonds: a metaphorical model for conceptualizing and treating codependency and other forms of emotional overinvesting. *American Journal of Psychotherapy,* 66(3), 259–278.

Davis, S. (2015). The "Strong Black Woman Collective": A developing theoretical framework for understanding collective communication practices of Black women. *Women's Studies in Communication,* 38(1), 20–35. doi:10.1080/07491409.2014.953714.

D.C. Department of Corrections (2014). *D.C. Department of Corrections Facts and figures.* Retrieved from http://www.dcdc.gov.

D.C. Housing Authority (n.d.). *Public Housing.* Retrieved from http://www.dchousing.org/topic.aspx?topid=3&AspxAutoDetectCookieSupport=1.

DC.gov (2001). *Department of Corrections.* Retrieved from http://doc.dc.gov/release/department-corrections-closes-final-prison-and-accomplishes-major-milestone.

Department of Labor Statistics (2016, March 17). *District of Columbia.* Retrieved March 17, 2001, from http://www.bls.gov/eag/eag.dc.htm Dennis, M.R. (2012). Do grief self-help books convey contemporary perspectives on grieving? *Death Studies,* 36(5). 363–418. Doi. 10.1080/07481187.2011.553326.

DeVuono-Powell, S., Schweidler, C., Walters, A., & Zohrabi, A. (2015). *Who pays? The true cost of incarceration on families.* Retrieved from Oakland, CA: Ella Baker Center, Forward Together, Research Action Design.

Discovery Communications (2010). *Investigation discovery uncovers true love with new series, PRISON WIVES, Starting Valentine's Day.* Retrieved from https://corporate.discovery.com/discovery-newsroom/investigation-discovery-uncovers-true-love-with-ne/

District of Columbia Corrections Information Council (2102). *Annual report fiscal year 2012.* Retrieved from http://www.cic.gov.

District of Columbia Corrections Information Council (2012). *Corrections Information Council fiscal year 2012 report.* Retrieved from http://www.cic.gov.

Dixon, P. (2014). The African American relationships and marriage-strengthening curriculum for African American Relationships Courses and Programs. *Journal of African American Studies,* 18(3), 337–352. doi:10.1007/s12111-013-9274-1.

Doka, K.J., Aber, R.A. (2002). Psychosocial loss and grief. In K. Doka (Ed.), *Disenfranchised grief* (pp. 217–250). Champaign, IL: Research Press.

Dolan, K., & Carr, J.L. (2015). The poor get prison: The alarming spread of the criminalization of poverty. Retrieved from http://www.ips-dc.org/wp-content/uploads/2015/03/IPS-The-Poor-Get-Prison-Final.pdf.

Dozier, R. (2010). The declining status of Black women workers, 1980–2002. *Social Forces,* 88(4), 1833–1858.

Dyer, J.W., Pleck, J.H., & McBride, B.A. (2012). Imprisoned fathers and their family relationships: A 40-year review from a multi-theory view. *Journal of Family Theory & Review,* 4(March 2012), 20–47.

Electronic FrountierFrontier Foundation (2016, April 29). *The hidden cost of JPay's prison email service.* Retrieved from https://www.eff.org/deeplinks/2015/05/hidden-cost-jpays-prison-email-system.

Evans, David R. (2017). Essential interviewing: A programmed approach to effective communication, 9th edition. [VitalSource Bookshelf Online]. Retrieved from https://bookshelf.vitalsource.com/#/books/9781305855977/

Federal Communications Commission (2013).

FCC Reduces high long-distance calling rates paid by inmates. Retrieved from https://www.fcc.gov/document/fcc-reduces-high-long-distance-calling-rates-paid-inmates.

Federal Prison Industries, Inc. (2015). *Unicore Fiscal year 2015 annual management report.* Retrieved from http://www.unicor.gov/publications/reports/FY2015_Annual MgmtReport.pdf.

Fenston, J. (2014, January 27). *Crack's rapid rise brought chaos to D.C.* Retrieved April 23, 2016, from http://wamu.org/news/14/01/14/crack_1.

Fishman, L. (1984). *Women at the wall: A study of prisoners' wives doing time on the outside.* Digital Library of Theses & Dissertations, Ipswich, MA.

Fitzgerald, J., & Vance, S.E. (2015). How today's prison crisis is shaping tomorrow's federal criminal justice system. *Federal Probation, 79*(2), 24–28.

Fornaci, P. (2010, May 5). *Housing of DC Felons far away from home: Effects on crime, recidivism, and reentry.* Retrieved May 26, 2014, from http://oversight.house.gov/wp-content/uploads/2012/01/20100505fornaci.pdf.

Franklin, C., & Pillow, W. (1995). Black male-black female conflict: Individually caused and culturally nurtured. In: *The black family: Essays and studies.* Robert Staples, 106–13. (5th ed.). Belmont, CA: Wadsworth.

Frost, J., Freillch, J., & Clear, T. (Eds.). (2009). *Contemporary issues in criminal justice policy:* Cengage Learning.

Gabriel, M.T., Criteli, J.W., & Ee, J.S. (1994). Narcissistic illusions in self-evaluations of intelligence and attractiveness. *Journal of Personality, 62*(1), 143–155. doi:10.1111/j.1467-6494.1994.tb00798.x.

Gambler, N. (2015). The secret shame of middle-class Americans. Retrieved from http://www.theatlantic.com/magazine/archive/2016/05/my-secret-shame/476415/

Glaser, B., & Strauss, A.L. (1967). *The discovery of grounded theory: Strategies for qualitative research.* New York: Aldine De Gruyter.

Go, A.S., Mozaffarian, D., Roger, V.L., Benjamin, E.J., Berry, J.D., Borden, W.B., et al. (2014). Heart disease and stroke statistics—2014 update: A report from the American Heart Association. Circulation, 29, e28–e292. doi:10.1161/01.cir. 0000441139.02102.80. Advance online publication.

GovTrack.us (2004). *H.R. 5963 (98th): Comprehensive Crime Control Act of 1984.* Retrieved from https://www.govtrack.us/congress/bills/98/hr5963#summary/library ofcongress.

Grim, R. (2016). *A Maryland lawmaker offers a radical new solution to the heroin crisis.* Retrieved from http://www.huffingtonpost.com/entry/dan-morhaim-heroin_us_56b3c342e4b08069c7a69b86.

Groom, N. (1991). *From bondage to bonding: Escaping codependency embracing biblical love.* Colorado Springs, CO: Navpress.

Guerra, M. (2013). *Fact sheet: The state of African American women in the United States (Center for American Progress).* Retrieved from https://www.americanprogress.org/issues/race/report/2013/11/07/79165/factsheet-the-state-of-african-american-women-in-the-united-states/

Gust, L. (2012). Can policy reduce the collateral damage caused by the criminal justice system? Strengthening social capital in families and communities. *American Journal of Orthopsychiatry, 82*(2), 174–180. doi:10.1111/j.1939–0025.2012.01156.x.

Gustavsson, N.S. (1991). The war metaphor: A threat to vulnerable populations. *Social Work, 36*(1), 277–278.

Haberstroh, S. (2005). Facing the music: Creative and experiential group strategies for working with addiction related grief and loss. *Journal of Creativity in Mental Health, 1*(3/4), 41–55. doi:10.1300/J456v01n03_03.

Hamilton, M.C. (1991). Masculine bias in the attribution of personhood: People = male, male = people. *Psychology of Women Quarterly, 15*(3), 393–402. doi:10.1111/j.1471–64 02.1991.tb00415.x.

Hammond, W. (2010). *Principles of strength-based practice.* Retrieved from http://www.ayscbc.org/Principles%20of%20Strength-2.pdf.

Harbeck, K.M. (2015). *Social disorganization theory. Research starters.* Retrieved from Research Starters, Ipswich, MA.

Harman, J.J., Smith, V., & Egan, L.C. (2007). The impact of incarceration on inmate relationship. *Criminal Justice and Behavior, 34*(6), 794–815. doi:10.1177/0093854807299543.

Harris, Y.R. (2013). *Children of incarcerated parents.* New York: Oxford University Press.

Harriston, K., & McCall, N. (1991). *D.C. neighborhood called war zone for drug gangs.* Retrieved May 25, 2016, from https://www.washingtonpost.com/archive/politics/1991/07/12/dc-neighborhood-called-war-zone-for-drug-gangs/d1a14865-e225-431d-9b50-b1aecd0456d9/

Hart-Johnson, A. (2014). *Symbolic imprisonment, grief, and coping theory: African American women with incarcerated mates* (Doctoral dissertation) Retrieved from ProQuest dissertations and Theses.

Hattery, A., & Smith, E. (2014). Families of incarcerated African American men: The impact on mothers and children. *The Journal of Pan African Studies, 7*(6), 128–153.

Hauswirth, K. (2015). *Codependency*. Retrieved from Salem Press Encyclopedia Of Health.

Hay House. *The power of I am*. Retrieved from http://www.drwaynedyer.com/blog/the-power-of-i-am/

Henrickson, H.C., Crowther, J.H., & Harrington, E.F. (2010). Ethnic identity and maladaptive eating: Expectancies about eating and thinness in African American women. *Cultural Diversity & Ethnic Minority Psychology, 16*(1), 87–93. doi:10.1037/a0013455.

Hewitt, R., Coak, H.. & Smale, R. (2004). I love you—neither do I: Co-dependent and abusive relationships of women clients on the addiction service. *Mental Health Practice, 7*(5), 30–32. Hortwitz, S. (2015). From a first arrest to a life sentence. Retrieved from http://www.washingtonpost.com/sf/national/2015/07/15/from-a-first-arrest-to-a-life-sentence/

Houston, M.S. (2014). Telling it just like it is: The tragicomedy of the 1965 Voting Rights Act. *Signs: Journal of Women in Culture & Society, 39*(3), 709–733.

Hsu, S., & Zauzmer, J. 2015). U.S. judge pauses at cutting sentence of D.C. drug lord's associate. Retrieved from https://www.washingtonpost.com/local/crime/a-kingpin-too-far-us-judge-pauses-at-reducing-sentence-of-dc-drug-lord/2015/09/06/925d9a7e-5001-11e5-9812-92d5948a40f8_story.html

Hunter, M. (2014). *Wayne Brady: "The young Black man is becoming an endangered species."* Retrieved from http://cnsnews.com/news/article/melanie-hunter/wayne-brady-young-black-man-becoming-endangered-species.

Infoplease (2013). *2013 median annual earnings by race and sex—Infoplease*. Retrieved from www.infoplease.com/us/census/median-earnings-by-race.html.

Jackson-Dwyer, D. (2014). *Interpersonal relationships [Vital Source Online]*. Retrieved May 21, 2016, from https://bookshelf.vitalsource.com/#/books/9781135102067/

Jeffries, D., & Jeffries, R. (2015). Mentoring and mothering Black femininity in the academy: An exploration of body, voice, and image through Black female characters. *The Western Journal of Black Studies, 39*(2), 125–133.

Johnson, R.E., Rosen, C.C., Chang, C. & Lin, S. (2015). Getting to the core of locus of control: Is it an evaluation of the self or the environment? *Journal of Applied Psychology, 100*(5), 1568–1578. Doi: 10.1037/apl0000011.

Jones, N. (2014). [Motion Picture]. New York, NY: One 9's.

Kara Kurt, G. (2012). The interplay between esteem self-esteem, feeling of inadequacy, dependency, and romantic jealousy as a function of attachment processes among Turkish college students. *Contemporary Family Therapy: An International Journal, 34*(3), 334–345. doi:10.1007/s10591-012-9185-7.

Kasparrian, A. (2016). *Why Trump's support for private prisons and mass incarceration should worry you*. Retrieved from https://www.rawstory.com/2016/04/why-trumps-support-for-private-prisons-and-mass-incarceration-should-worry-you/

Katz, M.H., & Piotrkowski, C.S. (1983). Correlates of Family role strain among employed Black women. *Family Relations, 32*(3), 331–339.

Katzen, A. (2013). African American men's health and incarceration: Access to Care upon reentry and eliminating invisible punishments. *Berkeley Journal of Gender, Law & Justice, 26*(2), 222–252.

Krysan, M. (2000). Prejudice, politics, and public opinion: Understanding the sources of racial policy attitudes. *Annual Review of Sociology, 26*(135),.

Ladson-Billings, G. (1996). "Your blues ain't like mine": Keeping issues of race and racism on the multicultural agenda. *Theory into Practice, 35*(1), 248–255.

Lal, S., Suto, M., & Ungar, M. (2012). Examining the potential of combining methods of grounded theory and narrative inquiry: A comparative analysis. *The Qualitative Report, 17*(41), 1–22. Retrieved from http://www.nova.edu/ssss/QR/QR17/lal.pdf.

Lamis, D.A., Wilson, C.K., Tarantino, N., & Kaslow, N. (2014). Neighborhood disorder, spiritual well-being, and parenting stress in African American women. *Journal of Family Psychology, 28*(6), 769–778. doi:10.1037/a0036373.

Lee, H., & Wildeman, C. (2013). Things fall apart: Health consequences of Mass imprisonment for African American women. *Review of Black Political Economy, 40*(1), 39–52. doi:10.1007/s12114-011-9112-4.

Levitt, S.D., & Dubner, S.J. (2005). *Freakonomics*. New York: HarperCollins.

Leys, Ruth. (2007). From guilt to shame. [VitalSource Bookshelf Online]. Retrieved from https://bookshelf.vitalsource.com/#/books/9781400827985/2016032307431687 0811939.

Ligett, A. (2015, December 11). *Washington, D.C., crime rate 2015; Amid gentrification, a public safety crisis worries some neighborhood leaders, police union*. Retrieved from http://www.ibtimes.com/washington-dc-crime-rate-2015-amid-gentrification-public-safety-crisis-worries-some-2220355.

Lowery, W. (2015). *Former inmates: Incarceration makes economic stability nearly impossible for our families*. Retrieved from https://www.washingtonpost.com/news/post-nation/wp/2015/09/15/former-inmates-incarceration-makes-economic-stability-nearly-impossible-for-our-families/

Macartne, S., Bishaw, A., & Fontenot, K. (2013, February). *Poverty Rates for selected detailed race and Hispanic groups by state and place: 2007–2011: American community survey briefs*. Retrieved from http://census.gov.

Mahoney, M., Bien, M., & Comfort, M. (2013). Adaptation of an evidence-based HIV prevention intervention for women with incarcerated partners: Expanding to community settings. *AIDS Education & Prevention, 25*(1), 1–13. doi:10.1521/aeap.2013.25.1.1.

Marans, D. (2015, November 4). *Black unemployment is highest in Washington, D.C.* Retrieved from http://www.huffingtonpost.com/entry/black-unemployment-washington-dc_us_563a2923e4b0411d306f00d7.

Marrone, R. (1999). Dying, mourning, and spirituality: A psychological perspective. *Death Studies, 33*(1), 495–519.

Martin, C. (2015). *12 zero tolerance policy incidents that were too ridiculous for words*. Retrieved from http://www.ijreview.com/2015/11/467823-12-zero-tolerance-policy-incidents-that-were-too-ridiculous-for-words/

Martin, T. (2002). Disenfranchising the brokenhearted. In K.J. Doka (Ed.), *Disenfranchised grief: New directions, challenges, and strategies for practice*. Champaign, IL: Research Press.

Mauer, M., & Chesney-Lind, M. (2002). *Invisible punishment: The collateral consequences of mass imprisonment*. New York: The New York Press.

Mechoulan, S. (2011). The external effects of Black male incarceration on Black females. *Journal of Labor Economics, 29*(1), 1–35. Retrieved from http://ezp.waldenulibrary.org/login?url=http://search.ebscohost.com/login.aspx?direct=true&db=bth&AN=57765613&site=eds-live&scope=site.

Merriam-Webster, Incorporated (2015). *Online dictionary*. Retrieved from http://www.merriam-webster.com/dictionary/Pyrrhic%20victory.

Messing, M. (1991, September 23). *D.C.'s war on drugs, why Bennett is losing*. Retrieved May 25, 2016, from http://www.nytimes.com/1990/09/23/magazine/dc-s-war-on-drugs-why-bennett-is-losing.html?page wanted=all.

Miller, L. (2015, May 22). *The psychological advantages of strongly identifying as biracial*. Retrieved June 24, 2016, from http://nymag.com/scienceofus/2015/05/psychological-advantages-biracial.html.

Monahan, J.L., Shtrulis, I., & Givens, S.B. (2005). Priming welfare queens and other stereotypes: The transference of media images into interpersonal contexts. *Communication Research Reports, 22*(3), 99–205. doi:10.1080/00036810500207014.

Mooney, C.G. (2013). *Theories of childhood* (2nd ed.). St. Paul, MN: Redleaf Press.

NAACP Legal Defense Fund (n.d.). *Kemba's story: Victimized by the war on drugs*. Retrieved from http://www.naacpldf.org/story/kembas-story-victimized-war-drugs.

National Conference of State Legislatures (2015, July 27). *Drug testing for welfare recipients and public assistance*. Retrieved from http://www.ncsl.org/research/human-services/drug-testing-and-public-assistance.aspx.

National Domestic Violence Hotline (n.d.). *"Why don't they just leave?"* Retrieved from http://www.thehotline.org/is-this-abuse/why-do-people-stay-in-abusive-relationships/

National Research Council (2014). *The growth of incarceration in the United States*. Washington, D.C.: The National Academies Press. Retrieved from http://www.nap.edu.

Nelson, G., & Prilleltensky, I. (2005). *Community psychology: In pursuit of liberation and well-being*. New York: Palgrave Macmillian.

Nelson, T.E., & Kinder, D.R. (1996). Issue frames and group-centrism in American public opinion. *The Journal of Politics, 58*(4), 1055–1078. doi: http://dx.doi.org/10.2307/ 2960149.

The New Yorker (2013). Slide show: Obama on The New Yorker's cover. Retrieved May 25, 2016, from http://www.newyorker.com/ news/news-desk/slide-show-obama-on-the-new-yorkers-cover.

Ng, I., Sarri, R., & Stoffregen, E. (2013). Intergenerational incarceration: Risk factors and social exclusion. *Journal of Poverty, 17*(4), 437–459. doi:10.1080/10875549.2013.833161.

Nkansah-Amankra, S., Agbanu, S.K., & Miller, R.J. (2013). Disparities in health, poverty, incarceration, and social justice among racial groups in the United States: A critical review of evidence of close links with neoliberalism. *International Journal of Health Services: Planning, Administration, Evaluation, 43*(2), 217–240.

Norton, M.I., & Francesca, G. (2014). Rituals alleviate grieving for loved ones, lovers, and lotteries. *Journal of Experimental Psychology, 143*(1), 266–272. doi:10.1037/a0031772.

Obamacare.net (2016). *2016 federal poverty level.* Retrieved March 2, 2016, from https:// obamacare.net/2016-federal-poverty-level/

Ocampo, C. (2015). "*Welfare queen" stereotype.*" *Salem Press Encyclopedia. Research Starters.*

O'Donohue, W., & Ferguson, K.E. (2001). *The psychology of B.F. Skinner.* Thousand Oaks, CA: Sage Publications, Inc.

Office of the Chief Financial Officer (2015). *Who stays in the district? Who leaves? Preliminary findings from D.C. tax filers from 2004.* Retrieved from http://cfo.dc.gov/sites/ default/files/dc/sites/ocfo/publication/ attachments/Family%20Structure%20Web %20Paper.pdf.

114 Congress (2015). *To provide access to medication-assisted therapy, and for other purposes.* Retrieved June 25, 2016, from http://www.markey.senate.gov/imo/media/ doc/2015-05-27-TREAT-Act-BillText.pdf.

Pettit, B., & Western, B. (2004). Mass imprisonment and the life course: Race and class inequality in U.S. incarceration. *American Sociological Review, 69*(1), 151–169.

Prince, L. (2008). Resilience in African American women formerly involved in street prostitution. *ABNF Journal, 19*(1), 31–36.

Prison Girlfriends and Wives (n.d.). Prison girlfriends and wives. *Pacific Standard, 9*(2), 11.

Prison Policy Initiative (2003). *Section III: The prison economy.* Retrieved from http://

www.prisonpolicy.org/prisonindex/prison labor.html.

Prison Policy Initiative (2015). *Prisons of poverty.* Retrieved from http://www.prison policy.org/reports/income.html.

Quereshi, A.I., Suri, F.K., Zhou, J., & Divani, A.A. (2006). African American women have poor long-term survival following ischemic stroke. Neurology, 67, 1623–1629.

Rees, D. (1971). The hallucinations of widowhood. *British Medical Journal, 4*(5778), 37–41.

Rice University Baker Institute for Public Policy (2010). *Century of lies 2010.* Retrieved from http://bakerinstitute.org/drug-policy-program/drug-truth-archive/century-of-lies/2010/

Roberts, D.E. (2002). *Shattered bonds: The color of child welfare.* New York: Civitas Books.

Robinson, J.N., Tidwell, D.K., Briley, C.A., Williams, R.D., Taylor, W.N., & Threadgill, P. (2015). Eve's apple: A faith-based nutrition education pilot program for African American women. *American Journal of Health Studies, 30*(2), 81–89.

Rogers, J.D. (2015). *Study claims marriageable men shortage only exists among Blacks and the highly educated.* Retrieved from http:// madamenoire.com/588720/study-claims-marriageable-men-shortage-only-exists-among-blacks-and-the-highly-educated/

Rosen, E., Ackerman, L., & Zosky, D. (2002). The sibling empty nest syndrome: The experience of sadness as siblings leave the family home. *Journal of Human Behavior in the Social Environment, 6*(1), 65–80.

Rosenthal, L., & Lobel, M. (2016). Stereotypes of Black American women related to sexuality and motherhood. *Psychology of Women Quarterly,* 1–14. doi: 10.1177/0361684315627 459.

Sakala, L. (2014). *Wisconsin profile.* Retrieved from http://www.prisonpolicy.org/profiles/ WI.html.

Sayegh, G. (2010). *After the Rockefeller drug laws: A new direction in New York and the nation.* Retrieved from http://www.drug policyorg.

Schept, J., Tyler, W., & Brisman, A. (2015). Building, staffing, and Insulating: An architecture of criminological complicity in the school-to-prison pipeline. *Social Justice, 41*(4), 96–115.

Schultz, A.J., Israel, B.A., Zenk, S.N., Parker, E.A., Lichtensteinc, R., Shellman-Weira, S., & Klem, L. (2006). Psychosocial stress and social support as mediators of relationships between income, length of residence and depressive symptoms among African American women on Detroit's eastside. *Social Science & Medicine, 62*(2), 510–522. doi:10.1016/j.socscimed.2005.06.028.

SecurusTechnologies (n.d.). *Rates.* Retrieved from https://securustech.net/web/securus/rates.

Semple, J. (1993). *A study of the Panopticon penitentary.* New York: Oxford University Press. Retrieved from https://books.google.com/books?id=ayjLuTdVkTYC&printsec=frontcover&dq=The+Panopticon&hl=en&sa=X&ved=0ahUKEwjY8p-CvMDKAhVEmh4KHSzDDOAQ6AEIKDAC#v=onepage&q=The%20Panopticon&f=false.

Siegel, L.J., & Welsh, B.C. (2012). *Juvenile delinquency: Theory, practice, and law* (11 ed.). Belmont, CA: Cengage Learning.

Slatton, B.C. (2009). *Deep frames, White men's discourse, and Black female bodies.* Retrieved from http://webcache.googleusercontent.com/search?q=cache:zqNKUaOM0uEJ:oaktrust.library.tamu.edu/handle/1969.1/ETD-TAMU-2009-08-7028+&cd=1&hl=en&ct=clnk&gl=us.

Staton-Tindall, M., Duvall, J., Stevens-Watkins, D., & Oscer, C. (2013). The roles of spirituality in the relationship between traumatic life events, mental health, and drug use among African American women from one southern state. *Substance Use & Misuse, 48*(12), 1246–1257. doi:10.3109/10826084.2013.799023.

Stroebe, M., Abakoumkin, G., Stroebe, W., & Schut, H. (2011). Continuing bonds in adjustment to bereavement: Impact of abrupt versus gradual separation. *Personal Relationships, 19*(2012), 255–266. doi:10.1111/j.1475-6811.2011.01352.x.

Stroebe, M., Stroebe, W., Van De Schoot, R., Schut, H., Abakoumkin, G., & Li, J. (2014). Guilt in bereavement: The role of self-blame and regret in coping with loss. *Plos ONE, 9*(5), 1–9.

Suburbanstats.org (2015). *Current population demographics and statistics for Washington, D.C., by age, gender and race.* Retrieved March 29, 2016, from https://suburbanstats.org/population/how-many-people-live-in-washington-dc.

Tate, M., Hart-Johnson, A., Esparaza, C., Grier, C., Graham, H., Mosman, Z., & Rhyanes, L. (2015). *The mass incarceration continuum: The human rights issue of the* 21st century. Retrieved April 2, 2016, from http://prisonersfamilyconference.org/wordpress/wp-content/uploads/2015/05/AinA-White-Paper-final-draft-10-12-15-Version-1.1.pdf.

Taylor, J.M., Gilligan, C., & Sullivan, A. (1995). *Between voice and silence.* Cambridge, MA: Harvard University Press.

Thompson, J. (2016). Eliminating zero tolerance policies in schools: Miami-Dade County public schools approach. *Bringham Young University Education & Law. No.2,* 325–349.

Thurston, W.E., & Vissandjee, B. (2005). An ecological model for understanding culture as a determinant of women's health. *Critical Public Health, 15*(3), 229–242. doi:10.1080/09581590500372121.

Turney, K. (2014a). The intergenerational consequences of mass incarceration: Implications for children's co-residence and contact with grandparents. *Social Forces, 93*(1), 299–327.

Turney, K. (2014b). Stress proliferation across generations? Examining the relationship between parental incarceration and childhood health. *Journal of Health & Social Behavior, 55*(3), 302–319.

Turney, K., Schnittker, J., & Wildeman, C. (2012). Those they leave behind: Paternal incarceration and maternal instrumental support. *Journal of Marriage and Family, 74*(1), 1149–1165. doi:10.1111/j.1741-3737.2012.00998.x.

Uncommon Knowledge Ltd (2001–2016). *All or nothing, or 'Black and White' thinking and depression.* Retrieved from http://www.clinical-depression.co.uk/dlp/understanding-depression/all-or-nothing-or-black-and-white-thinking-and-depression/

U.S. Census Bureau (2010). *The Black population: 2010. 2010 Census Briefs.* Retrieved from http://www.census.gov/prod/cen2010/briefs/c2010br-06.pdf.

U.S. Census Bureau (2012). *America's families and living arrangements, 2012. Table 1: Marital status of people 15 years and over, by age, sex, personal earnings, race and Hispanic origin/1,2012: Black alone.* Retrieved from http://www.census.gov/hhes/families/data/cps2012.html.

U.S. Department of Health and Human Services (2016). *Trends in teen pregnancy and childbearing.* Retrieved from http://www.hhs.gov/ash/oah/adolescent-health-topics/reproductive-health/teen-pregnancy/trends.html.

U.S. Department of Health & Human Services (2010). *Characteristics and financial circumstances of TANF recipients, fiscal year 2010*. Retrieved from http://www.acf.hhs.gov/programs/ofa/resource/character/fy2010/fy2010-chap10-ys-final.

U.S. Department of Justice. (2012). Arrests in the United States, 1990–2010. Retrieved from http://www.bjs.gov/content/pub/pdf/aus9010.pdf.

U.S. Department of Labor (2016). *Black women in the labor force*. Retrieved from https://blog.dol.gov/2016/02/26/black-women-in-the-labor-force/

VERA Institute of Justice (2015). *Incarceration's front door: The misuse of jails in America*. Retrieved from http://www.vera.org/sites/default/files/resources/downloads/incarcerations-front-door-report.pdf.

Vespa, J., Lewis, J.M., & Kreider, R.M. (2013, August). *America's families and living arrangements: 2012*. Retrieved from http://census.gov.

Walletpop Staff (2010). *25 most dangerous neighborhoods 2010*. Retrieved from http://www.aol.com/article/2010/10/04/25-most-dangerous-neighborhoods-2010/19651802/?gen=1.

Wilcox, W.B., & Wolfinger, N.H. (2016). *Religion, sex, love, and marriage, among African Americans and Latinos* (ed.). New York: Oxford University Press.

Wildeman, C. (2010). Paternal incarceration and children's physically aggressive behaviors: Evidence from the fragile families and child well-being study. *Social Forces, 89*(1), 285–309.

Wildeman, C. (2014). Parental incarceration, child homelessness, and the invisible consequences of mass imprisonment. *The Annals of the American Academy of Political and Social Science, 651*(1), 74–96. doi:10.1177/000 2716213502921.

Wooden, E.M., & O'Leary, K.D. (2006). Partner aggression severity as a risk marker for male and female violence recidivism. *Journal of Marital & Family Therapy., 32*(3), 283–296.

Woods, L., Lanza, S., Dyson, W., & Gordon, D.M. (2013). The role of prevention in promoting continuity of health care in prisoner reentry initiatives. *American Journal of Public Health, 103*(5), 830–838. doi:10.2105/AJPH.2012.300961.

Woods-Giscombé, C. & Black, A.R. (2010). Mind-body interventions to reduce risk for health disparities related to stress and strength among African American women: The potential of mindfulness-based stress reduction, loving-kindness, and the NTU therapeutic framework. *Complementary Health Practice Review, 15*(3), 115–131. doi:10.1177/1533210110386776.

Wright, P., & Wright, K. (1999). The two faces of codependent relating: A research-based perspective. *Contemporary Family Therapy: An International Journal, 21*(4), 527–546.

Wronka, J. (2008). *Human rights and social justice: Social action and service for the helping and health professions*. Thousand Oaks, CA: Sage Publications.

Index